CRITICAL ARCHITECTURE AND CONTEMPORARY CULTURE

CRITICAL ARCHITECTURE AND CONTEMPORARY CULTURE

Edited by

WILLIAM J. LILLYMAN

MARILYN F. MORIARTY

DAVID J. NEUMAN

New York   Oxford
OXFORD UNIVERSITY PRESS
1994

Oxford University Press

Oxford   New York   Toronto
Delhi   Bombay   Calcutta   Madras   Karachi
Kuala Lumpur   Singapore   Hong Kong   Tokyo
Nairobi   Dar es Salaam   Cape Town
Melbourne   Auckland
and associated companies in
Berlin   Ibadan

Library of Congress Cataloging-in-Publication Data
Critical architecture and contemporary culture / edited by
William J. Lillyman, Marilyn F. Moriarty, David J. Neuman.
p.   cm.   (Publications of the University
of California Humanities Research Institute)
Includes bibliographical references.
ISBN 0-19-507819-5
1. Deconstructivism (Architecture)
2. Architecture, Modern—20th century.
I. Lillyman, William J.
II. Moriarty, Marilyn F.
III. Neuman, David J.
IV. Series.
NA682.D43C75   1994
724'.6—dc20   92-22185

9 8 7 6 5 4 3 2 1

Printed in the United States of America
on acid-free paper

ACKNOWLEDGMENTS

This volume contains papers presented at the symposium "Postmodernism and Beyond: Architecture as the Critical Art of Contemporary Culture," held at the Beckman Center of the National Academy of Sciences and Engineering adjacent to the University of California, Irvine, on October 26–28, 1989. In addition to the sponsorship of the University of California, Irvine (particularly of Terence Parsons, Paul Sypherd, John Miltner, and Kathy Jones), we gratefully acknowledge the support of the Humanities Research Institute of the University of California and its directors, Murray Krieger and Mark Rose; the National Endowment for the Humanities; the Orange County Chapter of the American Institute of Architects; the Architecture Foundation of Orange County; Stanford University; Bernards Brothers Construction; the IBI Group; and Griffin/Related Properties. Roy Dormaier, his staff in the Office of Financial Planning, and various staff members in the Office of Physical Planning at UCI provided invaluable support through all stages of the project.

William Lillyman would also like to thank the Rockefeller Foundation for awarding him a residency at its Bellagio Study and Conference Center. It was there, in the center's untrammeled ambience, that the initial formulation of the symposium arose, a formulation that was to be much improved and made into a program through the involvement and insights of Marilyn Moriarty and David J. Neuman.

Irvine, Calif.   W.J.L.
Roanoke, Va.   M.F.M.
Stanford, Calif.   D.J.N.
March 1993

C O N T E N T S

V AFTER POSTMODERNISM

CRITICAL

ARCHITECTURE

AND

CONTEMPORARY

CULTURE

INTRODUCTION

The Search for Common Ground

MARILYN F. MORIARTY

ALTHOUGH A COLLECTION of essays cannot hope to duplicate the experience of the actual symposium "Postmodernism and Beyond," the selection and organization of these essays attempt to preserve the intellectual underpinnings that brought together architects, architectural historians, journalists, literary theorists, and a variety of humanists. A connection between architecture and literary theory had been heralded by the "Deconstructivist Architecture" exhibit at the Museum of Modern Art in New York in 1988; however, the exhibition catalogue offered a disclaimer: deconstructive architecture was seen as having emerged from an architectural tradition rather than from a philosophical or literary one. According to Mark Wigley, deconstructive buildings do not derive "from the mode of contemporary philosophy known as 'deconstruction.' They are not an application of deconstructive theory."[1]

Deconstruction, as a strategy of reading, locates the critical moment in a text when its narrative and rhetorical strategies exist at odds, so that neither predominates. Although the "meaning" of the text cannot be grounded on the authority of one element over another, deconstruction does not negate Meaning (as foundation, ground, nonnegotiable truth) but multiplies meanings. Deconstructive architecture and deconstructive theory would seem to be very different, the construction of texts a much different activity from the construction of edifices. Buildings, after all, must always have a foundation, for the ground is ever the *ground* there below one, solid, obeying the law of gravity. Gravity offers a clear point of reference, one might think, unless one questions this reference by shifting scale to a stellar point of view, as both Derrida and Lyotard do. According to Steven Taubeneck in the postscript to this volume, the theoretical shift in perspective that subverts the definition of an absolute ground (truth) describes the antifoundationalism characteristic of contemporary theory.

If gravity, like truth, were seen in absolute terms, how *could* one construct an architecture without foundation? The literary theorist J. Hillis Miller answers in chapter 1: deconstruction in architecture would "appropriate, displace, transfer, transform, decompose [the old architecture and its architectonic raison d'être], (though transformation and decomposition are not the same act) and above all read them, in the sense of bringing their principles to light." In other words, a deconstructive architecture would expose the architectural and philosophical premises that ground it.

But what gives Miller, a theoretician and literary critic, the right to speak about architecture—especially given the long philosophical tradition, starting with Plato, that articulates the difference between primary and derived forms of knowledge? One might reasonably extend the question: Who knows best about deconstructive architecture, about architecture in general? And who, therefore, may legitimately claim to speak of it as an object of knowledge? By what authority and on what grounds can architects, philosophers, critics, and the general public claim to speak knowledgeably about architecture and thus decide what constitutes architectural knowledge? Knowledge about architecture may be claimed from the theoretical and practical points of view. Although we all know that buildings stand, opinions vary as to what they *stand for*.

The reciprocity between architecture and literary studies is not, in fact, limited to a narrow exchange between deconstruction in theory and deconstruction in architecture: architectural and literary discourses have a long history of exchanging their metaphors. Language and philosophy, for instance, borrow founding metaphors from architecture: consider such commonplace expressions as these: "The theory needs more *support*. We need to *buttress*, or *shore up* a *shaky* theory which might easily *fall apart* under criticism."[2] Reciprocally, our sense of what architecture is and does derives in part from the *talk* about it. In the many phases of development from conception to completion, a building emerges from a web of discourse that explains what it could accomplish, should accomplish, did accomplish, and might accomplish. The completed building, the physically tangible, monumental *thing*, stands in the world extending an invitation to be commented on by users, the general public, critics, architects, and artists. Because we normally think that a building must *stand for* something, architecture can be defined in

Aaron Betsky's terms (chapter 5): "the physical housing of a public function and the simultaneous articulation of that function through a representational strategy." So although deconstructive architecture might emerge from within the architectural tradition, that tradition does not escape the problematic of representation, a problematic that in fact lays the ground for Wigley's disclaimer.

The talk about architecture, from within or without the tradition, tells us something about the extent to which architecture satisfies or disappoints an array of cultural expectations. This talk about architecture may take a number of forms: manifestos or other kinds of self-formulated explanations about the purpose and significance of architecture; philosophical writings that treat broader theoretical concepts; popular writings in journalistic organs like newspapers and magazines; conferences and symposia organized to discuss art; parody or satire, ways of criticizing art-about-art; references to "sister" arts. Because genres classify "subjects" along different lines, they offer relative rather than absolute standards of reference. To ask therefore, what architecture means requires some qualification and demands a confrontation with context.

The question What does architecture represent? emerged as a spirited and provocative one when it came indirectly to be reformulated as What *should* architecture represent? As The architect Robert Stern states in chapter 4:

> [A]rchitecture must be the reification of public values. A building must be a public act of communication: a coherent presentation, representation, reification not merely of program, function, or conventions belonging to the discipline itself, but also of the things that belong to the world outside it that it must serve, honor, and depict. . . . It is not the built version/illustration of a written text.

According to Stern, therefore, because architecture serves the world outside it, architecture stands accountable to the public authority that defines its function and purpose. But "public values" are usually not *anyone*'s values; these values often belong to a group or an elite that defines or circulates a selected range of values, usually its own. Betsky, for one, presents such an ideological analysis in chapter 5:

> Architecture is, in its essence, the representation of power. It houses the central institutions of any society, commands enormous physical resources, and imposes itself on the daily life of the user or observer as a physical fact. Therefore, architecture is always the built affirmation of the social, economic, and physical status quo, and in the activity of affirmation finds a representational role that is unique to its constitution.

Betsky's discussion of James Gamble Rogers offers a case in point of the way that structuring the Yale campus reinforces the image of the "Yale man."

Because architecture codifies established values (for better or worse), representation is not neutral. But the way that an artist or an architect *can* represent something does not emerge from a void: a history of style governs the codes and topics of expression. The session at the symposium "Architecture and Conventions" sought to explore the limitations placed on just such a history. Although typological forms may be remotivated, discrete buildings might assert a continuity or a confrontation with a received tradition; style thereby offers a way to interrogate the "statements" made by buildings. "Why, for example," asks Diane Ghirardo in chapter 6, "would Terragni, knowledgeable as he was about architectural history and typologies, want his Casa del Fascio to be based on the Venetian palace type?" Expressing a similar point of view from a different orientation in chapter 7, Frank Israel characterized his own work in terms of "modifications of original models, responses to existing contexts and buildings. Each project is an addition, a remodeling, or a renovation of something that existed prior to my coming into the picture."

The historical dimension introduced by the session on stylistic conventions focused controversy on the differences between formalist and ideological (historical) critiques. Although the distinction between such critiques is less straightforward than it might seem, this controversy rested on the traditional view that a formalist critique defines the object as timeless, self-enclosed, and apolitical; viewed in a historical context, the object takes on ideological significance. Although the politicization of the object comes through context, formalist interpretations never existed without an implicit one; contemporary theory has made context explicit to the point that context now becomes part of the object of critique.

Context specifies place and time, among other things. For many writers, history was one such contextual field, whether it was conceived as a history of style (form and content) or of political and historical circumstances. But historical retrospects differ in tone, ranging from nostalgia at the loss of the past to the joy at re-creating it. For the keynote speaker, architect Frank Gehry, history offered a topos of invention, a reservoir from which the contemporary architect might pick and choose spontaneously. Historical elements of style and form present themselves as found objects offering themselves for improvisation—another kind of everyday material like chain-link fencing. Although Gehry maintained that he attempted to get beyond history by resorting to primordial forms like the fish, a preference that might be construed as grounding in biological evolution, Gehry's pronouncement was not motivated by the wish to make any theoretical statement about history but instead offered the opportunity for play: "You can imagine the next move has to be gefilte fish" (chapter 10).

For Andrea Dean (chapter 8) in the session "Architecture and Society," sentimental nostalgia for the past is itself past, as architecture in the 1990s has become oriented to ecology, landscaping, and the users' needs. After the authority of the architect as social reformer declined in the 1960s, the role was refigured to implicate the architect in a more fully dialogic relationship with site and client. In a way that does not discount the difference between virtual and actual homelessness, Dean heralds the optimistic view that concern for global issues has directed architecture to a greater interest in community needs. Literally through dialogue, both Michael Wilford and Paul Zajfen illustrate Dean's observations by demonstrating the extent to which the programming process may embrace the practical needs of the user without forfeiting aesthetics. Although the firm of James Stirling Michael Wilford & Associates maintains a strong link with the client and with government planning agencies, Wilford asserts, "We practice architecture as an Art" (chapter 9).

No account of the relationship between representation and politics would be complete without acknowledging the references to Walter Benjamin's concept of the *aura,* a term evoking a complex view of the historicized work of art.[3] In dialogue with Benjamin, Peter Eisenman argued that architecture should be read in the context of an alternative aura: "Presentness [indicates] the possibility of another aura in architecture, one not in the sign or in being, but a third condition of betweenness. Neither nostalgic for meaning or presence nor dependent on them, this third, nondialectical condition of space exists only in an excess that is more, or less, than the traditional, hierarchical, Vitruvian preconditions of form" (chapter 3).

Jacques Derrida's work on the temporal dimension of the sign forces us to reevaluate the activity of signification because the sign always has at least a virtual capacity to differ from itself and consequently to defer any terminal or absolute meaning. In the context of this discussion, Derrida's work marks a turn away from our apprehension of historical time as a palpable and determinable body and a turn to the register of signification. In chapter 2, Derrida writes: "This question of history, understood as the history of spacing, as the spacing of time and voice, does not separate itself from the history of visibility (immediately mediate), that is to say from the entire history of architecture."

Derrida locates a critique of closed structures through his remarks on the future perfect. More than a grammatical tense, the future perfect describes a way of thinking about an end or telos as an issue ("result" and "subject") that attends the closure of time and space. From the standpoint of the future perfect, "what will have been" sees the building both as completed structure and as (Benjaminian) ruin, already created and fallen in the moment of its conceptualization from a projected future. The future perfect totalizes and structures time. What, Derrida asks Eisenman, would an architecture be that is not founded on such a metaphysical structure, an architecture that, "without holding, without standing upright, vertically, would not fall again into ruin?" In other words, what would an architecture be that did not unconsciously derive its constitution from a metaphysical understanding of language, as in the virtual construction of the future perfect, a state that can exist only in language?

The coordinates of space and time as a means to establish a baseline of reference figure significantly as well in philosopher Jean-François Lyotard's "Postmodern Fable on Postmodernity, or: In the Megalopolis" (chapter 11), his long-awaited commentary on postmodernism ten years after the publication of *The Postmodern Condition*. The parameters of time and space, Lyotard notes, rely on scale, depending on whether one chooses the life of a man or the life of a sun to define time and, therefore, to define closure. The millennial moment when the present rushes for the future (and the closure) it imagines (i.e., the future perfect) characterized a modernity that already included within it the possibility of postmodernity. The shift in scale or reference, accounted as the antifoundationalism in contemporary theory, was nascent in modernism:

> What is called the crisis of the fundamentals in the hard sciences and epistemology; the avant-garde in the arts and literature; the often disastrous efforts to create right- or left-wing alternatives to the liberal communities as well as the failure of such attempts; the social and economic crisis of 1920 to 1950, followed by the reorganization of communities on the international level after World War II—all this may be ascribed to postmodernity, but only to the extent that it posts in the foreground a lot of implicit or latent questions already present in modernity. As was previously said, it is a question of systems of reference, scale of measure, and determination of a zero point of observation.

Such complex responses to the issues embraced by representation, conventions, society, and structure point to the difficulties in locating a common ground. It may be clear how the search for common ground to some extent became a contest for mastery, for holding ground by securing context. Given these conflicting views in contention for possession of architectural knowledge, who can be credited with actually holding the ground? Did philosophy ultimately call architecture to account? Did architecture call philosophy to account? While the conference format seemed to privilege those most comfortable with the verbal arts, unsurprisingly the ground returned to the architects for whom the use of slides enabled the usurpation of the verbal by the visual. The very question of the ground might itself be subject to scrutiny, for this metaphor a priori privileges architectural discourse by using the metaphor of building.

It might seem that any closing of the ground between literary and architectural concerns would be impossible, the differences being irreducible. Rather than one particular Meaning to which all explanations might refer, the conference agenda produced a plethora of meanings.

What could all these writers have in common apart from the fact that they were in the same building?

This observation is less naive than it may appear.

"Building" might refer both to the architectural construction—the physical fact of the place—and to the "building" of intellectual exchange—the virtual place of a common discourse. How might one separate the actual fact of the event from the intellectual event that took place? The definition of common ground might fall back on the performativity of the situation itself, as place and persons came together to construct a significance both virtual and actual, abstract and concrete, to engage an issue (end or subject) that could not be apprehended in advance of its arrival, although the place could be drawn on a map. On such dialogic ground, claims to authority multiplied without mastery to produce a series of exchanges among persons, disciplines, and discourses. Without foundation, the ground of exchange became the ground *as* exchange.

NOTES

1. Mark Wigley, "Deconstructivist Architecture," in *Deconstructivist Architecture,* ed. Philip Johnson and Mark Wigley (Boston: Little, Brown, 1988). Published on the occasion of the exhibition "Deconstructivist Architecture" at the New York Museum of Modern Art, 23 June–30 August 1988. According to Wigley:

> It is the ability to disturb our thinking about form that makes these projects deconstructive. It is not that they derive from the mode of contemporary philosophy known as "deconstruction." They are not an application of deconstructive theory. Rather, they emerge from within the architectural tradition and happen to exhibit some deconstructive qualities. (10–11)

2. George Lakoff and Mark Johnson, *Metaphors We Live By* (Chicago: University of Chicago Press, 1980), 97–105.

3. The aura of a work of art comes from a complex relationship among the maker, the object, and the audience, such that the object bears the traces of its maker that confer on it the authenticity of the original. See Walter Benjamin, "The Work of Art in the Age of Mechanical Reproduction," in *Illuminations,* trans. Harry Zohn, ed. and introduction by Hannah Arendt (New York: Schocken Books, 1969), 220–21.

I

ARCHITECTURE AND THEORY

Beginning from the Ground Up

J. HILLIS MILLER

WHAT IN THE WORLD might be meant by "deconstructive architecture": And why in the world, if there is such a thing, which is by no means certain, should we want such a thing here at the University of California, Irvine, for example, or on any other American campus? Why should we, for example, want a building here designed by Peter Eisenman, who, by the way, strenuously resists the word phrase "deconstructive architecture"? What would it mean, intellectually, institutionally, politically, to have one? What does it mean, politically, educationally, institutionally, intellectually, that we have the great array of postmodern buildings that we do have? These buildings, I should say, are by no means homogenous in their meaning and function. They incarnate in steel, concrete, and glass the warfares within postmodern or post-postmodern or a modern architecture, its fissures and tensions.

"Deconstructive architecture" seems almost a contradiction in terms, an oxymoron, like heavy feathers or light lead. Architecture, as its name implies, is a fabric or structure that is founded, that is built according to a basic principle, that has a foundation or base, that incarnates a meaning, that is solidly planted, posited, instituted at one particular historical moment in one particular place to serve a particular social, community, institutional, or family end. The word "architect" comes from the Greek *arkhitekton* (master builder), from the Greek *arkhein* (to begin, rule), plus *tekton* (carpenter, craftsman).

To build a temple, a family dwelling, a place of business, a theater, a school, a bridge, a library, a museum, a research laboratory, or a hospital is an act of foundation almost as performatively original and originating, almost as much a beginning, as to promulgate a declaration of independence or a constitution. In both cases, the help of the gods is traditionally invoked. How could we, without God's help, construct an edifice that would stand? Does not the Bible tell us so? *Nisi Dominus aedificaverit domum:* "Except the Lord build the house, they labor in vain that build it" (Psalms 127:1).

The youthful Paul Valéry, in his "Paradoxe sur l'architecte" (1891), imagined the great architect to come who will make an edifice in porphyry or marble that is the analogical equivalent of a great work of music, a symphony of Beethoven, or a page of *Tannhäuser*. Such a master of correspondence will be able to build a symphony in stone because "il aura bu le lait d'une Déesse [he will have drunk the milk of a Goddess]."[1] And much later, in the dialogue *Eupalinos ou l'architecte* (1921), the architect, for Valéry, or for Válery's Socrates, is the archetypal example of the artist who repeats, continues, and completes God's work of creation: "But the constructor whom I am now bringing to the fore . . . takes as the starting point of his act, the very point where the God had left off. . . . Here I am, says the Constructor, I am the act."[2]

For Martin Heidegger in "Bauen Wohnen Denken," on the other hand, building seems to go the other way. It does not so much begin where God left off, as invoke and install the gods in an earthly habitation that *gathers [versammelt]*. An edifice—for example, a bridge over a stream—does not just take up space in a certain location. It gathers space into a landscape, that is, a humanly significant configuration, around it, and so joins earth, sky, divinities, and mortals:

> The bridge swings over the stream "with ease and power." It does not just connect [*verbindet nicht nur schon*] banks that are already there. The banks emerge as banks only as the bridge crosses the stream. . . . With the banks, the bridge brings to the stream the one and the other expanse of the landscape lying behind them. It brings stream and bank and land into each other's neighborhood [*in die wechselseitige Nachbarschaft*]. The bridge *gathers [versammelt]* the earth as landscape around the stream. . . . The bridge *gathers [versammelt]* to itself in *its own* way earth and sky, divinities and mortals.[3]

Traditionally, we signal the solemnity of the act of building by a ceremonious laying of a cornerstone, inscribed with a date and an authorizing name, with appropriate speeches, and by acts of sacrifice and of invocation or blessing, as in the laying of the foundation stone of Charlotte's summer house in chapter 9 of Goethe's *Die Wahlverwandtschaften*. This episode admirably exemplifies this tradition of establishing a foundation in the present moment that at the same time both is a memorial and looks forward to the future in a hierarchically ordered structure of beginning, stratified and differentiated building, end, and underlying ground that finds its analogue in the shapeliness of the edifice itself. "Three things have to be taken into account when erecting a building," says the mason in his speech at the laying of the stone:

> that it is standing on the right spot, that the foundations are sound, that it is well constructed. . . . [T]his foundation stone [*Grundstein*] is to be a memorial stone [*Denkstein*] also. Here in these hollow spaces we shall place various objects as witnesses to a distant posterity [*eine entfernte Nachwelt*]. . . . We found this stone for eternity, to ensure the enjoyment of this house to its present and future possessors [*Besitzer*] for the longest possible time.[4]

And the mason says, among other things, something exceedingly odd, but that prepares for Jacques Derrida's remarks in chapter 2 about the ruin. The very act of making the laying of the foundation stone an act of memory and commemoration presupposes, metaleptically, an anticipation of the moment when "that which has not yet even been built" will "all . . . be destroyed again."[5] The act of building, in this tradition of architecture, presupposes as a future anterior, the moment when the building will become a ruin.

Architecture, in short, according to a long and puissant tradition in the West, is the incarnation and material embodiment, in visible, resistant, tangible stone, wood, or glass, of the whole system of logocentric metaphysics. As Derrida says in "Point de folie—maintenant l'architecture," architecture is "the last fortress of metaphysics [*dernière forteresse de la métaphysique*]."[6]

It would seem impossible to detach architecture in the West from this tradition. As soon as you build, you build under the aegis of metaphysics, reinstitute it, reinstall it, found it anew, reaffirm its millennial hegemony. A nonlogocentric building, it seems, would not be a building at all. It would be no longer governed by the arch authority of origins, means, and ends, the organic enclosure of spaces into entrances, rooms, and levels for a certain civic or private purpose that defines in its essence what we mean by buildings and a building, the act and the product.

Deconstruction in architecture, nevertheless, contests and transforms this powerful structuring system. Of all the forms of "deconstruction" active today—in law, theology, literature, philosophy, politics, ethics, even painting and music—none, it could be argued, is more fundamental and more likely to meet with resistance, or more likely to be misunderstood, than the architectural one. The resistance in this case not only takes the form of ideological assumptions that are so firmly rooted that to change them would seem like the end of everything rational, natural, and to be taken for granted, but also is embodied in the solidity of all those structures of wood, stone, concrete, and glass with which we are surrounded and that speak to us over and over again some form or other of that set of assumptions I have called, in shorthand, "logocentric metaphysics." Architecture, moreover, both institutional and domestic, is embedded in a particularly complex and resistant way in the surrounding political, economic, financial, governmental, environmental, technoscientific, and institutional power structures, in all those laws, regulations, codes, conventions, restraints, and strictures that begin to operate as soon as the first discussions about a new building are held and the preliminary drawings made. By comparison, anyone is relatively free to write an essay or a poem, paint a painting, or compose a quartet without interference, partly because these acts are considered to be relatively trivial in our society. But building a building is another thing.

What, then, is it, or what are *they,* that constitute "deconstructionism in architecture." They do *not* mean a purely negative work of destruction, the making of buildings that are uninhabitable, without shapeliness or utility, without principle or end, without any active inherence in the productive activities in history, politics, or praxis of all kinds, surrounding and traversing the sites where the buildings stand. Such a purely negative work would only be another form of what it contests, just as nihilism in whatever form is only a species of metaphysics. Such an architecture would be instantly recuperated within the system, the architectonics, that it would negate. And the power of recuperation and the reassimilation by logocentric architectonics of even the most apparently radical forms of architecture should never be underestimated. Says Derrida of the *folies* of Bernard Tschumi:

> Nothing here of that nihilistic gesture which would fulfill a certain theme of metaphysics; no reversal of values aimed at an unaesthetic, uninhabitable, unusable, a-symbolical and meaningless architecture, an architecture simply left vacant after the retreat of the gods and men. . . . Deconstructions would be feasible if they were negative, if they did not construct, and above all, if they did not first measure themselves against institutions in their solidity, *at the place of their greatest resistance:* political structures, levers of economic decision, the material and phantasmatic apparatuses which connect state, civil society, capital, bureaucracy, cultural power and architectural education—a remarkably sensitive relay; but in addition those which join the arts, from the fine arts to martial arts, science and technology, the old and the new.[7]

Nor will a deconstructive architecture liberate architecture from traditional meanings and traditional norms of human inhabitability in order to produce a purely abstract and dehumanized play of volumes, planes, surfaces, textures, and ornaments that would pretend to be a "pure architecture," referring only to itself and to its own immanent laws. That too would be to submit to a familiar form of metaphysics, the aesthetic ideology of the work of art that is without purpose or end, or is its own end, abstracted from the personal, domestic, institutional, and social realms of ends and uses. No, the deconstructionisms in architecture that are beginning to emerge, for example, in the work of Eisenman and Tschumi, are above all active, affirmative, productive, transformative. This architecture does not destroy, but works and makes, or it contests only as it works and makes. I can only briefly sketch here the characteristics of this working and making.

First, this new architecture does not so much destroy or negate the old architecture and its architectonic raison d'être (it cannot be destroyed) as appropriate, displace, transfer, transform, decompose them (though transformation and decomposition are not the same act) and above all read them, in the sense of bringing their principles to light, just like those writings by Goethe, Valéry, and Heidegger I began by citing. Since those principles "go without saying," to enunciate them, as Goethe, Valéry, and Heidegger do, to bring them to light, is to "deconstruct" them, just as these new buildings do in playing on and against our assumptions of what a building must be like to "*look* like architecture."[8]

Second, the actual buildings that result from these new architectural designs are only a stage in a potentially endless series of drawings, schemes, elevations, models, sketches. And the traces of these earlier and later stages remain—for example in the form of drawings inscribed in the bottom of a swimming pool, or in the form of a model of one stage of the house design placed outside the house and periodically burned and replaced, as Peter Eisenmann imagined for House X, or in the form of a lyre within a lyre in the plans for the Choral Work, the garden of metal and stone for La Villette in Paris, designed by Eisenman and Derrida in "collaboration." The lyre is an overdetermined pun (liar, layer, lyric), but also objectifies the hidden reference to the *chora* of Plato's *Timaeus*, with its sieve or sifter filtering the primal elements as they fall, giving them the *clinamen* necessary to turn aleatory chance into programmed configurations.

Third, as the example of the lyre indicates, this new architecture will not only critically read the old, but itself be not a monumental book in stone, but rather a text in progress to be actively read as it is inhabited or used, mixing language, architectural forms and textures, and even those allusions to music that charmed Paul Valéry.

Fourth, as the perpetually transformative, transferring, differentiating, dissociating, decomposing, recomposing nature of this new architecture indicates, it is without fixed origin, end, organic continuity, narrative hierarchical, or dialectical form. It has no discernible immovable ground plan as foundation. It resolutely resists totalization. There is no cornerstone laying at the inception of these buildings. They establish and invite interruptions, discontinuities, dissociations. As Peter Eisenman puts this in *House X*,

In all of this, the order of relationships is neither sequential nor regular. The forms interlock, separate, and overlap in a complex hierarchy that cannot be arranged to conform to a simple taxonomy, nor strong together in any linear, progressive concatenation. The parts remain suspended relativistically as in a DNA chain, in which partial orders become self-sustaining and replicating totalities. While our perceptual mechanisms seem conditioned to search for a whole, coherent conception, struggling to "unlock" by the secrets of House X some mental addition or subtractions, each time something fits together in space something else falls apart.[9]

Fifth, I have said "establish and invite." Another way to put this is to say that this new architecture is performative and participatory. It is oriented toward the *not yet* of an unknown and unknowable future, rather than casting in concrete already fixed civic or domestic meanings. Such a building invites those who use it to give it meanings, performatively, in the shape of those promises that are always in one way or another a response to a call from the hidden Other who interpellates me and calls on me to invent that Other.

It is easy to see, finally, why we should wish to have such buildings at UCI. A university, especially a state university, is a locus where all those political, governmental, ideological, economic, psychological, artistic, technological, and bureaucratic forces converge. It is obviously one of those places of "greatest resistance" of which Derrida speaks. The danger is that the buildings of the university would incarnate, would cement in solid, perdurable form, the old presuppositions. On the other hand, since UCI is a new university, we are building its structures from the ground up—structures in both the material and the organizational senses. This means that we have extraordinary opportunity, an opportunity not offered to older universities that are already materially *there,* to make our buildings conform to the image of a great teaching and research university that is in constant process, constantly permutating or reinventing itself, where no department, school, or research unit can think of itself as fixed for all time. We need buildings that will allow us to respond to rapid changes taking place in every discipline, so we can keep at the frontier, where the action is—so we can make the action. We need buildings that will encourage or even seem to necessitate, though not program or prescribe in any predictable way, the productive and transformative mobility that characterizes the most important work in all fields in the university today.

NOTES

1. Paul Valéry, "Paradoxe sur l'architecte" (1891), in *Oeuvres,* ed. Jean Hytier (Paris: Gallimard, 1960), 2:1403; translated in *Dialogues,* trans. William McCausland Stewart, Bollingen Series xlv-4 (New York: Pantheon Books, 1956), 181.

2. Valéry, *Dialogues,* 147, 148; "Mais le constructeur que je fais maintenant paraître . . . prend pour origine de son acte, le point même où le dieu s'était arrêté. . . . Me voici, dit le constructeur, je suis l'acte" (Valéry, *Oeuvres,* 2:144, 145).

3. Martin Heidegger, "Building Dwelling Thinking," in *Poetry, Language, Thought,* trans. Albert Hofstadter (New York: Harper & Row, 1971), 152, 153; "Bauen Wohnen Denken," *Vorträge und Aufsätze* (Pfullingen: Neske, 1967), 2: 26, 27.

4. Johann Wolfgang von Goethe, *Elective Affinities,* trans. R. J. Hollindale (Harmondsworth: Penguin, 1983), 82–83, 84, 85; *Die Wahlverwandtschaften* (Munich: Deutscher Taschenbuch Verlag, 1975), 55, 56, 57.

5. Goethe, *Elective Affinities,* 85; *Die Wahlverwandtschaften,* 57.

6. Jacques Derrida, "Point de folie—maintenant l'architecture," in *Psyché: Inventions de l'autre* (Paris: Galilée, 1987), 482, translated in Bernard Tschumi, *La Case Vide; La Villette 1985; Folio VIII* (London: Architectural Association, 1986), 9.

7. Derrida, "Point de folie," 487–88; Tschumi, *La Case Vide,* 11, 15.

8. Peter Eisenman, *House X* (New York: Rizzoli, 1982), 44.

9. Ibid., 160.

T W O

Letter to Peter Eisenman

JACQUES DERRIDA

12 October 1989

MY DEAR PETER,

I am simultaneously sending this letter, with the cassette that accompanies it, to Hillis, who is to talk with us during the anticipated meeting. As he will also "moderate" and lead it, but for other reasons as well, Hillis is therefore, along with you, the first addressee of these questions. He understands the labyrinth better than anyone else, as we all know. And what I'm going to say to you probably will reverberate in a sort of labyrinth. I am entrusting to the recording of the voice or letter that which is not yet visible to me and cannot guide my steps toward an end/exit, and can barely guide them toward an *issue*. I'm not even sure myself if what I'm sending you holds up. But that is perhaps by design, and related to precisely what I plan to speak to you about. In any case, I very much regret having to deprive myself of this meeting with you, the two of you, all of you.

Now don't worry, I'm not going to argue with you. And I'm not going to take advantage of my absence, not even to tell you that you perhaps believe in it, *absence,* too much. This reference to absence is

Translated by Hilary P. Hanel.

perhaps one of the things (because there are others) that most troubled me in your discourse on architecture, and if that were my first question, you could perhaps profit from my absence to speak about it a little, about absence in general, about the role that this word, "absence," will have been able to play at least in what you believed you could "say," if not "do," with your architecture. One could multiply examples, but I am limiting myself to what you say about the presence of an absence in *Moving Arrows Eros and Other Errors,* which concerns Romeo's château, "a palimpsest and a quarry," etc. This discourse on absence, or the presence of an absence, perplexes me, not only because it bypasses so many tricks, complications, traps that the "philosopher," especially if he is a bit of a dialectician, knows only too well and fears to find you caught up in again, but also because it has authorized many religious interpretations, not to mention vaguely Judeo-transcendental ideologizations, of your work. I suspect a little that you liked and encouraged these interpretations even as you discreetly denied it with a smile, which would make a misunderstanding a little more or a little less than a misunderstanding. My question has to do not only with absence or the presence of absence, but with God. Voilà, if I didn't come it isn't just because I'm tired and overworked—held up in Paris—but precisely to have the opportunity to directly ask you a question about God that I would never have dared to do in Irvine if I had been present in person; instead, I'm glad that this question has come to you by way of this voice, that is to say on tape. The same question brings up others, a whole group of closely related questions, for example, at the risk of shocking you: whether it has to do with houses, museums, or university research laboratories, what distinguishes your architectural space from that of the temple, indeed of the synagogue (by this word I mean a Greek word expressing a Jewish concept)? Where will the break, the rupture have been in this respect, if there is one, if there was one, for you and other architects of this period with whom you feel yourself associated? I remain very perplexed about this subject; if I had been there, I would have been a difficult interlocutor. If you were to construct a place of worship, Buddhist for example, or a cathedral, a mosque, a synagogue (hypotheses that you are not obliged to accept), what would be your primary concern today? I allude shortly to Libeskind's project in Berlin for the Jewish Museum. We spoke about this the other morning in New York, but let's leave that aside for the moment.

Naturally this question concerns also *your* interpretation of *chora* in "our" "work," if one can say our work "in common" in quotation marks. I am not sure that you have detheologized and deontologized *chora* in as radical a way as I would have wished (*chora* is neither the void, as you sometimes suggest, nor absence, nor invisibility, nor certainly the contrary, whence—and this is what interests me—a large number of consequences follow). It is true that for me it was easier, in a certain way, since I didn't have anything to "do" with it and couldn't have done anything with it; that is to say, for the city of Paris, for La Villette, the little city; you see what I mean (and that, perhaps, is the whole difference between us), but I would like you to say something to our friends in Irvine, while speaking to them of the difference between our respective relations to discourse on the one hand, and to the operation of architecture, to its realization, on the other. Profit from my absence in order to speak freely. But don't just say anything, because, since everything today is recorded, and memory, always the same, is no longer the same at all, I would know everything you will have said in public. I have had the feeling, and I believe that you said it somewhere, that you have judged me too reserved in our "choral work," a little bit absent, entrenched in discourse, without obliging you to change, to change place, without disturbing you enough. No doubt there would be a great deal to say on this subject, which is complicated because it is that of the place (*chora*) and of displacement itself. If I had come, I would have spoken perhaps of my own displacement in the course of "choral work," but here it is you who must speak. Therefore, tell me if, *after* Choral Work (as you yourself said in Irvine in the spring), your work in effect took a new direction and engaged itself in other paths, what then has happened? What is this time for you, this history? How does one determine the boundaries of it or put rhythm into it? When did we begin to work together, if we ever did, on this Choral Work that is not yet constructed but that one sees and reads everywhere? When will we stop?

All this brings me directly to the next question, which also concerns a certain absence. Not my absence today in Irvine, where I would have liked so much to see you again along with other friends—even more so since I had been one of those who wished for and prepared this meeting (and I must ask you to forgive me and to make others forgive me)— but another absence, like the shadowed sound of the voice, you see what I mean by this. What relations (new or archi-ancient, in any case different) does architecture, must architecture, particularly yours, carry on, must it carry on with the voice—the range of the voice, but also therefore with telephonic machines of all sorts that structure and transform our experience of space every day? This is certainly a question of quasi-immediate telephonic address—quasi-immediate, I emphasize— but also one of telephonic archivation, as is the case right here, with the spacing of time that telephonic archivation supposes and structures at the same time. If one can imagine a whole labyrinth-like history of architecture, guided by the entwined thread of this question, where would one be today, and where would you be tomorrow?

This question of history, understood as the history of spacing, as the spacing of time and voice, does not separate itself from the history of visibility (immediately mediate), that is to say, from the entire history of architecture; it is so great that I won't even dare touch upon it, but will "address" this question, as you say in English, through economy and metonymy, in the form of a single word, glass (*Glas*).

What about glass in your work? What do you say about it? What do

you do with it? How should we talk about it? In optical terms or in
tactile terms (in regard to tactility, it would be good if, continuing what
you were saying the other morning in New York, you would speak to
our friends of the erotic uses, of the calls of desire, do I dare say of
the sex appeal of the architectural forms about which you think, with
which you work, to which you give yourself up? Whether its directions
(paths) are new or not, does this seduction come as a supplement into
the bargain, as a "premium of seduction," precisely that, or a "premium of pleasure"? Or is it essential? Or the premium itself essential?
But then, what would the premium itself be? Subsidy/Bonus? For the
author of *Moving Arrows Eros and Other Errors,* what is the relation between the premium and the rest in the calculating and negotiations of
the architect? As my American students sometimes disarmingly ask me,
Could you elaborate on that? After this long parenthesis on your desire, I
return now to my question about glass, which is not perhaps so far
removed. What terms can we use to speak about glass? Technical and
material terms? Economic terms? Terms of urbanism? Terms of social
relations? Of transparency and immediacy, of love or the police, of the
border, which is perhaps erased, between the public and the private,
etc.? "Glass" is an old word. Am I wrong if I believe that you are interested in glass, perhaps even like it? Are we concerned with only new
materials that resemble but no longer are glass, etc.? Before letting you
speak about glass, I bring up a text by Benjamin, *Erfahrung und Armut,*
Expérience et pauvreté, that I'm sure you know (it also concerns architecture and was published in 1933, which, in Germany and elsewhere, is
not just any date). From it I cite only the following, which our friends
will certainly want to hear you comment on:

> But Scheerbart—to return to him—most values that his people—and ac-
> cording to their model, his fellow citizens—live in apartments corre-
> sponding to their rank: in houses of moving and slippery glass, like those
> that Loos and Le Corbusier have since erected. Not for nothing is glass
> such a hard, smooth material to which nothing can attach itself. And a
> cold, concise material as well. Things made of glass have no aura (*Die
> Dinge aus Glas haben keine "Aura"*). In general, glass is the enemy of se-
> crecy. It is also the enemy of possession. The great poet André Gide once
> said: "Each thing I wish to possess becomes opaque for me." (Here we
> return to the question of desire and glass, of the desire of glass: I have
> elsewhere tried to follow this experience of desire as the experience of
> glass in Blanchot, especially in *La Folie du jour* and in *L'Arrêt de mort.*) Do
> people like Scheerbart dream of glass masonry (*Glasbauten*) because they
> have recognized a new poverty (*Bekenner einer neuen Armut*)? But perhaps
> a comparison here will reveal more than the theory. Upon entering a
> room of the 1980s, despite "the comfortable intimacy" (*Gemütlichkeit*) that
> may reign there, the strongest impression will be: "you have nothing to
> look for here." You have nothing to look for here because there is not
> any ground here on which the inhabitant would not already have left his
> trace: knickknacks on shelves, doilies on the armchair, sheer curtains at
> the windows, or the fire screen in front of the fireplace. A beautiful word

from Brecht helps us go far, farther: "Erase your traces!" (*Verwisch die Spuren!*) says the refrain of the first poem in "Anthologie pour les habitants des villes" ("Anthology for the Residents of Cities"). . . . Scheerbart and his glass and the Bauhaus and its steel have opened the way: they have created spaces in which it is difficult to leave traces. After all that has been said, declares Scheerbart twenty years later, we can easily speak of a "glass culture" (*Glaskultur*). The new environment of glass will completely change man. We can only hope now that the new glass culture will not encounter too many opponents.

What do you think, Peter, of these propositions? Would you be an "opponent," a supporter? Or, as I suppose, but perhaps wrongly, neither one nor the other? In any case, could you say something about it, and why?

Benjamin's text speaks, as you have seen, of "new poverty" (a homonym, if not a synonym, for a new expression, a new French concept, to designate a wandering group of poor people, indeed of the "homeless," that is irreducible to categorizations, classifications, and former localizations of marginality or of the social ladder: low income, the proletariat as a class, the unemployed, etc.). And the new poverty—the one about which Benjamin speaks, not the other—is "our" future, already even our present. From this fascinating text, which is politically ambiguous and must not be too fragmented, I extract the following:

> Scheerbart is interested in knowing what our telescopes, airplanes, and rockets do to men of the past in transforming them into completely new creatures, worthy of notice and affection. Furthermore, these creatures already speak in an entirely new language. And what is decisive (*das Entscheidende*) in this language is the tendency toward the Arbitrary Construct (*zum willkürlichen Konstruktiven*), a tendency that particularly resists the organic. It is by virtue of this tendency that the language of these men, or rather of Scheerbart's people, cannot be confused with any other; because these people challenge this principle of humanism, the resemblance to human beings. Even in their proper names. . . . Poverty of experience (*Erfahrungsarmut*): one must not take this to mean that these men desire a New Experience. No, they want to liberate themselves from experience, they want a world in which they can get their poverty recognized—outer and eventually also inner poverty—in such a pure and distinct way that something decent may come of it. And they are not always ignorant and inexperienced. One can say the opposite: they have "gobbled up" (*gefressen*) all that, "culture" and "man," to the point of satiety and fatigue. . . . We have gotten poor. We have abandoned one part after another of the heritage of humanity, and often we have had to pawn it for a hundredth of its value, in order to receive as an advance the small change of the "Present" (*des "Aktuellen"*). In the door stands economic crisis, and behind it the shadow of the war to come. Today, to attach oneself to something has become the business of the small number of the powerful, and God knows if they aren't more human than the majority, who for the most part are more barbarous, but not in the good

sense (*nicht auf die gute Art*). The others, however, must settle in once again, and with Little. They relate it to the men who created the Fundamentally New (*das von Grund auf Neue zu ihrer Sache gemacht*), and who founded it upon understanding and self-denial. In its buildings (*Bauten*), paintings, and histories, humanity prepares to outlive (*überleben*) culture, if necessary. And most important, humanity does this while laughing. Perhaps this laughter here and there sounds barbarous. Good (*Gut*). Therefore, let he who is an individual (*der Einzelne*) occasionally give a little humanity to the mass, which one day will return it to him with interest.

What do you think of this text, Peter, in particular of a poverty that should not *cause* another one to be forgotten? What do you think of these two barbarities that must not be confused and, as much as possible—is it possible?—must not be allowed to contaminate each other? What do you think of what Benjamin then called the "present" and of his "small change"? What, for you, would be "good" barbarity in architecture and elsewhere? And the "present" [*l' "actuel"*]? I know that there is a present-dayness [*actualité*] you do not want, but what (today? tomorrow?) best breaks with it? And you who want to remove architecture from the measure, even from the scale, of man, how do you understand this (in Benjamin's sense) "destructive" discourse in the mouth of "these people [who] challenge this principle of humanism, the resemblance to human beings. Even in their proper names"?

Therefore, Peter, I would like—and your listeners in Irvine, I imagine, will perhaps like—to hear you speak about the relations between architecture today and poverty, all kinds of poverty, the one Benjamin speaks of and the other; about the relations between architecture and capital (the equivalent today of the "economic crisis" that in 1930 stood "*in der Tür,*" in the doorway); about the relations between architecture and war (the equivalent today of the "shadow" and of what "comes" with it); about the scandals surrounding public housing, and "housing" in general (not without recalling what we have both said, and which was a little too complicated for a letter, about the habitable and the inhabitable in architecture); and the "homeless," "homelessness" today in the United States and elsewhere.

This letter is already too long. I shall speed up a little to schematically link other questions or requests to the preceding ones. I cited this text by Benjamin, among other reasons, to lead you to ruin and destruction. As you know, what he says about "aura" destroyed by glass (and by technology in general) is articulated in a difficult discourse on "destruction." In the *Trauerspiel* (and certainly elsewhere, but I don't remember where), Benjamin talks about the ruin, especially about the "baroque cult of the ruin," "the noblest matter of baroque creation." In the photocopied pages I am sending you, Benjamin declares that for the baroque architects, "the ancient inheritance is comparable, in each of its components, to the elements from which they concoct the new totality. No, they build it. Because the achieved vision of this new thing is just that: the ruin . . . the work of art confirming itself as ruin. In the allegoric edifice of the *Trauerspiel*, these ruined forms of the salvaged work of art have always already come unfastened." I won't say anything about Benjamin's concept of the ruin, which is also the concept of a certain mourning in affirmation, indeed the salvation of the work of art, but I will use this as a pretext to ask you the following: (1) Is there a relationship between your writing of palimpsest, your architectural experience of memory (for example, in *Choral Work*, but also everywhere else) and "something" like the ruin, which is no longer a thing? In what respect would you say, and would you say, that your calculation of memory is not baroque in this Benjaminian sense, despite some appearances? (2) If all architecture is finite, if it therefore carries within itself the traces of its future destruction, the future perfect of its ruin, according to modes that are original each time, if it is haunted, indeed signed, by the spectral silhouette of this ruin, at work even in the pedestal of its stone, in its metal or glass, what would bring the architecture of "this time" (just yesterday, today, tomorrow; use whatever words you want, "modern," "postmodern," "post-postmodern," or "amodern," etc.) back to the ruin, to the experience of "its own" ruin? In the past, great architectural inventions constituted their essential destructibility, even their fragility, as a resistance to destruction or as a monumentalization of the ruin itself (the baroque according to Benjamin, is it not?). Is a new figure of the ruin to come up already sketching itself in the design of the architecture that we would like to recognize as the architecture of our present, of our future, if one can still say that, in the design of your architecture, in the future perfect of its memory, so that it already draws and calculates itself, so that it already leaves its future trace in your projects? Taking into account what we were saying previously about Man (and God), will we still be able to speak of "the memory of man," as we say in French, for this architecture? In relation to the ruin, to fragility, to destructibility, in other words to the future, could you come back to what we were discussing the other morning in New York with regard to excess and "weakness"? Every time excess presents itself (but it never presents itself except above and beyond ontological oppositions), I for my part hesitate to use words of force or of weakness. But it is certainly inevitable as soon as there is announcement. This is merely a pretext so that *you* can talk about it, you and Hillis.

Finally, from fragility I turn to ashes, for me the other name, or the surname, for the (nonessential) essence of the step, of the trace, of writing, the place without place of deconstruction. There where deconstruction inscribes itself. (In "Feu la cendre"—excuse my reference to something dating from nearly twenty years ago—this thinking of ashes, like the trace itself, was principally destined, or rather delivered, to the "burn-everything" and to the "holocaust.") To return to our problem and to hear again the fragile words "fragility," "ashes," "absence," "invisibility," and "Jewish" or non-Jewish architectural space, what do you think of the Berlin Museum Competition, which we also discussed the other morning in New York? In particular, what do you think of the words of Libeskind, the "winner" of the "competition," in a recently published interview in the journal of the Columbia architecture school? Here, I must content myself with quoting:

> And in turn, the void materializes itself in the space outside as something that has been ruined, or rather as the solid remainder of an independent structure, which is a voided void. Then there is a fragmentation and a splintering, marking the lack of coherence of the museum as a whole, showing that it has come undone, in order to become accessible, functionally and intellectually. . . . It's conceived as a museum for all Berliners, for all citizens. Not only those of the present, but those of the future and the past who must find their heritage and hope in this particular form, which is to transcend passive involvement and become participation. With its special emphasis on housing the Jewish Museum, it is an attempt to give a voice to a common fate—to the contradictions of the ordered and disordered, the chosen and the not chosen, the vocal and the silent. In that sense, the particular urban condition of Lindenstrasse, of this area of the city, becomes the spiritual site, the nexus, where Berlin's precarious destiny is mirrored. It is fractured and displaced, but also transformed and transgressed. The past fatality of the German Jewish cultural relation to Berlin is enacted now in the realm of the invisible. It is this invisibility which I have tried to bring to visibility. So the new extension is conceived as an emblem, where the invisible, the void, makes itself apparent as such. . . . It's not a collage or a collision or a dialectic simply, but a new type of organization which is really organized around a void, around what is not visible. And what is not visible is the collection of this Jewish Museum, which is reducible to archival material, since the physicality of it has disappeared. The problem of the Jewish Museum is taken as the problem of Jewish culture itself—let's put it this way, as the problem of an avant-garde of humanity, an avant-garde that has been incinerated in its own history, in the Holocaust. In this sense, I believe this scheme joins architecture to questions that are now relevant to all humanity. What I've tried to say is that the Jewish history of Berlin is not separable from the history of modernity, from the destiny of this incineration of history; they are bound together. But bound not through any obvious forms, but rather through a negativity; through an absence of meaning and an absence of artifacts. Absence, therefore, serves as a way of binding in depth, and in a totally different manner, the shared hopes of people. It is a conception that is absolutely opposed to reducing the museum to a detached memorial.

Once again void, absence, negativity in Libeskind, as in you. I leave you alone to deal with these words, dear Peter, dear Hillis, I will tell you what I think some other time, but I suggested what I think at the beginning. Once again I have said too much and naturally I take advantage of my absence. I confess it; it is a sign of love. Forgive me, you and Hillis, and ask our friends, your listeners, to forgive me for not being there to speak with them and listen to you.

P.S. 1. This tape was recorded and this transcription finished when I read at the end of an interview (in a special edition of the Spanish magazine *Arquitectura* [270] devoted to "Deconstruction"—that's the title of the introduction) the following lines from you which were already anticipating my questions:

> I never talk about Deconstruction. Other people use that word because they are not architects. It is very difficult to talk about architecture in terms of Deconstruction, because we are not talking about ruins or fragments. The term is too metaphorical and too literal for architecture. Deconstruction is dealing with architecture as a metaphor, and we are dealing with architecture as a reality. . . . I believe Post-Structuralism is basically what I mean by Post-Modernism. In other words, Post-Modernism is Post-Structuralism in the widest sense of the word.

I certainly believe that I would *not* subscribe to *any* one of these statements, to *any* one of these 7 sentences, neither to 1, nor 2, nor 3, nor 4, nor 5, nor 6, nor 7. But I cannot explain it here, and truly, I never talk much *about* Deconstruction. Not spontaneously. If you wish, you could display 1, 2, 3, 4, 5, 6, 7 before the listeners and try to convince them by refuting the contrary propositions, or you could leave out this p.s.

P.S. 2. I was, of course, forgetting the fundamental question. In other words, the question of foundation, of what basically *[au fond]* you do with the foundation, or with the foundation in your architectural design. Let's talk basically about the Earth itself. I have questioned you directly about God and Man. I was thinking about the Sky and the Earth. What does architecture, and primarily yours, have to see and do with experience, that is to say with trips, outside of Earth? Then, if we don't give up architecture, and I don't think we will, what effects does this possibility have on the "design" itself of terrestrial architecture? Regarding what is now a definite possibility of leaving the terrestrial soil, will we say of the architecture of a rocket and of astronomy in general (already announced by literature, at least, long before becoming "effective") that they dispense with foundations and thus with "standing up", with the "standing up," with the *vertical* stance of man or of the *building* in general? Or will we say that these architectures still calculate foundations, and that calculation remains a terrestrial difference, which I somewhat doubt? What kind of architecture, without holding, without standing upright, vertically, would not fall again into ruin? How do all these possibilities and even questions (those of *holding up, holding together, standing*, or *not*) *record* themselves, if you think that they do? What traces are they already leaving in what you would build right now on earth, in Spain or Japan, in Ohio, in Berlin, in Paris, and tomorrow, I hope, in Irvine?

Lettre à Peter Eisenman

JACQUES DERRIDA

le 12 octobre 1989

MON CHER PETER,

J'envoie simultanément cette lettre, avec la cassette qui l'accompagne, à Hillis, qui devait s'entretenir avec nous au cours de la séance prévue. Comme il devait aussi la "modérer" et l'animer, mais pour d'autres raisons aussi, Hillis est donc avec vous "the first addressee" de ces quelques questions. Il s'y entend mieux que quiconque en labyrinthe, comme chacun sait. Or ce que je vais vous dire résonnera peut-être dans une sorte de labyrinthe. Je confie au "record" de la voix ou de la lettre ce qui ne m'est pas encore visible et ne peut guider mes pas vers une issue, à peine vers une *"issue."* Ce que je vous envoie, je ne suis même pas sûr que cela "tienne-debout," *that it holds up.* Mais, c'est peut-être â dessein—et de cela même que j'entends vous parler. En tout cas, je regrette beaucoup de devoir me priver de cette rencontre avec vous, vous deux, vous tous.

Maintenant, ne vous inquiétez pas, je ne vais pas vous faire une scène. Et je ne vais pas abuser de mon absence, même pas pour vous dire que vous y croyez peut-être trop, à l'*absence.* Cette référence à l'absence est peut-être une des choses (car il y en a d'autres) qui m'ont le plus gêné dans vos discours sur l'architecture et si c'était là ma première question,

29

vous pourriez peut-être profiter de mon absence pour en parler un peu: de l'absence en général, du rôle que ce mot, "absence," aura pu jouer au moins dans ce que vous avez cru pouvoir "dire" sinon "faire" de votre architecture. On pourrait en multiplier les exemples, mais je me limite à ce que vous dites de la "presence of an absence" dans *Moving Arrows Eros and Other Errors*, à propos du château de Roméo, "a palimpsest and a quarry," etc. Ce discours de l'absence ou de "the presence of an absence" me laisse perplexe, non seulement parce qu'il fait l'économie de tant de ruses, de complications, de pièges que le "philosophe," surtout s'il est un peu dialecticien, connaît trop bien et craint de vous y retrouver "caught up in," mais aussi parce qu'il a autorisé beaucoup d'interprétations religieuses, pour ne pas dire d'idéologisations confusément judéo-transcendantales de votre oeuvre. Je vous soupçonne un peu de les avoir aimées et encouragées, ces interprétations, même en le déniant discrètement d'un sourire, ce qui ferait du malentendu un peu plus ou un peu moins qu'un malentendu. Ma question ne porte donc pas seulement sur l'absence ou la présence de l'absence mais sur Dieu. Voilà—si je ne suis pas venu, ce n'est pas seulement parce que je suis fatigué et surmené, *held up in Paris*, mais juste pour avoir la chance de vous poser directement une question sur Dieu, ce que je n'aurais jamais osé faire à Irvine si j'y avais été présent en personne, mais j'aime que cette question vous arrive par cette voix, je veux dire sur cassette. La même question en porte d'autres, toute une assemblée de questions fidèlement associées, par exemple, au risque de vous choquer: qu'il s'agisse de maisons, de musées ou de laboratoires de recherche universitaire, qu'est-ce qui distingue votre espace architectural de celui du temple, voire de la synagogue (j'entends ce mot comme un mot grec au service d'un concept juif)? Où aura été la rupture à cet égard, s'il y en a une, s'il y en eut une, chez vous et chez d'autres architectes de ce temps avec lesquels vous vous sentiriez en bonne compagnie? Je reste très perplexe à ce sujet et si j'avais été là, j'aurais été un interlocuteur difficile. Si vous construisiez un lieu de culte, par exemple boudhiste, ou une cathédrale, une mosquée, une synagogue (hypothèses que vous n'êtes pas obligé d'accepter), quel serait votre souci principal aujourd'hui? Je ferai tout à l'heure allusion au projet de Libeskind à Berlin autour du Jewish Museum. Nous en avions parlé l'autre matin à New York, mais laissons pour l'instant.

Naturellement cette question concerne aussi *votre* interprétation de *chora* dans "notre" "travail," si on peut dire entre guillemets, notre travail "commun." Je ne suis pas sûr que vous ayez dé-théologisé et dé-ontologisé *chora* de façon aussi radicale que je l'aurais souhaité (*chora* n'est ni le vide, comme vous le suggérez parfois, ni l'absence, ni l'invisibilité: ni bien sûr le contraire, d'où, et c'est ce qui m'intéresse, un grand nombre de conséquences). Il est vrai que pour moi, c'était plus facile, d'une certaine manière, je n'avais rien à en "faire," et n'aurais rien pu en faire; c'est-à-dire vis-à-vis de la ville de Paris, pour La Villette, la petite ville; je veux dire (et c'est peut-être, entre nous, toute la différence), mais j'aimerais que vous en disiez quelque chose à nos amis de Irvine, en leur parlant de la différence de nos rapports respectifs au discours d'une part, à l'opération de l'architecture, à sa mise en oeuvre d'autre part. Profitez de mon absence pour parler librement. Enfin, ne dites pas n'importe quoi, car tout étant aujourd'hui "recorded" et la mémoire, la même toujours, n'étant plus du tout la même, je saurais tout ce que vous aurez dit publiquement. J'ai eu le sentiment, et je crois que vous l'avez dit ici ou là, que vous m'avez jugé trop réservé, dans notre "choral work," un peu absent en somme, retranché dans le discours, sans vous obliger à changer, à changer de place, sans vous déranger assez en somme. C'est sans doute vrai, il y aurait beaucoup à dire à ce sujet, qui est compliqué, car c'est celui de la place (*chora*) et du déplacement même. Si j'étais venu, j'aurais peut-être parlé de mon propre déplacement au cours de "choral work" mais ici, c'est vous qui devez parler. Alors dites-moi, si, *après* Choral Work (comme vous le disiez vous-même à Irvine au printemps), votre travail a pris en effet un nouvel élan et s'est engagé dans d'autres voies, que s'est-il passé? Quel est pour vous ce temps? cette histoire? Comment la délimiter ou la rythmer? quand avons-nous commencé de travailler ensemble, si nous l'avons jamais fait, à ce Choral Work qui n'est pas encore construit mais qu'on voit et qu'on lit partout? quand cesserons-nous?

Ceci me conduit directement à la question suivante. Elle concerne aussi une certaine absence. Non pas la mienne aujourd'hui à Irvine où j'aurais tant aimé vous revoir avec d'autres amis, d'autant plus que j'avais été de ceux qui avaient souhaité et préparé cette rencontre (et je vous demande donc de me pardonner et de me faire pardonner par les autres) mais l'absence, comme l'ombre portée de la voix, vous voyez ce que j'entends par là. Quels rapports (nouveaux ou archi-anciens, différents en tout cas) l'architecture, exemplairement la vôtre, entretient-elle, devrait-elle entretenir avec la voix, la portée de voix mais aussi, donc, avec les machines téléphoniques de toute sorte qui structurent et transforment chaque jour notre expérience de l'espace. Question de l'adresse téléphonique quasiment immédiate, bien sûr, quasiment immédiate, je souligne, mais aussi de l'archivation téléphonique, comme c'est le cas ici même, avec l'espacement du temps que cela suppose et structure à la fois. Si on peut imaginer toute une histoire labyrinthique de l'architecture guidée par le fil tressé de cette question, où en serait-on aujourd'hui, et demain, et vous?

Cette question de l'histoire, comme histoire de l'espacement, comme espacement du temps et de la voix, ne se sépare pas de l'histoire de la visibilité (immédiatement médiate), c'est-à-dire de toute l'histoire de l'architecture; je n'oserai pas même l'effleurer tant elle est énorme, mais je l' "addresserai," cette question, comme vous dites en anglais, par économie et par métonymie, sous la forme d'un seul mot, le verre (*Glas, glass*).

Quoi du verre dans votre oeuvre? Qu'est-ce que vous en dites? Qu'est-ce que vous en faites? Comment en parler? en termes d'optique ou en termes tactiles (à propos de tactilité, ce serait bien si, prolongeant ce que nous disions l'autre matin à New York, vous parliez à nos amis des ruses érotiques, des appels de désir, oserai-je dire du sex-appeal des formes architecturales auxquelles vous pensez, vous travaillez, vous vous livrez? Que ses voies soient nouvelles ou non, cette séduction vient-elle en supplément, par-dessus le marché, comme "prime de séduction," justement, ou "prime de plaisir"? Ou bien est-elle essentielle? A moins que la prime ne soit elle-même essentielle? Mais que serait alors la prime elle-même? La récompense? Quel est, pour l'auteur de *Moving Arrows Eros and Other Errors*, le rapport entre la prime et le reste, dans le calcul et dans les négotiations d'architecte? *Could you elaborate on that*, comme me demandent parfois de façon désarmante mes étudiants américains?)? Je reprends donc ma question après cette longue parenthèse autour de votre désir, ma question sur le verre qui n'est peut-être pas si éloignée. En quels termes parler du verre? En termes de technologie et de matériaux? d'économie? d'urbanisme? de rapports sociaux? de transparence et d'immédiateté, d'amour ou de police, à la frontière peut-être effacée entre le public et le privé, etc.? Et puis, "verre" est un vieux mot, et si je crois que vous vous intéressez au verre, que vous l'aimez peut-être, est-ce que je me trompe? S'agit-il seulement de matières nouvelles qui ressemblent au verre mais n'en sont plus, etc.? Avant de vous laisser parler sur le verre, je rappelle un texte de Benjamin, *Erfahrung und Armut, Expérience et pauvreté*, que vous connaissez sûrement (il concerne aussi l'architecture et fut publié en 1933, ce qui n'est pas n'importe quand, en Allemagne et ailleurs). J'y prélève seulement ceci que nos amis aimeront sans doute vous entendre commenter:

> Mais Scheerbart—pour en revenir à lui—attache le plus grand prix à ce que ses gens—et, d'après leur modèle, ses concitoyens—soient logés dans des appartements correspondant à leur rang: dans des maisons de verre mobiles et coulissantes, telles que Loos et Le Corbusier en ont érigées depuis. Le verre n'est pas pour rien un matériau si dur et si lisse, sur lequel rien ne s'accroche. Un matériau froid et sobre, aussi. Les choses en verre n'ont pas d' "aura" (*Die Dinge aus Glas haben keine "Aura"*). Le verre est en général l'ennemi du secret. Il est aussi l'ennemi de la possession. Le grand poète André Gide a dit un jour: "Chaque chose que je veux posséder me devient opaque." (Nous revenons ainsi à la question du désir et du verre, du désir de verre; j'avais essayé ailleurs de suivre cette expérience du désir comme expérience du verre chez Blanchot, notamment dans *La Folie du jour* et dans *L'Arrêt de mort*.) Les gens tels que Scheerbart rêvent-ils de bâtisses en verre (*Glasbauten*) pour avoir reconnu une nouvelle pauvreté (*Bekenner einer neuen Armut*)? Mais peut-être une comparaison ici en dira plus que la théorie. Qu'on entre dans la chambre des années 80, et, malgré, "l'intimité confortable" (*Gemütlichkeit*) qui y règne peut-être, l'impression la plus forte sera: "tu n'as rien à chercher ici." Tu n'as rien à chercher ici, car il n'est pas d'emplacement, ici, où l'habitant

n'aurait déjà laissé sa trace: sur les corniches par des bibelots, sur le fauteuil rembourré par des napperons, aux fenêtres par des rideaux de transparents, ou encore devant la cheminée par l'écran du poêle. Un beau mot de Brecht aide ici à aller loin, plus loin: "Efface tes traces!" (*Verwisch die Spuren!*), dit le refrain du premier poème de l' "Anthologie pour les habitants des villes." [. . .] Scheerbart et son verre, et le Bauhaus et son acier ont ouvert la voie: ils ont créé des espaces dans lesquels il est difficile de laisser des traces. Après tout ce qui a été dit, déclare Scheerbart il y a de cela vingt ans, nous pouvons bien parler d'une "culture du verre" (*Glaskultur*). Le nouveau milieu de verre changera l'homme complètement. Et il ne reste plus maintenant qu'à souhaiter que la nouvelle culture du verre ne rencontrera pas trop d'opposants.

Que pensez-vous, Peter, de ces propositions? Seriez-vous un "opposant," un partisan? Ou, comme je le suppose, mais peut-être à tort, ni l'un ni l'autre? dans tous les cas, pourriez-vous dire en quoi et pourquoi?

Ce texte de Benjamin parle littéralement, vous l'avez vu, de "nouvelle pauvreté" (homonyme, sinon synonyme d'une nouvelle expression, d'un nouveau concept français, pour désigner un ensemble errant de pauvres, voire de "homeless," irréductible aux catégorisations, aux classifications et aux localisations anciennes de la marginalité ou de l'échelle sociale: les bas revenus, le prolétariat comme classe, les chômeurs, etc.). Et la nouvelle pauvreté, celle dont parle Benjamin, non l'autre, serait "notre" avenir, déjà notre présent. De ce texte fascinant, politiquement si ambigu, et qu'il ne faudrait pas trop fragmenter, j'extrais encore ceci:

> Scheerbart s'est intéressé à la question de savoir ce que nos télescopes, nos avions et nos fusées font des hommes d'autrefois en les transformant en créatures entièrement nouvelles, dignes d'être remarquées et aimées. D'ailleurs, également, ces créatures parlent déjà dans une langue entièrement nouvelle. Et ce qui dans cette languAge est Décisif (*das Entscheidende*), c'est la tendance a l'Arbitraire Constructif (*zum willkürlichen Konstruktiven*); tendance qui s'oppose nommément à l'organique. C'est par cette tendance que la langue des hommes ou plûtot des gens de Scheerbart ne peut être confondue avec aucune autre; car ces gens récusent la ressemblance aux humains—ce principe de l'humanisme. Jusque dans leurs noms propres. . . . [. . .] Pauvreté d'expérience (*Erfahrungsarmut*): on ne doit pas comprendre par là que les hommes aient un désir d'Expérience Nouvelle. Non, ils désirent se libérer des expériences, ils désirent un monde dans lequel ils puissent faire reconnaître leur pauvreté—l'extérieure et finalement aussi l'intérieure—de façon si pure et distincte qu'il en sorte quelque chose de convenable. Et ils ne sont pas toujours ignorants et inexpérimentés. On peut dire le contraire: ils ont "bouffé" (*gefressen*) tout cela, la "culture" et l' "homme," jusqu'à en être rassasiés et fatigués. [. . .] Pauvres nous sommes devenus. De l'héritage de l'humanité nous avons abandonné une part après l'autre, et nous avons dû souvent la gager au Mont-au-Piété au centième de sa valeur, pour recevoir comme avance la petite monnaie de l' "Actuel" (*des "Aktuellen"*). Dans l'embrasure de la porte

se tient la crise économique, derrière elle, une ombre, la guerre qui vient. S'accrocher est aujourd'hui devenu l'affaire du petit nombre des puissants, et Dieu sait s'ils ne sont pas plus humains que le grand nombre; en majorité plus barbares, mais pas de la bonne manière (*nicht auf die gute Arte*). Les autres, cependant, doivent emménager une nouvelle fois et avec Peu. Ils s'en rapportent aux hommes qui ont fait du Fondamentalement Nouveau (*das von Grund auf Neue zu ihrer Sache gemacht*), et qui l'ont fondé sur la compréhension et le renoncement. Dans leur bâtiments (*Bauten*), leurs tableaux et leurs histoires, l'humanité se prépare à survivre (*überleben*), s'il le faut, à la culture. Et le principal, c'est qu'elle le fait en riant. Peut-être ce rire ici et là sonne-t-il barbare. Bon (*Gut*). Puisse donc celui qui est un seul (*der Einzelne*) donner parfois un peu d'humanité à cete masse qui, un jour, le lui rendra avec usure. (Traduction française inédite de P. Beck et B. Stiegler)

Que pensez-vous de ce texte, Peter, en particulier d'une pauvreté qui ne *devrait* pas en faire oublier une autre? des deux barbaries, qu'il ne faut pas confondre, et autant que possible—est-ce possible?—ne pas laisser trop se contaminer entre elles? Que pensez-vous de ce que Benjamin appelait alors l'actuel et de sa "monnaie"? Que serait la "bonne" barbarie, pour vous, en architecture et ailleurs? Et l'"actuel"? Je sais qu'il y a une actualité dont vous ne voudriez pas, mais qu'est-ce qui rompt le mieux (aujourd'hui? demain?) avec cette actualité? Et vous qui voulez soustraire l'architecture à la mesure de l'homme, à son échelle même, comment entendez-vous ce discours "destructeur," au sens de Benjamin, dans la bouche de "ces gens [qui] récusent la ressemblance aux humains—ce principe de l'humanisme. Jusque dans leurs noms propres . . ."?

J'aimerais donc, Peter, et vos auditeurs à Irvine, je le suppose, aimeront peut-être que vous parliez alors au passage des rapports entre l'architecture, aujourd'hui, et la pauvreté, toutes les pauvretés, celle dont parle Benjamin et l'autre, entre l'architecture et le capital (l'équivalent aujourd'hui de la "crise économique" qui se tenait en 1930 *"in der Tür,"* dans l'embrasure de la porte) entre l'architecture et la guerre, l'équivalent aujourd'hui de l'"ombre" et de ce qui "vient" en elle), les scandales des logements sociaux, le "housing" en général (non sans rappeler ce que nous avons dit, l'un et l'autre, et qui fut un peu trop compliqué pour une lettre, de l'habitable et de l'inhabitable en architecture), et les "homeless," la "homelessness," aujourd'hui, aux Etats-Unis et ailleurs.

Cette lettre est déjà trop longue. J'accélère un peu pour enchaîner schématiquement d'autres questions ou demandes à ce qui précède. J'ai cité ce texte de Benjamin, entre autres raisons, pour vous conduire à la ruine et à la destruction. Comme vous savez, ce qu'il dit de l'"aura" détruite par le verre (et par la technique en général) s'articule dans un discours difficile sur la "destruction." D'autre part, dans le *Trauerspiel* (et sans doute ailleurs, mais je ne me rapelle plus), Benjamin parle de la ruine, notamment du "culture baroque de la ruine," "la matière la plus noble de la création baroque." Il déclare que pour les baroques, "l'héritage antique est comparable, dans chacune de ses parties, aux éléments à partir desquels ils concoctent la totalité nouvelle. Non: ils la construisent. Car la vision achevée de cette chose nouvelle, c'était cela: la ruine. [...] L'oeuvre s'affirme comme ruine. Dans l'édifice allégorique *Trauerspiel,* ces formes ruinées de l'oeuvre d'art sauvée se détachent clairement depuis toujours." Je me dirai rien de ce concept benjaminien de la ruine, qui est aussi le concept d'un certain deuil dans l'affirmation, voire le salut de l'oeuvre, mais j'en prendrai prétexte pour vous demander ceci: 1. Y a-t-il un rapport entre votre écriture du palimpseste, votre expérience architecturale de la mémoire (par example dans *Choral Work,* mais aussi partout ailleurs) et "quelque chose" comme la ruine qui n'est plus une chose? En quoi diriez-vous, et le diriez-vous, que votre calcul de la mémoire n'est pas baroque en ce sens benjaminien, malgré quelques apparences? 2. Si toute architecture est finie, si donc elle porte en elle, selon des modes chaque fois originaux, les traces de sa destruction à venir, le futur antérieur de sa ruine, si elle est hantée, voire signée par la silhouette spectrale de cette ruine, à l'oeuvre dans le socle même de sa pierre, dans son métal ou son verre, qu'est-ce qui rapporterait encore l'architecture de "ce temps" (juste hier, aujourd'hui, demain; servez-vous des mots que vous voudrez, moderne, post-moderne, post-post-moderne ou a-moderne, etc.) à la ruine, à l'expérience de "sa propre" ruine? Dans le passé, les grandes inventions architecturales organisaient leur destructibilité essentielle, leur fragilité même, comme une résistance à la destruction ou comme une monumentalisation de la ruine même (le baroque, n'est-ce pas, selon Benjamin). Une nouvelle figure de la ruine à venir se dessine-t-elle déjà dans le dessein de l'architecture que nous voudrions reconnaître comme celle de notre présent, de notre avenir, si on peut encore dire cela, dans le dessein de votre architecture, dans le futur antérieur de sa mémoire tel qu'il se dessine ou se calcule déjà, tel qu'il laisse déjà sa trace d'avenir dans vos projets? Compte tenu de ce que nous disions plus haut de l'Homme (et de Dieu), pourra-t-on parler encore pour cette architecture de "mémoire d'homme," comme on dit en français? A propos de la ruine, de la fragilité, de la destructibilité, donc de l'avenir, pourriez-vous revenir sur ce que nous disions l'autre matin à New York de l'excès et de la "faiblesse" (weakness")? Chaque fois que l'excès s'annonce (mais il ne se présente jamais qu'au-delà des oppositions ontologiques), j'hésite pour ma part à me servir des mots de force ou de faiblesse. Mais c'est sans doute inévitable dès lors qu'il y a de l'annonce. Ceci n'est qu'un prétexte pour que *vous* parliez, Hillis et vous.

Enfin de la fragilité, je passe à la cendre, l'autre nom ou le surnom pour moi de l'essence (non-essentielle) du pas, de la trace ou de l'écriture, le lieu sans lieu de la déconstruction. Là où elle s'écrit (Dans "Feu la cendre," pardonnez-moi cette référence à ce qui remonte à près de 20 ans, cette pensée de la cendre, comme la trace même, était nommément destinée ou plutôt livrée au "brûle-tout" et à l' "holocauste"). Pour revenir sur nos pas, et réentendre les mots fragiles de "fragilité," de "cendre," d' "absence," d' "invisibilité," d'espace—"juif" ou pas—de l'architecture, que pensez vous de "The Berlin Museum Competition" dont nous avions aussi parlé l'autre matin à New York? Que pensez-vous en particulier de ces mots de Libeskind, le "winner" de la "competition," comme dit le journal de l'école d'architecture de Columbia qui vient de publier une interview de lui? Je dois me contenter ici de citer:

> And in turn, the void materializes itself in the space outside as something that has been ruined, or rather as the solid remainder of an independent structure, which is a voided void. Then there is a fragmentation and a splintering, marking the lack of coherence of the museum as a whole, showing that it has come undone, in order to become accessible, functionally and intellectually. . . . It's conceived as a museum for all Berliners, for all citizens. Not only those of the present, but those of the future and the past who must find their heritage and hope in this particular form, which is to transcend passive involvement and become participation. With its special emphasis on housing the Jewish Museum, it is an attempt to give a voice to a common fate—to the contradictions of the ordered and disordered, the chosen and the not chosen, the vocal and the silent. In that sense, the particular urban condition of Lindenstrasse, of this area of the city, becomes the spiritual site, the nexus, where Berlin's precarious destiny is mirrored. It is fractured and displaced, but also transformed and transgressed. The past fatality of the German Jewish cultural relation to Berlin is enacted now in the realm of the invisible. It is this invisibility which I have tried to bring to visibility. So the new extension is conceived as an emblem, where the invisible, the void, makes itself apparent as such. . . . It's not a collage or a collision or a dialectic simply, but a new type of organization which is really organized around a void, around what is not visible. And what is not visible is the collection of this Jewish Museum, which is reducible to archival material, since the physicality of it has disappeared. The problem of the Jewish Museum is taken as the problem of Jewish culture itself—let's put it this way, as the problem of an avant-garde of humanity, an avant-garde that has been incinerated in its own history, in the Holocaust. In this sense, I believe this scheme joins architecture to questions that are now relevant to all humanity. What I've tried to say is that the Jewish history of Berlin is not separable from the history of modernity, from the destiny of this incineration of history; they are bound together. But bound not through any obvious forms, but rather through a negativity; through an absence of meaning and an absence of artifacts. Absence, therefore, serves as a way of binding in depth, and in a totally different manner, the shared hopes of people. It is a conception that is absolutely opposed to reducing the museum to a detached memorial.

Encore le vide, l'absence, la négativité, chez Libeskind comme chez vous. Je vous laisse vous débrouiller tout seul avec ces mots, cher Peter, cher Hillis, je vous dirai ce que j'en pense une autre fois, mais je l'ai suggéré en commençant. J'ai encore trop parlé, et naturellement, j'abuse de mon absence. Je l'avoue, en signe d'amour. Pardonnez-moi,

Hillis et vous, et demandez à nos amis, à vos auditeurs, de me pardonner de ne pas être là pour parler avec eux et pour vous écouter.

P.S. 1. Cette cassette était enregistrée et cette transcription achevée quand j'ai lu à la fin d'une interview (dans le numéro spécial de la revue espagnole *Arquitectura* [270] consacré à "Deconstrucción"—c'est le titre de l'Introduction) ces lignes de vous qui allaient déjà à la rencontre de mes questions:

> I never talk about Deconstruction. Other people use that word because they are not architects. It is very difficult to talk about architecture in terms of Deconstruction, because we are not talking about ruins or fragments. The term is too metaphorical and too literal for architecture. Deconstruction is dealing with architecture as a metaphor, and we are dealing with architecture as a reality. . . . I believe Post-Structuralism is basically what I mean by Post-Modernism. In other words, Post-Modernism is Post-Structuralism in the widest sense of the word.

Je crois bien que je *ne* souscrirais à *aucun* de ces statements, à *aucune* de ces 7 phrases, ni à 1, ni à 2, ni à 3, ni à 4, ni à 5, ni à 6, ni à 7. Mais je ne peux pas l'expliquer ici, et moi, vraiment, I never talk much *about* Deconstruction. Pas spontanément. Si vous le souhaitiez, vous pourriez, démontrer 1, 2, 3, 4, 5, 6, 7 devant les auditeurs, essayer de les convaincre en réfutant les propositions contraires—ou laisser tomber ce post-scriptum.

P.S. 2. J'oubliais la question fondamentale, bien sûr. Autrement dit celle du fondement, de ce que vous faites au fond du fondement ou de la fondation dans votre dessein architectural. Parlons au fond de la Terre même. Je vous ai interrogé sans détour sur Dieu et sur l'Homme. Je pensais au Ciel et à la Terre. Qu'est-ce que l'architecture, et d'abord la vôtre, aurait à voir et à faire avec l'expérience, c'est-à-dire avec le voyage frayant sa voie hors de la Terre? Si on ne renonce pas alors à l'architecture, et je crois qu'on n'y renonce pas, quels sont les effets, dans le "design" même de l'architecture terrestre, aujourd'hui, de cette possibilité? De cette possibilité désormais assurée de quitter le sol terrestre: Dira-t-on de l'architecture d'un fusée et de l'astronautique en général (annoncé déjà par la littérature, au moins, bien avant de devenir "effective") qu'elles se passent de fondations et donc de "tenir-debout," du "tenir-debout," du *"standing-up,"* de la station *verticale* de l'homme ou du *building* en général? ou bien qu'elles les calculent encore et que le calcul reste une différance terrestre—ce dont je doute un peu? Que serait une architecture qui, sans tenir et sans tenir debout, à la verticale, ne tombe pas encore en ruine? Comment toutes ces possibilités et même ces questions (celles du *holding up, holding together, standing*—or not) s'*enregistrent*-elles, si vous pensez qu'elles le font? quelles traces laissent-elle déjà dans ce que vous construiriez en ce moment sur terre, en Espagne ou au Japon, en Ohio, à Berlin, à Paris, et demain, je l'espère, à Irvine?

Post/El Cards:
A Reply to Jacques Derrida

PETER EISENMAN

Dear Jacques,

After many months I find the time and the calm distance to reply to your extraordinary letter. I was pleased that you would take the time to write a letter of such energy and length, but also disturbed by what I perceived as an implied criticism in your words. At the symposium, I was also quite literally left speechless by your questions, questions that I could not answer personally, questions that, indeed, must be directed to architecture for a reply.

Why was I so stunned, so taken aback? Perhaps on first thought because I felt in your criticism a rejection of my work. However, after many rereadings, I no longer feel that same rush of defensiveness but rather a certain exhilaration, a certain sense of an *other* freedom. Why? Because in a way you are right. Perhaps what I do in architecture, in its aspirations and in its fabric, is not what could properly be called deconstruction. But things are not quite so simple: if my work is not something, then it raises questions as to what it is not! In attempting to interrogate what it is not, I will not give an answer to all your questions. Indeed, I do not think that the spirit of your letter was one of inquisition. Rather, your questions seem to outline a provocative framework for thinking about architecture. So I will attempt to follow suit, to elaborate through questions yet another framework, or perhaps a post/work, for architecture.

A question, in one sense, is a frame for an answer, a frame for a discourse that may not be the discourse of the reply. Thus I will use your three numbered questions (only two of which are actually numbered, question 3 beginning with the word "finally") as posts to support me (or perhaps as the cards I might play). Indeed, knowing your fondness for precision and numbers, should I inquire further as to what happened to the missing 3, which is, after all, a reflection of the letter *E!?*

How, for example, does one respond to such questions as "Do you believe in God?" or "What do you think of a culture of glass?" or "What about the homeless?" without sounding either evasive or irrelevant? How does one assert that certain urgent problems such as homelessness or poverty are no more questions of architecture than they are of poetry or philosophy, without sounding callous? These are indeed human problems, but poetry and philosophy are not the domains in which they will be solved. In that sense, such issues are no more relevant than my inquiring about your own domestic, suburban home in relationship to your work. Yet if I fail to answer, others will ask why. No answer will be interpreted as an answer: as a refusal to answer or an inability to answer or a lack of concern to answer, but never the real answer. The real answer: that to answer is impossible in the medium either of letter or of glass.

Your questions probably require a volume, several volumes, inscribed for you. Perhaps with that you, too, would be led to "ruin and destruction." But if I do not answer some of your questions, it is not through lack of time, interest, or compassion, but rather because the questions, perhaps, cannot be answered in architecture.

I publish this letter with yours because I think that every architect should witness philosophy against the wall, all architects should have to answer for themselves some of your questions. And possibly some day you, too, will problematize architecture in your discourse and thus be forced to answer these same questions. I wonder in passing if the fact of your questions points to problems that architecture poses for something that is now named deconstruction and for the "you" that may now have become the aura of Jacques Derrida. Therefore, my response may be less to answer the specific questions, frames, and frame-ups that you have proposed than to place my cards on the table, cards that, perhaps, cause you some fraction of dis/ease.

Jacques, you ask me about the *supplement* and the *essential* in my work. You crystallize these questions in the term/word/material *glas/s.* You glaze over the fact that your conceptual play with the multifaceted term *glas* is not simply translatable into architectural glass. One understands that the assumptions of the identity of the material glass and your ideas of *glas,* in their superficial resemblance of letters, is precisely the concern of literary deconstruction; but this becomes a problem when one turns to the event of building. This difference is important. For though one can conceptualize in the building material glass, it is not necessarily only as you suggest—as an absence of secrecy, as a clarity. While glass is a literal presence in architecture, it also indexes an absence, a void in a solid wall. Thus glass in architecture is traditionally said to be both absence and presence.

Yes, I am preoccupied by absence, but not in terms of this simple presence/absence dialectic, as you might think. For me as an architect each concept, as well as each object, has all that is *not* inscribed within it as traces. I am preoccupied with absence, not voids or glass, because architecture, unlike language, is dominated by presence, by the real existence of the signified. Architecture requires one to detach the signified not only from its signifier but also from its condition as presence. For example, a hole in a plane, or a vertical element, must be detached not only from its signifier—a window or a column—but also from its condition of presence—without at the same time causing the room to be dark, or the building to fall down. This is not the case in language, where you and I can play with *glas* and *post, gaze* and *glaze,* precisely because of the traditional dialectic of presence and absence.

It is improbable to effect in architecture what you do in language. Opacity is the possibility of the poetic in language. It screens the distance between sign and signifier. Opacity and density are possible in glass, even in clear glass, which, in your quotation, is "the enemy of secrecy." The textuality of glass in architecture is different from the textuality of *glas,* the letters *g, l, a, s.* Modes of translation from one language to another, from one syntax to another, can do things with the word *glass* that architecture cannot. For that matter, the hinge between Derridean thought and architecture is neither in glass nor in ash (gash or ass may be better). It would be naive to think so, particularly in the face of your work. It is no longer possible to simply accept naïveté in your thought about architecture, or in thought in general about architecture. One may have started there. Yet that *there,* which is not the *there* of my architecture, is difficult because it is dominated by what is already there in architecture: another tradition of sign and signified. Your idea of glass is eminently transparent, whereas there is no transparency in your *glas,* perhaps only *verre* and no truth *(-)itas.* Wordplay that produces both opacity and transparency in language has no easy equivalent in architecture. The closest, perhaps is the classical ideal of virtual space, or the Gestalt of figure/ground. Even so, neither of these concepts moves architecture from its belief in the theory of origins to something *other.* Only when the thought-to-be-essential relationship of architecture to function is undermined—that is, when the traditional dialectical, hierarchical, and supplemental relationship of form to function is displaced—can the condition of presence, which problematizes any possible displacement of architecture, be addressed. It is not that there is no possibility of deconstruction in architecture, but it cannot simply take issue with what you have called the metaphysics of presence. In my view, your deconstruction of the presence/absence dialectic is inadequate for architecture precisely because architecture is not a two-term but a three-term system. In architecture, there is another condition, which I call *presentness*—that is, neither absence nor presence, form nor function, but rather an excessive condition between sign and being, As long as there is a strong bond between form and function, sign and being, the excess that contains the possibility of presentness will be repressed. The need to overcome presence, the need to supplement an architecture that will always be and look like architecture, the need to break apart the strong bond between form and function, is what my architecture addresses. In its displacement of the traditional role of function, it does not deny that architecture must function, but rather suggests that architecture may also function without necessarily symbolizing that function.

All these issues pale by comparison to differences on the question of aura. You want no aura, or the deconstruction of aura, and I want this aura that is the aura of the third—this excess that is presentness. My architecture asks, Can there be an *other* in the condition of aura in architecture, an aura that both is secret and contains its own secret, the mark of its absent openness? This may involve the difference between the thing as word and the thing as object, between language and architecture. Unlike language, which is understandable through the gaze alone, in architecture there is no such thing as the sign of a column or a window without the actual presence of a column or a window. Both the gaze and the body are implicated by the interiority of architecture. This interiority, this necessity to enclose, is not found in language or even in painting or sculpture. Thus you may be right that architecture strives for an aura, one having nothing to do with the text, or good or bad, or truth or God, but nevertheless with something that needs to be explained.

Presentness is the possibility of another aura in architecture, one not in the sign or in being, but a third condition of betweenness. Neither nostalgic for meaning or presence nor dependent on them, this third, nondialectical condition of space exists only in an excess that is more, or less, than the traditional, hierarchical, Vitruvian preconditions of form: structure, function, and beauty. This excess is not based on the tradition of plenitude, but rather is the condition or possibility of presentness. This condition of aura is perhaps something that also remains unproblematized in your work, despite your protestations to the contrary. I believe that by virtue of architecture's unique relationship to presence, to what I call presentness, it will always be a domain of aura. After all, aura is presence of absence, the possibility of a presentness of something else.

I say this because when I read your work on Valerio Adami, I am fascinated by your discourse, yet when I look at the painting, I find it lacking: it lacks the aura possible in marking a surface with lines, paint, color, texture, and so on. I feel the same way about psychoanalysts who put symbolic and ritualistic drawings and paintings in frames on the walls of their offices and think of them (because they are framed) as art. While these works may have psychological content and intent, they are, for me, illustrated psychology, not art. They are not analytic or critical in the terms of their own medium, either painting or drawing. No matter how important your thoughts on Adami are, he remains unimportant for me as an artist when compared with, say, Jasper Johns, because of this very lack of aura. Now you probably believe that this painterly aura I speak of is one of secrecy and distance, a traditional aura of an original work ripe for deconstruction. But I am not talking about this kind of Benjaminian aura—the aura of metaphysical fullness—but rather of an *other* aura evolving from the remainder of the here and now after its deconstruction: presentness, not the presence of the work. Traditional architecture collapses presentness into presence and has always viewed their separation as dangerous. In my view, the most virulent translation of undecidability in architecture rests on this point.

My architecture holds that architecture could write something else, something other than its own traditional texts of function, structure, meaning, and aesthetics. So, as you have observed, it always has strived, implicitly, for this other aura. Now it is one thing to speak theoretically about these matters, and it is another thing to act on them. You see, Jacques, when you leave your own realm, when you attempt to be consistent, whatever that might mean in architecture, it is precisely then that you do not understand the implications for deconstruction in architecture—when deconstruction leaves your hands. For me to toe the party line is useless; for in the end, Jacques, you would be more unhappy with an architecture that illustrates deconstruction than with my work, wherein the buildings themselves become, in a way, useless—lose their traditional significance of function and appropriate an other aura, one of excess, of presentness, and not presence. No amount of talking about presence, or of wordplay between *presence* and *present*, can create such an aura that distances architecture in building from the past and future of building. In the end, my architecture cannot be what it should be, but only what it can be. Only when you add one more reading of my work alongside yours of it in pictures and texts—that is, a reading in the event of a building—only there will you see the play between presence and presentness, only then will you know whether I have been faithful.

Yet I remain yours faithfully,
Peter Eisenman

II

ARCHITECTURE AND REPRESENTATION

On Representation

ANN BERGREN

REPRESENTATION IS a topic at the heart of theory and practice of architecture in the Western world, ever since Plato in his dialogue *Timaeus* made the creator of the universe an architect: Demiurge. This Demiurge creates the world by building sensible material copies or representations of the eternally existing forms. Representation presents itself whenever we think of architecture as embodying an idea.

This section is designed to explore representation in architecture by addressing these questions among others: Does or should architecture represent something? What does or should it represent? How do contemporary views of representation relate to architecture?

To discuss this topic we have two men, Robert Stern and Aaron Betsky. Robert Stern is a professor of architecture, and has been so at Columbia since 1970. He has been awarded numerous design honors, written several books, and organized many symposia and exhibitions, including "The Presence of the Past" at the Southern California Institute of Architecture (SCIARC) in 1980. His work is recognized around the world.

Aaron Betsky is a contributing editor to *Metropolitan Home*. You may have read his essay in the recent issue of *Metropolitan Home* that concentrated on L.A. and architecture. He is a visiting instructor at California Polytechnic University of Pomona. He teaches at SCIARC, both theoretical studios and theoretical seminars. He is also the managing editor of the California Office of *Art Coast Magazine*.

F O U R

The Postmodern Continuum

ROBERT A. M. STERN

WHEN I WAS ASKED to participate in the symposium "Postmodernism and Beyond" I was surprised; at first glance, so many of the others asked to take part seemed to be from the "Beyond," a place from which I am surely not. But then I realized that Peter Eisenman, Frank Gehry, and I have everything in common, especially when we are confronted with critics who make it clear what we in our different ways do is wrong and who lump together in one group the various of us anyway. However, it is not the point of the talk to criticize the critics.

Nor probably should it be to attempt once again to define the term "postmodernism," yet such a redefinition seems to be needed, given that it has come to be so widely adapted and so carelessly applied. It is true that the term "postmodernism," though an encompassing one, has by its very nature degenerated into a simple catch-all. In truth, the term is one that, though broad, is fairly precise, standing as it does for a complex set of values and beliefs that were initially articulated amid a rather precisely defined set of circumstances. While it may not have meant much of anything in the late 1970s to certain critics, the term "postmodernism" did mean a great deal to those who did the most to popularize it: to me and Charles Jencks, and to Peter Eisenman, despite his subsequent, ongoing critique of some of the ways its leading proponents have traveled. And it was a rebellious term—the rallying

point for much-needed artistic change representing a profound reaction to a stultifying situation in architecture and the other arts. While
all of us have gone our different ways, some even to the "beyond," I
would argue, we share the postmodernist experience. It was our liber-
ation, and, try as some may to be free of the term, in each of our ways
I believe we are still postmodernists. When "postmodernism" was adopted
as a term in the late 1970s, it already had behind it a certain history.[1]
Arnold Toynbee had used the term in the 1950s in *A Study in History*,
and Joseph Hudnut, the rather underappreciated dean of the Harvard
Graduate School of Design, had used it right after World War II, as he
struggled to articulate a locally appropriate approach to the European
modernism that was rather unquestioningly being adapted by American architects.[2] Hudnut hinted at a new synthesis, between European
ideals and American circumstances; his suggestive ramblings seemed
very intelligent to me in the late 1960s, when I came upon his essays
for the first time.

   At the risk of boring the reader with things I have probably said
before, I would like to try to prepare a very simple, basic, common
postmodernist ground that has helped guide me in my work as an architect. In 1977 I published a brief article, "At the Edge of Post-
Modernism," in which I suggested that there were three stylistic hallmarks of the postmodernist position: contextualism, allusionism, and
ornamentalism.[3] In it I also attempted to put forward what I then believed and still believe to be the essential characteristics of the movement as a whole—its rejection of modernism, and in particular late
modernism, with its claims that an ahistorical, non- or self-referential
essentially materialistic view of architecture was the exclusively appropriate position for contemporary architects. "Post Modernism," I wrote,

> recognizes that buildings are designed to mean something, that they are
> not hermetically sealed objects. Post-Modernism accepts diversity; it pre-
> fers hybrids to pure forms, it encourages multiple and simultaneous
> readings in its effort to heighten expressive content. Borrowing from forms
> and strategies of both the Modern movement and the architecture that
> preceded it, it declares the past-ness of both. The layering of space char-
> acteristic of much Post-Modernist architecture finds its complement in
> the overlay of cultural and historical references in the elevations. For the
> Post-Modernist, "More is More."[4]

   More than a decade later, I still believe in that definition; but while
many observers continue to see postmodernism as just another of today's style-isms, I increasingly see it, and the work that since the mid-
1970s has emerged in accord with its principles, as much more than
that, as, in fact, nothing short of a balm that permits modern architecture to heal the wrenching wound caused by modernism. In making
this claim, I use the term "modern," correctly I believe, as a broad term
describing the postmedieval era, and I use a much less encompassing

term, "modernism," to describe a movement within the modern, a movement prevalent in the first half of the twentieth century in architecture, the other plastic arts, and, to a lesser extent, literature, a movement to create a self-referential, autonomous art, a movement that, for architects at least, is inherently contradictory, given the public character of building. Given that modernism, despite its claim to autonomy, relies on a critique of the modern, even the most extreme proponents of its non- or self-referential approach such as Peter Eisenman are modern architects (and, as I tried to argue in the essay "Doubles of Post-Modernism," Eisenman is in effect a kind of excessive contrary-minded postmodernist as well).[5] We are therefore all moderns; but we are not all modernists.

To be modern is to have a sense of the pastness of the past and to value, even idealize, various aspects of the past. Over time, certain moments in history take on almost fixed values and come to be emulated, or at least referred to, as ideals. And in our work, our thinking, our discourse on architecture, we are all connected to a long tradition. For those of us operating in the West, that tradition ultimately grows out of the Greco-Roman classical world. Our modern world and our way of working in the modern world as architects began in the late medieval/early Renaissance period, when the classical past was rediscovered in relationship to an emerging individuality of culture, language, which we call the vernacular. These terms, the "classical" and the "vernacular," are very important for me and, I believe, for any architect interested in locating contemporary work within the wider context of history and culture, as well as within the physical context of a specific place. While, taken as a whole, the classical is too complex to discuss in such a format as this, it is not a love of flowers on stone walls or ornamental systems, no matter how beautiful, that establishes classicism's authority, though they surely contribute to it. Classicism's hold over all of us grows out of its much deeper values and our much deeper sense of loss.

The column is the principal element in the classical language, symbolizing at once both the erect human being and the tree. Grids of columns are like groves of trees, an analogy made even more explicit by ornamentation representing nature. The columns and lintels together with the secondary elements that constitute the orders are not only the grammar of the classical language, not only a codified system of tectonic composition, but also a highly suggestive representational vocabulary that has the capacity to embrace, or should I say articulate, many meanings for the culture as a whole. Principally the orders represent the human form in nature. They have been claimed to suggest gender.[6] A complex, visually engaging set of forms, the classical orders manage to distill, encapsulate, and communicate an archetypal concept of the natural and man-made world in a way that most people, even those without special education, can empathize with. Classicism succeeds because it is a language capable of infinitely complex permutations; its vocabulary is endlessly expressive and deep-seated; it is abstract and real.

To talk of a "vernacular" architecture or culture is to talk of one that grows up in a reasonably straightforward way out of a set of local conditions solving problems of shelter and communication in a more or less nonself-conscious way: a vernacular grows out of a local soil that nourishes a local flavor; it offers simple solutions simply arrived at. A true vernacular is timeless in the very best sense of the word; it evolves but does not "develop." A vernacular architecture is a "native" and a "naive" architecture, one in which there is a common agreement about form. Building is added to building to create a coherent, nearly uniform environment encompassing the public and the private realms. Though traditional vernacular towns like Portofino near Genoa grew over a long time, they seem all of a piece because they are so natural to their place. This sense of ineffable inevitability has been increasingly held in high esteem in the modern period as, increasingly, high cultures have become national, or even international, rather than local, synthetic rather than organic, individualistic rather than communal. The loss of the vernacular goes hand in hand with the growth of the modern, as opposed to the ancient or the medieval culture, characterized as it is by the depersonalized, delocalized production of both goods and learning. As we have lost the vernacular, we have come to value it all the more: to idealize it, to lift it to a status comparable to that of the classical.

Palladio was in many ways the first "modern" architect, by bringing together, through misunderstanding and understanding, the two seemingly contradictory strains of building culture, the high classicism of the ancient world and the everyday vernacular of the local peasantry. Palladio juxtaposes but does not homogenize the high and the low, the ideal and the real. Palladio was the first to give lithic expression to the most important new social fact of the modern era, the emergence of the middle class. Palladio's Villa Barbaro combines the simple directness of the vernacular, the local materials, the humble functional program, with the middle-class emphasis on individuality and its penchant for self-declaration. At Villa Barbaro, Palladio elevates the ordinary realm of the farm to that of the public realm of the town. Villa Barbaro is not just a house: it is a place and a proclamation. A farm building for a disfranchised urbanite, it is the exemplar of a new ideal: the suburban life, an ideal central to our experience to this day.

Palladio also misunderstood creatively, or just stupidly—I'm not sure which—the meaning of the Roman temple, which he took to be a model for the Roman house, elevating the form of the single-family house to a hitherto unknown symbolic level, transforming ordinary shelter into an inhabited shrine consecrated to the family, to its material possessions, and to the place of the family in the larger order of things. In so

Villa Barbaro, Maser, Italy (Andrea Palladio, ca. 1549/1551–1558). (Courtesy Robert A. M. Stern Architects Archives [Slide Collection])

doing, Palladio combined the private and the public, the profane and the sacred, as never before.

In the early nineteenth century, when the mass production of goods first became practical, the traditional vernacular was threatened as a means of production and as form-giver to the man-made landscape. As factories began to threaten the traditional life and physical structure of vernacular towns and villages, in keeping with the modern tendency to idealize that which is lost, the vernacular was elevated to the level of an ideal, comparable to that of classicism itself; it was assigned a moral value, that of "honesty." Craft was elevated into creed. To a surprising extent as a result of this trend, the high architecture of the medieval world has come to enjoy a status comparable to that of the classical, as a kind of quintessential vernacular—but that is another point.

Now some would argue that the emergence of the machine in the early nineteenth century transformed both ordinary building and symbolic architecture, and indeed transformed culture as a whole, bringing to birth a condition apart from the postmedieval situation and, it is argued, one that puts the true beginning point of the modern somewhere between the late eighteenth and the mid-nineteenth centuries. Those who would so argue fail to see nineteenth- and twentieth-century architecture in a sufficiently broad perspective: they fail to understand the work of the recent past in relation to the complex modern matrix as a whole. The most destructive form of modernist exclusivity takes a fiercely materialistic view of architecture and adopts the Crystal Palace (Joseph Paxton, 1851), as emblematic of the break between the Renaissance tradition, to which they deny the term "modern," and modernism, to which they arrogate the term "modern." To see the realization of the Crystal Palace in 1851 as the breaking point between the Renais-

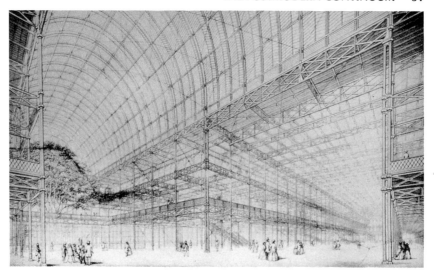

Crystal Palace, London (Joseph Paxton, 1851). (Courtesy Robert A. M. Stern Architects Archives [Slide Collection])

sance tradition and what comes after is not only to rob the modern of its early history and thereby its full meaning, but also to confuse instrumentalities with instruments. Unquestionably, the Industrial Revolution had a profound effect not only on architecture but on all the aspects of civilization; so too did the emergence of mass democracy, which began to take root in Western countries at about the same time. But though these twin phenomena profoundly altered the basic structure of the modern condition, they were not a break with it; rather, they were an outgrowth of it, a direct consequence of it even, heralding the full-fledged emergence of the secular world of the bourgeoisie. The modernists, having elevated the craft vernacular to the level of an ideal, sought to create out of the machine and its processes a new vernacular. What was needed was a new synthesis that would at once replace the faltering local craft vernacular with one based on the machine, and sustain the authority of the vernacular by virtue of association with the classical. Instead, modernism sought to create a new, purely materialistic language of form. In trying to free architecture from all responsibility to traditional culture, to clear the way for a new world order of its own devising, modernism lost sight of architecture's fundamental responsibilities. With modernism, the horse sought to drive the cart.

As I see it, the Crystal Palace means just about the opposite of what the antitraditionalist modernists believed. Those who saw the messages of its form as the triumph of utility over symbol failed to look at the building very carefully. Close inspection of the Crystal Palace will find that, except for its use of new construction techniques, it is a very traditional building; it is in fact a grand Roman public building of the imperial era translated into glass, metal, and wood. It is a building that in every respect, starting with its name, is intended to represent inherited ideals and adapt them to modern conditions. In this sense, it is a modern building in the full sense of that word, designed to be "read" by the public in terms of prior experience. It is new—that is, up to date—and it is modern. It is a palace, but a palace of glass. It is not a homogenization of old and new, or an obliteration of the old in favor of the new; it is a balanced juxtaposition in the modern tradition of Palladio; that is why it is so aptly named—Crystal Palace!

Inside, the Crystal Palace reveals itself not only as a vast enclosure for sheltering myriad objects gathered together for public education, but as an internalization of public life on an unprecedented scale; it was the first building realized on the scale of mass democracy. It is classical not because Paxton wasn't very good or very smart or very creative, or because he hadn't been able to figure out how to erase what he knew from the past, but simply because Paxton wasn't interested in creating a new language of architecture; such would not serve his purpose. His job was to say new things with the language architects already had, the language most people in his audience could understand. And use of the classical enabled Paxton and his patron, Prince Albert, to establish connections with time-honored, ongoing values amid the utter confusion of a plethora of objects that the machine made possible. This was exactly the program that Prince Albert had given the commission when he organized the display house in the Crystal Palace. This great building, this Crystal Palace, reifies a set of traditional values in the face of something new; it celebrates the new but does not succumb to it.

Mies van der Rohe is the critical architect of the modernist movement. While it is clear now that Mies's attempt to invent an ahistorical vocabulary of form and to combine it with a classical grammar—in short, to create a mechanoclassicism—was doomed, the cultural circumstances of its formulation were utterly logical. By the early 1900s many artists in the western European tradition, particularly those in northern Europe, felt that the modern program had run its course: that its architecture and urbanism were doomed only to repeat themselves and could no longer clear new aesthetic ground. The tragic stalemate of World War I only served to confirm them in this belief, and the revolutionary politics that evolved to bring the war to closure for a short time encouraged some few among these to claim a new millennium. In this context, Mies's postwar skyscraper projects were perfect—tectonically and formally convincing articulations of the modernist program applied to a new building type, the skyscraper, which was consecrated to the overthrow of the traditional urban order while accommodating all the functional requirements of a new organizational elite.

Although Mies went further than any other architect in lifting the machine vernacular to the level of exalting architectural art, his work failed to replace that of traditional classicism or the traditional vernac-

Glass skyscraper project (Ludwig Mies Van Der Rohe, 1920–1921).
(Courtesy Robert A. M. Stern Architects Archives [Slide Collection])

ular in the public esteem. This is particularly true in England and even more so in the United States, where the machine, the handmaiden of material progress that put these two nations on top of the economic heap, was seen by many as a negative force destroying not only the physical landscape but also the very social underpinnings of daily life. As a result, England and America have refused to mytholigize the machine; though they have enjoyed the benefits of industrialization, they have seen firsthand its terrible capacity for physical and psychological destruction. With no common history except for the natural history of the continent, and no native architecture except that of the Amerindian, whose culture was disdained, the United States has experienced the conflict between the machine and the natural environment on an unprecedented scale. So it is not surprising that as Americans took hold of their continent and prospered, largely through the instrumentality of the machine, they did not turn to the machine for cultural sustenance but to its opposites—to nature and to the preindustrial world, to natural history and architectural history. So it is that those moderns who have had the longest-lived, most direct, intimate, and pervasive experience of the machine culture, the English and the Americans—those who were the first to have it and gained so much in material wealth from it—were also those most antipathetic to the modernist program and least willing to accept the argument that the brave new world of factory tectonics was superior to the traditional workshop world it replaced. To those who participated in the machine world on a day-to-day basis, architecture became increasingly sacred as an artifact of traditional culture, maybe even of myth. For the Anglo-American, architecture had to be much more than the *Bauen* beloved by Mies: architecture had to transcend materiality to become a symbolic-cultural act.

If Mies's vision for the modern was a noble failure, Jefferson's was a noble success. Jefferson saw architecture as the representation of ethical ideals, ideals that he believed essential for the success of the nascent American culture. Jefferson transferred these ideals, and the architectural forms that were their environmental representation, to the American continent through a process of symbolic appropriation, one that has continued to characterize American culture to this day. The young Henry James commented on this and offered what was perhaps the first and certainly the clearest articulation of this process, when in 1867 he wrote,

> I think that to be an American is an excellent preparation for culture. We have exquisite qualities as a race and it seems to me that we are ahead of the European races in the fact that more than any of them we can deal freely with forms of civilization not our own, can pick and choose and assimilate and, in short, aesthetically, etc., claim our property wherever we find it.

Five years later, he commented a little more on the subject when he said, "[I]t is a complex fate being an American, and one of the responsibilities that it entails is fighting against superstitious evaluation of Europe."[8]

As I see it, it is distinctly different to be an American architect than to be a Continental European architect, even to this day, and for this reason, the postmodernism that has emerged since the 1970s has come from the United States. As an architect, I have seen it as my mission to try to express, to represent, the values of American culture as I see them; not to impose values on it. I'm fascinated more and more with Jefferson, of course, because he so brilliantly used architecture as a means of reflecting and influencing the direction of culture. Some say he was an amateur, a term used as a negative criticism. But I think amateurism is, in a sense, the highest way of doing things. As an ama-

University of Virginia, Charlottesville, Virginia (Thomas Jefferson, 1743–1826). (Courtesy Robert A. M. Stern Architects Archives [Slide Collection])

teur, Jefferson understood that it was not the tectonic but the symbolic possibilities of architecture that were the first magnitude of importance. He used architecture as a part of a larger view of culture, not as a substitute for it. When he lived in Paris in the 1780s, he saw culture as a whole; he saw the new classicism and distilled it, formed lessons, and brought them back. But this use he put them to, first at Monticello and then at the University of Virginia, revealed him no more copyist, or even one engaged in a simpleminded act of transference, but a profound celebrant of architecture as an embodiment of human value across time.

At the University of Virginia, through a process of design and representation, Jefferson defined what American urbanism might be. He defined it by creating the great lawn, flanked by pavilions and the gardens and secondary pavilions behind, all combining to form what he called an academic village. No complex was an exact model for it; indeed, there was no such planned idealized aggregation anywhere. Jefferson created a dream world so fundamental to the modern condition of mass democracy that today it is correctly perceived as a type. He lined his village lawn with professors' houses, each of which confronted the greensward with a pedimented order from a classical building of antiquity so that both professors and students could study the classical world, not only through books, not only through its verbal language, but through its architectural language or at least a pretty fair simula-

tion of it. This was not done merely for the sake of an abstract learning, but so that the forms as well as the ideas of the classical world
would be taken up by the students after leaving the university. Jefferson capped his composition not with a religious building, but with a
library that is a half-scale version of the Pantheon in Rome. How significant was that functional transformation: in Jefferson's time, the Roman Pantheon was a religious building, a Catholic church, and before
that a sacred building to the Roman gods. Jefferson's Virginia Pantheon was a library. The choice of model seems very deliberate, rendering a point obvious by the transference of purpose and meaning
from the realm of the spirit to the realm of the mind; in the new secular society, the building says, learning will be the new religion. So the
building dedicated to education is an act of education as well; it is
something that, in satisfying a real need, elevates utility to the level of
symbolic discourse.

Now comes the question: Are buildings just sheds waiting to be decorated or nipped a bit here and tucked a bit there to give them a "look"
appropriate to a particular place or a particular program? No, they are
not—at least, not quite. Every building is a unique undertaking—not
just from the functional point of view, but also from its formal language. I believe that architecture cannot just be about program or ge-
ometry. It must be more. Every architect must come to terms with that;
but that "more" must come from the circumstances outside the building itself. While some would say it can come from the architect's inner
psyche, I would say that, given architecture's public nature, it would
better come from the context of the place, of the culture. Each new
building has an obligation to comment on and contribute to the wider
public realm. The place, its culture, and its physical history, as well as
the requirements and the ideals of the client—all these are the text of
architecture. If one is serious about this idea of building as public text,
one cannot content oneself with the too-easy task of seeing architecture
as lithic autobiography.

In any case, though I sometimes write a book or the odd article in a
journal, I don't think of myself as a theorist, but as an architect who
tries to design buildings with some meanings attached. And I would
like to conclude with that in mind, to try to discuss the work, or the
meanings, in the hopes of revealing one, but by no means the only,
way to formulate and fulfill a postmodernist approach. So I would conclude by discussing a building my colleagues and I have recently completed, one that illuminates the possibilities inherent in the story-telling
approach I mentioned earlier and, as well, casts light on the complex
circumstances that both distance modern American architecture from
and connect it with, that of the Western European tradition as whole.

The Mexx building in Voorschoten, Netherlands (1985–1987), brought
to my mind many of the issues that I have tried to raise in this discussion: in particular, the distinction between the American perception

Mexx International, international headquarters, Voorschoten, Netherlands (Robert A. M. Stern Architects, 1985–1987). (Courtesy Peter Aaron/ESTO)

Mexx International, international headquarters, Voorschoten, Netherlands (Robert A. M. Stern Architects, 1985–1987). (Courtesy Peter Aaron/ESTO)

and the European perception of modernism. Our clients, a company designing and manufacturing high-style, streetwise clothing for the young and hip, acquired a landmark building of the 1850s that had been built as a silversmith's factory and was now derelict. Redesigned and doubled in size, it now serves as our client's business headquarters and design center. Working in Holland as an architect, not visiting as a tourist, forced me to come to grips directly with a dilemma that was surely central to the incandescent Dutch modernism of the early twentieth century: the sense of aesthetic and environmental completeness that one gets while wandering through cities like Amsterdam and Delft. American architects have never had this problem. We are lucky if we have three blocks of anything consistent and fine. Though giving rise to pleasurable sensations, such completeness also creates anxieties for the architect. What to do in a built world that seems so perfect and complete? Surely if I were an architect raised in such an environment, as Mies or Rietveld were, it would drive me nuts. It surely would have a seriously inhibiting influence. In our individualistic age, such an environment seems to give rise not to the question, What can a single architect contribute?, but to one that is ultimately destructive: What can an architect do to it?

The question was the same for me as I contemplated so much that was fine and finished. But my response was distinctly different. For me the challenge was one of evolution, not revolution. To develop my approach, I first turned to history in order to better understand the situation in Holland. In the early part of this century, modernism in Holland took two distinct directions: the abstract formulation of De Stijl and the expressive functionalism of constructivism. De Stijl was painterly; constructivism was tectonic. Gerrit Rietveld's Schroeder House (1924) was the quintessential work of De Stijl, like a painting one can walk through. But bring your own hammer, screwdriver, and paintbrush, because it is always falling apart when you are there! It always needs a little fixing up. It is not at all about Bauen. But it is not about the public realm either—it totally contradicts the environment around it as it defies the very materiality of construction itself. It is an art object placed in the town; it is not a building in the conventional sense of the term, but a construct that uses the excuse of habitation to make a statement about pure aesthetics, albeit a very powerful one, a brilliant one, one that gives me much pleasure, but one that is not, in the most fundamental sense, architectural.

J. A. Brinkman and L. C. Van der Vlugt's Van Nelle factory (1927–1930), designed with Mort Stam, is, on the other hand, a great building, one deeply rooted in machine-inspired tectonics, being entranced by the assembly-line processes that it is conceived to accommodate. While the aesthetic effects of the Schroeder House are precisely calculated, those of the Van Nelle factory seem to have been arrived at more freely; it is a building that overflows with exuberance, even wit. It seems full

Schroder House, Utrecht, Netherlands (G. T. Rietveld, 1924). (Courtesy Robert A. M. Stern Architects Archives [Slide Collection])

Van Nelle factory, Rotterdam, Netherlands (Brinkman & Van der Vlugt, 1927–1930). (Courtesy Robert A. M. Stern Architects Archives [Slide Collection])

of activity, of life, celebrating not only the new building technology, or the production processes that are its raison d'être, but also the pleasure it brings to the workers, bathed in natural light. The particularities of the program, rather than a self-conscious aesthetic, are the inspiration for the design, so full of life with its chutes stretching across voids, its conning-tower tearoom, its easy volumetric juxtapositions. True, as a self-contained large-scale industrial complex, it does not have to take on the issue of local context. So it is not fair to make too much of it in contrast to Schroeder, but the differences are there to make for points of comparison.

In any case, the building we put together for Mexx restores the old and creates something new, but something that seeks to grow out of the liberating constructivism of Van Nelle rather than the hothouse aesthetics of Schroeder. Ours is, in a way, an effort to establish the lost history of the original building, which, like the company that built it, stagnated in the early twentieth century. We restored the exterior of the old building, but its ground-floor interiors, probably never much to begin with and ruined when we found them, were reconfigured for use as an executive suite, with ceilings shaped to coddle the precious Dutch light. Design studios were located above in the atticlike spaces on the second floor. As one moves from the old building to the new, the transition is not abrupt but gradual, as if the building had a "natural" history.

To make it clear that this "history" was consciously evolved, fragments of the walls of the original building were reproduced as detached elements framing the outdoor courtyard, suggesting the interweaving of aesthetics across time, as if a much larger traditional building had been partially demolished to introduce such environmental benefits of the twentieth century as superabundant natural light and intimacy between inside and out. But the "new" elements are intended to be distinctly Dutch, incorporating the free curves and joyous mechanomorphology that I admire at Van Nelle and in the work of the engineer-architect Sybold van Ravestyn. So, although Mexx may seem at first glance out of keeping with my recent work, or at least my work in America, the ideas that influenced its shaping are not; it is a building about other buildings and about its place in its landscape and in its culture. If it succeeds as architecture, it does so because it is a building that gives environmental and cultural pleasure, not merely as abstract composition or form, but as a representation of shared experience and shared values; it builds on the past, drawing modernism into the wider family of the modern.

The problem has been the same for me since I was a beginning architect, working in the studio space that had been created on the top floor of Louis Kahn's Yale University Art Gallery. Out the window Yale's skyline lay before me, with its wonderful Gothic-style buildings, widely admired by "real" people, but condemned by architects as irrelevant expressions of a somewhat laughable past. For me, these wonderful structural/conceptual hybrids, dismissed as "girder Gothic," exerted a strong pull away from the direction of contemporary work. Despite teachers and many of my fellow students who said, "You can't do those any more," I began to wonder about the events that had caused architecture to so change in the twenty or so years between the time when the last of those Yale buildings had been built and the time when I enrolled as a student. My book on George Howe, begun while I was still a student at Yale but not published until fifteen years later, was a direct product of my curiosity about this revolution in taste.[9] Economic depression, a world war, and a sense of cultural inferiority had all combined to rob American and most other Western architects of the courage to continue their dialogue with the past. It was not only better to "make it new,"[10] to use Ezra Pound's phrase, it was essential. The world, I was told, had so dramatically changed that only little flat-roofed boxes would do; modern architecture, it would seem, could only be defined as buildings your mother and practically everyone else hated. In order to be good, one had to be hated. Deep down, I never wanted to be that different; I wanted to be an architect who made things better, not different, or at least not different merely for being different. But it took quite a while to be the architect I wanted to be, rather than the one that prevailing taste said I should be. First Vincent Scully and then Paul Rudolph and then Robert Venturi taught me how to look at the buildings of the past, and in those buildings I saw something that I could not see in the work of my own time, something that I thought worth holding on to, something that had values the "new" did not have on its own. So I tried to make buildings that are old and new.

Architecture is at its best, it seems to me, when it digs deep into culture in order to affirm, and sometimes even to reestablish, values and ideals. It is not enough for buildings to express the architect's tortured soul or psyche, or the painstaking processes of design that lead to the final product, or some abtruse literary theory or compositional game. This is not to say that the house of architecture is not big enough to include those things. But at its most basic, architecture must be the reification of public values. A building must be a public act of communication: a coherent presentation, representation, reification not merely of program, function, or conventions belonging to the discipline itself, but also of the things that belong to the world outside it that it must serve, honor, and depict. It must be in its essence a portrait of places, of cultures, of beliefs, and of dreams. Architecture must be more than the lithic representation of the private fantasies or inner demons of the architect. It is not the built version/illustration of a written text. Architecture is the most public of all the arts. The most obdurate of the arts. It is also the least personal of the arts. It is not at its best when pursued as an instrument of radical change. This is not to say that it cannot contribute to society's gradual evolution, but that its ways are more conservative. It must comprehend the meaning of the past in order to move on. And so I could reaffirm—if not for you, at least for myself—that the task of architecture is not to represent a collapse of values or the crisis of our times. What time in history has not had a crisis? Or at least thought that it did not? So I would reaffirm for myself that it is not appropriate for the architect to arrogate to himself the self-delusory belief that he can give form to the spirit of his own time. Every architect, if he has a bigger idea than just simply getting the job and building the building, must have a sense of a larger purpose. But that purpose seems to most properly lie in the realm of narrative rather than autobiography, representation rather than illustration. The architect may best be suited to represent what he sees and what he knows from what is around him, and to use what he sees and knows from what is around him, as well as what he knows from the past, to give new work resonance. I believe architecture is a story-telling art, a narrative. The story I seek to tell is that of America, or more precisely what it means to be an American, whether an American in America or an American abroad. Architecture has played a special role in the continual struggle of Americans to define who they are; given the vast emptiness of our continent, and our shared experience as aliens nearly all, we search for a collective identity. As we face the challenge of creating a history and culture for ourselves, we necessarily appropriate the forms and symbols of the past, raising them to mythic proportions. If we are at all good at what we do, we also make them our own.

NOTES

1. For a discussion of the varieties of postmodernism, see Robert A. M. Stern, "Doubles of Post-Modernism," *Harvard Architectural Review* 1 (Spring 1980): 74–87.

2. The term "postmodernism" seems to have been initiated by Joseph Hudnut in "The Post-Modern House," *Architectural Record* 97 (May 1945): 70–75, which was reprinted in Hudnut, *Architecture and the Spirit of Man* (Cambridge, Mass.: Harvard University Press, 1949), 109–19. Its earliest influential use was in Arnold J. Toynbee, *A Study in History* (New York: Oxford University Press, 1954), 8:338.

3. Robert A. M. Stern, "At the Edge of Post-Modernism: Some Methods, Paradigms and Principles for Architecture at the End of the Modern Movement," *Architectural Design* 47 (April 1977): 274–86.

4. Ibid., 286.

5. Stern, "Doubles of Post-Modernism," 66.

6. For an extensive discussion of the origin of the orders, including the gender issue, see George Hersey, *The Lost Meaning of Classical Architecture* (Cambridge, Mass.: MIT Press, 1988), 53–67, 79–90; John Onians, *Bearers of Meaning* (Princeton, N.J.: Princeton University Press, 1988), 33–36.

7. Henry James to Thomas Sergeant Perry, 20 September 1867, quoted in

Henry James' Letters, ed. Leon Edel (Cambridge, Mass.: Belknap Press of Harvard University Press, 1974), 1:77.

8. Henry James to Charles Eliot Norton, 4 February 1872, quoted in Edel, *Henry James' Letters,* 1:274.

9. Robert A. M. Stern, *George Howe: Toward a Modern American Architecture* (New Haven, Conn.: Yale University Press, 1975).

10. Ezra Pound, *Make It New: Essays* (London: Faber & Faber, 1934).

F I V E

James Gamble Rogers and the Pragmatics of Architectural Representation

AARON BETSKY

THE QUESTION of representation, like that of language, is a difficult one to pose in the case of architecture, for the simple fact that a building inserts its physicality in place of its signification. In fact, a building does not in and of itself represent or speak about anything. Meanings must be, and inevitably are, brought to the actual construction by interpretation and use.[1] The building is, in the most literal sense of the word, structure. While one might argue that this interpretation begs exactly the difference between building and architecture[2] or that the condition of exile from spoken language makes architecture a more potent critique of accepted norms of cognitive control,[3] the question of the necessity of actual building still arises, since the imaginative constructs of interpretation remain within the realm of pictorial or linguistic representation. That realm has little need of the elaborate constructs of building. When does one then need a building for the task of representation, or when do buildings form the only adequate medium for representation?

Representation in architecture assumes the need to represent something in such a way that a building is uniquely suited to that act and cannot be replaced by two-dimensional means, solely with iconography or with mute form. This is the case when that which is represented is a set of vaguely defined values that cannot be articulated in text, that cannot be overtly stated, and that must be validated or realized through the act of construction. These circumstances can be found when the effective elite of any society, which coheres because of a shared belief system and retains its control by that same method, needs to affirm that power. Architecture is, in its essence, the representation of power. It houses the central institutions of any society, commands enormous physical resources, and imposes itself on the daily life of the user or observer as a physical fact. Therefore, architecture is always the built affirmation of the social, economic, and physical status quo, and in the activity of affirmation finds a representational role that is unique to its constitution. I therefore propose to examine one particular body of work that had the peculiar need to articulate the value system of the effective elite of America. In so doing, it helped to ensure the continuation of this group's rule through the institutions housed by this architecture.

I must note that I am in this instance decidedly not interested in the oppositional role of architecture. In fact, architecture has always been in a difficult position in the theory of a critical or avant-garde art. The role of the oppositional art object for at least the past two hundred years has been to stand apart from the society in which it is created, in order to represent or express certain values of that society. The traditional role of criticism has then been to interpret the object and thus make it an operative part of the culture once again. This neat nineteenth-century circle of representation and interpretation has always, however, found its hardest test case in the architectural object. From Ruskin to Hegel, philosophers have claimed architecture to be either the final *Gesammtkunstwerk* that sums up the expressive abilities of art or the nadir of creation, that place where art loses all its transcendent abilities and disappears into the fabric of the world.[4] As already noted, architecture cannot be an object apart from society. Architecture, understood as the representative housing of the central institutions of society, is, as Mario Gandelsonas has written, a double representation. It both presents itself as physical structure—defying gravity, keeping out the rain, and organizing various functions in a map (plan) of their relations—and presents us with a set of planological relationships, or a face or façade, a picture of that which is not there. These double representations cancel each other out except when there are discrepancies, a deliberate state that is, in reality, difficult to achieve. This is what sets architecture apart and leads to the seemingly inescapable dilemma of the avant-garde architect: his (rarely her) creation is in the best position to act as a critical instrument exactly because of its inescapable power, reality, and integration, but because of this integration it cannot separate itself from already existing power structures. This situation has been further complicated by the rapid disappearance of physical reality as a controlling factor in the production and consumption cycle, an evanescence caused by the increasing efficiency of technology. The ideological mirror of this development is, as Manfredo Tafuri has pointed out, the disappearance of the necessity of architecture in its aesthetic dimensions—that is, as something needed to put a face on capitalism.[5]

I am therefore not going to discuss the avant-garde. Rather, I am interested in what I see as one of the moments in twentieth-century architectural history when one particular architect, working with one particular group of clients, represented exactly the position of architecture as the physical composition and validation of otherwise unstated beliefs, so that the nature of architecture as representation can be better understood. The architect James Gamble Rogers (1867–1943) is representative of the role of American architecture in making physical, and then maintaining, the economic and social status quo of this country. His buildings for such institutions as the University of Chicago, Yale, Northwestern, Columbia, and New York University express in stone the values of the effective elite educated there. Beyond such mirroring, they also employ elaborate strategies of plan, façade, and massing in order to create a representation of a model world governed by the members and values of that elite.

James Gamble Rogers had the task of giving form to several of those institutions that were dedicated exactly to the teaching or passing along of those values, at a time when the effective elite of this country was forced to clarify its values in response to social and economic changes threatening its control over the economic and ideological bases of the United States.[6] The methodology of this architecture, from plan configuration to compositional technique to stylistic usage, is governed by its ability to make physical the belief system, mythology, and working methods of this country's effective elite, a group made up of future members of the productive sector (executives), its functionaries (lawyers), and its ideologues (humanists, divines). The same changes already alluded to, the change in the ethnography of America, the streamlining of the economy, and the perfection of the middle-class compromise that allowed this country to avoid class warfare—made this kind of architecture unnecessary after the 1930s, and Rogers's career is marked by the disappearance of architecture as an autonomous act in his later buildings.[7]

Born in 1867, James Gamble Rogers came from a fairly well-to-do southern family that owned considerable property outside of Lexington, Kentucky. His father fell on hard times after the Civil War and joined the immigration to Chicago.[8] There, James Gamble Rogers grew up in a middle-class neighborhood and received a scholarship to attend Yale. Once in New Haven, he immersed himself not in scholarly pursuits, but in living out the myth of the Yale man. He was popular, famous as a joker and a baseball player.[9] He saw Europe not on the grand tour, but on a promotional tour with the baseball team. At Yale, he was part of a new class of sons of self-made men from the "West" who were reinvigorating the hitherto closed East Coast establishment.

It was their needs that later substantially changed the Yale curriculum. In return, Yale introduced them to a code of ethics, a shared cultural heritage, a manner of behaving, and a set of shared rituals that allowed them to bond and rule: they became Yale men, representatives of an articulate, self-re-creating ruling elite.[10] In practical terms. Rogers became acquainted with the right kind of people—future clients.

But Yale was only one of the two sources for his career. The other was the place in which he had grown up and first found employment, Chicago. At some point, Rogers had decided to become an architect. He returned to Chicago after his graduation to work for the man who played a central role in setting the tone for rebuilding most of Chicago after the great fire of 1871, William LeBaron Jenny. Jenny was trained not as an architect, but as an engineer, and prided himself on the creation of a series of buildings that represented structural reality. Jenny, his employees, and his students, who together formed what is known as the "Chicago School" in American architecture, gave physical form to the particular economic and social logic of the capital city of the American West.[11] They built monuments for the men who transformed the seemingly endless human and natural resources of the country into consumer goods, and their buildings were governed by the same rational bravura that marked the economic endeavors of that city.[12] The values inherent in this brawny elite's behavior were different from those of the East Coast elite, and it would be the task of the thinkers, politicians, artists, and architects of James Gamble Rogers's generation to meld those values—a process celebrated, but not finished, at the Columbian Exposition of 1893, where Frederick Jackson Turner talked of the closing of the frontier and Henry Adams thought he saw American thought tending toward unity.[13]

Rogers was a successful member of this firm and later claimed to have helped obtain one of its largest commissions, all the while learning the pragmatics of his trade.[14] He then moved on to the largest architecture firm in Chicago, Burnham and Root, where he became superintendent of building for the Ashland Block, probably because he was connected with the developers of that building.[15] Just as that firm started on the design of the Columbian Exposition, Rogers left at the tender age of twenty-seven to prepare plans for his own skyscraper. Then, just when he appeared set to become a successful, if not particularly outstanding, designer of speculative office buildings, he left for Paris to study at the Ecole des Beaux-Arts. At the Ecole he was a distinguished, if not great, student who created buildings that could best be said to be representative of the work done in that *étalier* at that time.[16]

He returned to Chicago five years later and found that he now had two things going for him. First, he was trained as a classical architect and, through his Yale connections, was part of the cultural elite of Chicago. Second, he was a businessman who understood the ways of the world: his first designs were rows of houses prepared for developers he knew from his old neighborhood. He continued to design small office buildings and apartment buildings that, through a combination of Tudor, Arts and Crafts, and Colonial motifs, created a composite image of home in the suburbs out of mass-produced materials. Rogers also made good use of his Yale connections and married the daughter of the second president of the Chicago Stock Exchange, thereby entering a very powerful clan of families that included the Farwells, who financed Marshall Field. Through his new in-laws he met the McCormicks, the Fields, and many other wealthy Chicago families. He moved to the suburbs, changed his church from Baptist to Presbyterian, and started building houses for a new clientele. These structures were large boxes onto which Rogers added overscaled porches and entrance motifs to signal the grandeur of the edifice.[17]

At this point, James Gamble Rogers was no more than an average self-made architect. The combination of his middle-class, middle-American background and his experiences in France and New Haven, however, were also representative of a nascent class of leaders in business, finance, and culture. In his first institutional commission, Rogers tapped into a school of thought that was to give a coherent ideology to that class.

In 1901 Rogers was asked, through his friendship with the McCormick family, to design the first School of Education for the University of Chicago. The School of Education was a joint project of John Dewey and Colonel Francis Parker. Together, these founding lights of American pragmatism founded a school that was supposed to educate students through experimentation and hands-on involvement.[18] The architecture of the school was meant to be a model of the real world. It was to articulate the realities of everyday life and, by the very act of articulation and composition, give them meaning. As James pointed out in an article he wrote about the design of the School of Education, that meaning could never be separated from the actual representation. It was an intrinsic part of the building, just as the education lessons were to be embedded in actions.[19]

The School of Education at the University of Chicago was designed in Neo-Gothic because that was the mandated style of the university, but the skin was thrown loosely over an organization of spaces that combined extreme practicality—to the point that parts of the school consciously resembled a factory—with an ordering system derived from the teachings of the Ecole des Beaux-Arts. Of special interest, however, is the fact that the axial progression that one would expect to find in a Beaux-Arts building was cut short, and the building was actually organized around a double-loaded corridor running at right angles to the direction of entrance. In other words, James Gamble Rogers denied the idea that one could understand the building from one viewpoint, which would lead one from the entrance to the most important programmatical element, and from there to the subsidiary elements. The

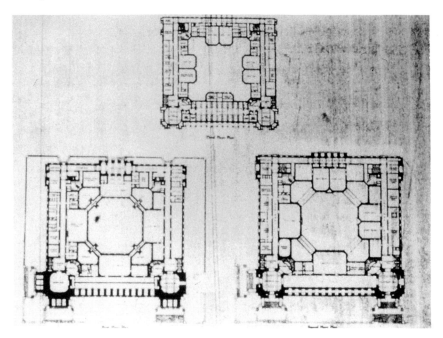

Shelby County Courthouse, Memphis, Tennessee. Plans (James Gamble Rogers, 1906–1909). (Courtesy *Architectural Record*)

building made no a priori sense in plan, and its façade did not show a hierarchy of spaces. It was organized functionally and experientially in a series of shifting spaces that had absolutely no grand focal point. This *parti* was to be a theme in Rogers's work for the remainder of his career. It marks a refusal of representation in plan and façade in favor of an experiential integration of functional elements.

If the School of Education commission connected Rogers with the philosophical and educational wing of the reformist tide then sweeping the country, the series of post offices and courthouse buildings he designed in Memphis, New Orleans, and New Haven between 1905 and 1915 made him part of the political side of that movement. Each of these buildings was the result of a City Beautiful or political-reform movement, and each was meant as a rational, businesslike monument to renascent civic virtues.[20] Their façades cast the institutions in the image of classical order, an agreed-on language of civic decorum, while their plans were tightly packed organizations of often disparate functions (both the New Orleans and the New Haven structures combined first-floor post offices with second-floor court rooms). Once again, the central axis was absent, and once again movement through the buildings was marked by a series of episodic events composed almost like a collage. These institutions represented the power of a rational government, firmly in the hands of white, mainly Anglo-Saxon men, to control and order American society. They appeared as isolated moments of control but, unlike their counterparts by more traditional Beaux-Arts-trained architects, that authority was broken down in both their massing and their internal organization in favor of functional adjacencies and a sensual composition that validates the institution through its appeal not to abstract theories, but first, to rational decision-making processes derived from a study of business practices and, second, to the relationship between the body and the physical world. As such, they were architectural equivalents for the victory of reform movements, pragmatism, and the emergence of the corporate culture that marked the reign of Teddy Roosevelt, Andrew Carnegie, J. P. Morgan, and John D. Rockefeller.[21]

James Gamble Rogers finally secured his already burgeoning career when he received his first commission from a central member of that emerging elite, Edward S. Harkness. Harkness had the good fortune that his father was the only man willing to back John Rockefeller from the very beginning, and the family fortunes rose with that of the Rockefellers. Edward Harkness never worked a day in his life, but managed to give away the (at that time astounding) sum of $160 million through the Commonwealth Fund, which was established for—in the necessarily vague locution of his class—"the welfare of mankind."[22] In interviews, Harkness explained that he saw his task as converting the great wealth he had been given to create structures of coherence that would allow people first to understand the modern world governed by the kind of corporations creating his wealth, and then to thrive in that environment. He started by funding Presbyterian churches and missions, moved on to fund the lion's share of Yale's building program between 1915 and 1930, and then became the second largest benefactor of hospitals and clinics around the country.[23]

James Gamble Rogers first designed a townhouse off Fifth Avenue for Harkness. This modest-looking but sumptuous palazzo was entered through a suppressed grand entrance, after which one had to shift three times before reaching the actual foyer. The remainder of the house was organized around a double-loaded corridor. The façade was notable in that it was divided into bays marked by capitals, showing that this was a grand building, but there were no accompanying columns. The representation had become completely subsumed into the actual fabric of the building.[24]

After the death of his brother in 1916, Edward Harkness became the sole executor of the family estate, and his first act was to donate to his alma mater, Yale university, the funds for a large complex of dormitories and a memorial tower. He reserved the right to choose his own architect, and his selection of his friend and golfing partner James Gamble Rogers, along with the great popular success of the resulting Harkness Memorial Quadrangle, set Rogers on the way to becoming the university architect. It also allowed him to become the designer of many other major school buildings and campuses.[25] The task faced by

Harkness Memorial Quadrangle (Branford College), Yale University, New Haven, Connecticut (James Gamble Rogers, 1917–1921). (Aaron Betsky)

Rogers was to create the first major, planned residential expansion for an institution that, until then, had known exactly what it was about and therefore had had no need to express itself through carefully designed structures. Yale was experiencing tremendous growth and an influx of a new type of student who had to be surrounded by and taught the Yale myth in a more forceful manner than an informal architecture and the teaching practices of the seventeenth, eighteenth, and nineteenth centuries had allowed. The new building was therefore supposed not only to house these new students, but also to become a crystallization of Yale.

When James Gamble Rogers presented his scheme to the Yale Corporation, he chose two formats. One was an impressionistic clay model that he said was supposed to give a sense of the atmosphere of the building. In fact, the whole building was designed to create a romantic but vague sensibility. Rogers hired a renderer to be the chief designer of the project. The other format he presented was the plan of a single unit: a living room with a fireplace flanked by two bedrooms. Rogers then explained how, out of the rational assemblage of this basic unit, a large complex could be created. It would be rational and efficient, yet would be broken up around discrete courtyards, entryways, and episodes. The building was, in other words, not designed in terms of a central idea or a grand façade. Rather, it was meant to be assembled out of functional units that were then transformed in order to evoke the seamless, tradition-bound, and sensual world of Oxbridge. Thus the myth of a vested commonality central to the institution was validated and made real.

Precedent was important, but that did not mean that Rogers felt constrained to operate within the parameters of style. He thought the "Gothic" would work best not only because it was a style that marked the best buildings of Oxbridge, but also because it was a flexible compositional field.[26] Just as he had adapted Beaux-Arts planning to Chicago rationalism, so Rogers here rationalized the stylistic conventions by assembling a scrapbook of architectural elements from all over the world. These pieces were the tricks of the trade: the screens, columns, and windows that gave the buildings he admired their character. The scrapbook became a pattern language for the Memorial Quadrangle, a reference book much like a construction manual.[27]

The pieces were then assembled as episodes around the stacks of rooms, thus giving the efficient dormitory a representative exterior. The rows of rooms were massed into ranges that rose from north to south and made a bulwark out of the city side of the grouping. They were punctuated with towers and arched entryways. Bay windows and arches, buttresses and finials were treated as extensions of the walls that focused the eye in a rhythm of articulation unmatched by most other American Neo-Gothic structures. Finally Rogers, with the help of the university secretary, devised a narrative to organize these disparate episodes in courtyards named for the places where Yale had been located, entryways named for great Yale graduates, and a tower in the middle displaying statues of all the great minds of Western civilization in order of importance. Thus out of the very placeness of Yale its grandeur rose in a tower celebrating the abstraction of thought coming out of the community below, a movement paralleled by the ever-increasing abstraction of the architecture as it reached the top of the tower.

Branford College, as it later came to be known, created a home for and a representation of the Yale myth. It did so by cladding an apartment building with references to a tradition assembled in collaged episodes and then subjected to a master narrative. Beyond its specific function, however, it was also a shining village on top of the hill, another version of the New Jerusalem of which the Puritans had dreamed. It was a model community organized around a church (the dining hall), which was both the place of internal acculturation into shared values and its signal to the outside world; it was organized around a village green that was a courtyard of contemplation, a place where values could be judged; and it presented a rampart of faith to the outside world. This protected and idealized village was completely cut off from the surrounding reality of the city, and the closely set buttresses and relatively unarticulated walls of the exterior made the buildings' function as bastion clear. Inside, this model world was presented as an informal, understated romance. The courtyards were never crossed down the middle, but were entered from corners, allowing the full picture of the village of forms to spread out before the eye. Nothing was formalized in terms of axis. Everything was a collage, a rambling composition that surrounded you on all sides.

James Gamble Rogers eventually designed eight residential colleges for Yale, all funded by Edward Harkness. These colleges were conscious attempts to revive the communality that had marked Yale before the Civil War. They were meant to be the core of the college, and their architecture was intended to represent the values and internal constitution of the institution.[28] They were extraordinarily successful, and became models for the design of institutional learning all around the country. This program of building was, moreover, a fully conscious one. The president of Yale, James Angel, was a pupil of John Dewey; together with the head of the corporation's building committee and Rogers's in-law, John Farwell, and Harkness and Rogers himself, he represented the infusion of "western" men, money, and ideas into the eastern seaboard. Together, they actively campaigned for the "college system." This assimilation, along with the insistence on clothing the pragmatic, rational image of Yale in a historically governed and sensually realized architecture, marked the integration of midwestern, corporate energy into the existing social and economic power structure. Yale, along with Princeton and the University of Chicago, engendered the vernacular of elite education, and its architecture realized a prototype or representative community that continues to serve as the remembered utopia governing the actions of those members of the effective elite who bonded there.

James Gamble Rogers's other masterpiece at Yale, and perhaps his most successful single design, is the Sterling Memorial Library. This building does have a central axis, laid out by Bertram Goodhue before his death in 1925. Rogers ended the navelike axis with a crossing circulation corridor over which a portrait of alma mater presides. The building was wholly organized around this hall, which explained the building, made its collections available in the card catalogues, and allowed one to reach all the subsidiary spaces. But beyond this episode of logic, one found a rambling agglomeration of different junctions. Rogers here created a pavilionized structure articulating each of the various ways in which one could attain knowledge. In addition to the nave and the separate main reading room attached to its flank, there was a monastic courtyard for contemplation, a completely devolved rarebook room, a reading room near the front for those poorer people who used the library as commuters, carefully paired with the Linonia & Brothers reading room housing an old Yale collection. The reading rooms ranged from functional containers whose wood wainscotting mimicked the carved stone Gothicism of the overall structure, to rooms that re-created the richness of a late medieval English country house.

All these separate episodes for the assimilation of knowledge, each

Sterling Memorial Library, Yale University, New Haven, Connecticut (James Gamble Rogers, 1925–1928). (Aaron Betsky)

designed in a slightly different variation on an amalgamation of Romanesque, Gothic, and Renaissance styles, supported the stacks. This tower of knowledge was both a skyscraper and a fifteen-story block containing 6 million volumes and showing itself off to the back of the complex as a large box. The very curious superimposition of a skyscraper on a warehouse on top of a rambling complex was made coherent only through an iconography to which one was introduced at the front door. It was a display of learning and knowledge, featuring both different forms of writing and printing, and a selection of heroes in the quest for understanding the world that culminated at the very doors of Sterling Memorial Library. The building thus was about knowledge; it organized and was representative of it.

The use of Neo-Gothicism as a style was deliberate. For some theoreticians of the Gothic, such as Violet-le-Duc, the style represented structural honesty and clarity, while for the likes of Ralph Adams Cram, it represented the sanctity of tradition.[29] For Rogers and his clients, it probably meant both. By employing a Gothic that Rogers said was "as near to modern as we dared make it," he acknowledge the realities of construction and sought not to express but to represent them in the malleable skin of stone.[30] Rogers also felt that the style would allow Yale to "develop its own traditions," drawing on the example of Oxbridge, but evolving it into its own unique mythology.[31] The style thus represented both the progressive rationality of the university in its desire to be structurally honest, ever more abstract, and even streamlined,

Yale Law School, Yale University, New Haven, Connecticut (James
Gamble Rogers, 1927–1931). (Aaron Betsky)

and the mythic base for an institution such as Yale. This merger was
justified by an appeal to comfort, sensuality, and a picturesque coher-
ence that would make the whole cohere and communicate. The result
was the formation of what might be called a Collegiate Gothic, a style
to represent the self-renewal of the effective elite of this country.

The style was elaborated in several residential colleges at Yale, but
also in the Law School and the Hall of Graduate Studies, both completed in the early 1930s. The Hall of Graduate Studies was even more
"modern" than Sterling, rising in streamlined brick forms toward a
positively Jazz Age pyramidical roof. This development of the Collegiate Gothic was appropriate for that part of the university that prided
itself on its rational research rather than on its collegiate conviviality.
The Law School, on the other hand, was meant to evoke London's rambling Inns of Court, and thus was designed as a collage of some of the
same courtyards, rambling dormitory wings, dormers, bay windows, and
arched openings that formed the language of the dormitories. Onto
this pseudomedieval village a direct replica of the chapel at King's College in Cambridge, here secularized into a library, was imposed. The
iconography of the building, from the overall composition down to
stained-glass windows in the library celebrating the industries of America, in fact spoke of the melding of the traditions of jurisprudence with

the rational pursuit of justice in the modern world. The building thus represented the hopes of the effective elite that traditional forms of judicial control could be continued even in the face of a then stormy process of modernization.

Collegiate Gothic was not the only style in which James Gamble Rogers could achieve this kind of synthesis. His later works at Yale were carried out in what might be called a Collegiate Georgian. The last three residential colleges he designed—Davenport, Pierson, and Timothy Dwight—were located on the periphery of the Yale campus. They were thus meant to evoke that part of Yale that was part of this New England community, while still maintaining some of the aspects of the fortress that the buttressed battlements of the Collegiate Gothic buildings had created. The Collegiate Georgian used some of the same techniques of pseudoscientific assemblage, functional grouping, picturesque massing, and conscious mythmaking that had dictated the design of the earlier colleges, but in the more minimal, sparse mode that seemed to come naturally out of the adaptation of this style. The colleges thus appeared as more functional barracks, resembling their poorer cousins at Harvard, and pointed the way toward the disappearance of architecture as a representational language in later buildings at Yale.

These two "Collegiate" styles became the staples of Rogers's practice. While some of his clients preferred the Collegiate Georgian because of its direct reference to old New England virtues, made famous by Santayana and very popular among the pupils of pragmatism then running many of the institutions for which Rogers was designing, others demanded the grandeur of the Collegiate Gothic.[32] Such was the case in the design of what was arguably (before lamentable additions and renovations) Rogers's finest campus building outside of Yale, the Deering Library at Northwestern University. It was a concatenation of stone buttresses containing a glass cage and mounting a high ridge at the front of the campus. Despite its monumental presence, the central axis again dead-ended right past the front door. One had to turn, move upstairs, and circulate along a cross-axis. The building exhibited frontality, but no central hierarchical massing. Rogers had in fact originally designed the building in Collegiate Gothic, but the university president, a former advertising teacher, thought that Gothic would be easier to sell to donors.[33] Rogers left all the massing the same and merely changed the appearance of both interior and exterior. As at the Sterling Library, the style was then tied to the content through an elaborate iconography. The result is once again a representation of the merger between the acquisition of knowledge and the myth of the institution, literally framing the transmission of knowledge in a historically validated and contemporarily functional structure that is realized as a picturesque composition.[34]

This is the vernacular that James Gamble Rogers developed for the effective elite of this country. Some of the institutions for which he

Deering Library, Northwestern University, Evanston, Illinois (James Gamble Rogers, 1929–1931). (Aron Betsky)

designed remain as central representations of that elite: the Taft School, St. Paul's School, the downtown campus of Northwestern University, New York University, and Columbia University. Perhaps the most skillful of his collegiate work is to be found at the Colgate-Rochester Theological Seminary, a group of brick Collegiate Gothic buildings "echeloned in depth" on a ridge overlooking Rochester, New York. Designed for a client who consciously desired a Puritan "city on a hill," the complex contains a choreography of spaces that refuse a stable viewpoint, and creates a continually shifting composition.[35] All the hallmarks of Rogers's technique are found there, from the long cross-axes to the pavilionized functions, but the richness of assemblage here reached the point that it caused the client to compare it to the work of Jung, Heisenberg, and Santayana, claiming that Rogers's work somehow showed that the most modern discoveries about the unknowability of the physical universe validated the notion of God.[36] Here, Rogers's architecture potentially pointed to a style that could follow pragmatism into embracing the modern physics, radical social theory, and anticlassical aesthetics that were the hallmark of the eastern establishment, the Christian wing of the New Deal. Unfortunately, Rogers was too old or too unaware to follow this direction, and the remainder of his career took a very different tack.

The tragedy of James Gamble Rogers is that his representations were valid for the effective elite only at that point where it isolated itself into bastions of self-definition and regeneration. When he was forced to insert himself into an urban situation, he often failed miserably, as can be seen in the uncomfortable behemoths he designed near the end of

New Schoolhouse, St. Paul's School, Concord, New Hampshire (James Gamble Rogers, 1935–1937). (Aaron Betsky)

Colgate-Rochester Theological Seminary, Rochester, New York (James Gamble Rogers, 1930–1932). (Aaron Betsky)

his career for New York University's School of Education and Columbia University's Butler Library.[37] But beyond the physical context, the
theoretical context for his constructions had also changed. His later
works were designed for institutions much less exuberant and much
less interested in representing themselves. In fact, Rogers received most
of his later commissions merely as part of a package of donations from
Edward Harkness to the institutions in question.

By the mid-1930s, moreover, the bulk of Rogers's practice no longer
involved the design of colleges; he was designing hospitals. Though his
first essays in this field still held on to the need to clad such institutions
in an appropriate garb, mass them in a picturesque manner, and develop an iconography for them, the logic of these enterprises tended
to defeat this kind of traditional architectural thinking. Rogers was proud
of the fact that Columbia-Presbyterian Medical Center in New York,
his first major hospital complex and perhaps the largest commission of
his career, was designed by a team of specialists in answer to technical
needs.[38] Architecture played only a subsidiary part in representing a

Columbia-Presbyterian Medical Center, New York (James Gamble
Rogers, 1925–1927). (Courtesy *Architectural Record*)

complex program that defied compositional clarity. The composition Rogers did derive from these demands was then disciplined by the site, so that the medical skyscrapers were intended to look like man-made extrusions of the cliffs on which they were situated. Architecture as representation here started to disappear into context and function. The towers of the Columbia-Presbyterian Medical Center towered over the cliffs in interlocking wings of yellow brick, each defined by the particular needs of its internal arrangements, each built up through a weaving of horizontal and vertical articulation to create a tapestry of gridded containment, and each almost unornamented. Contemporary descriptions of the buildings emphasized their modernity, their efficiency, and their appropriateness to the kind of high-tech operation they housed, rather than the beauty or sophistication of the structure itself.[39] As Rogers continued to add to the complex, the buildings in fact became more and more streamlined, abstract, and massive, until his son was given the honor of helping to bury the original towers with ever more anonymous hulks.[40]

His last two major works, Abbot Hall for the downtown campus of Northwestern University, and the original Memorial Sloan-Kettering Cancer Center in New York, reflect how far Rogers had come from the representational strategies of his Collegiate Gothic and Georgian modes. Abbot was a stone-clad slab set into the city with no apparent relationship to the surrounding buildings. Its base was a *Moderne* essay whose curved corners expressed only movement. From there, the building massed up in a series of carefully balanced but wholly abstract setbacks, ornamented only by triangular bay windows that were angular, geometricized cousins to the elaborate curved bays that were a hallmark of Rogers's Collegiate Gothic buildings. Sloan-Kettering took the dispersal of the central axis one step further, merging the cross-axis with the organizing central courtyard into a web of circulation that connected the warren of treatment rooms and offices. Both buildings hovered uncomfortably between expressing their functional characteristics and a kind of monumental modern reductivism familiar from the large public works projects of the period.[41] These are monumental structures, but they do not represent a central part of our society. They were merely places of service, integral parts of the working of the institution. They had no need to represent what they were about and thus had no need to develop the vernacular toward their own mythological projection.

By the time James Gamble Rogers died in 1947, there was very little need for architecture because the effective elite had little need to justify itself. It had become an integral and indistinguishable part of the working of society and could not but remain anonymous—an anonymity celebrated in the glass and steel boxes of the next twenty years, and only recently broken through in the reuse of the historical form as part of advertising.

The lessons of the architecture of James Gamble Rogers lie not only

Memorial Sloan-Kettering Cancer Center, New York (James Gamble Rogers, 1936–1939). (Courtesy Memorial Sloan-Kettering Cancer Center)

in the beauty and sophistication of the architecture itself. Rogers no doubt created some of the most successful educational designs in the history of this country, and made a significant contribution to the development of Neo-Gothic and Neo-Georgian styles. But what is much more important is the status of this work as nonexceptional. Its deliberate use of revival styles and its pseudoscientific arrangement of the elements of those styles were governed by three factors. First, the functional requirements of the buildings were allowed to govern the composition of the whole. Second, a picturesque strategy then molded that composition into a series of episodes or vignettes that were defined not by an overall perspective on the project, but by the experience of each part. Finally, an ornamental iconography gave literal meaning to the whole. This was thus an architecture that was representational in three senses. First, it gave a physical shape to the functions housed. Second, it did so in a way governed by issues of pictorial representation. Third, it couched that making-present of the institution in a referential language that meant to represent the meaning of the whole. In the combination of these techniques, it managed to be more than a mute building, becoming instead an articulation of the hidden values and structure of the effective elite. Its power as architecture derives wholly from this function.

Rogers's clients were institutions that saw it as their primary task to represent the importance of knowledge not as an abstract pursuit, but as the organization of the resources of the world toward a productive end. That knowledge had to be attained, preserved, and passed on within a carefully framed structure. It was the property of a small group of people who could use their knowledge of the world to control reality. In so doing, these institutions fixed the methods by which American society could be controlled; knowledge within a framework of carefully defined values replaced pure force as the methodology of social division. The architecture of these institutions represented knowledge and at the same time provided the physical realization of that framework.

The question of representation in architecture thus turns on the question of what is being represented and why. I would contend that architecture only exists when two factors are united: the physical housing of a public function and the simultaneous articulation of that function through a representational strategy. Without the latter, one is confronted with pure building produced by a service industry. Without the former, one may be engaging in architectural investigations, but they remain forms of criticism outside the realm of building. The central dilemma that arises from this situation is that it makes it almost impossible not to create an architecture that is the built affirmation of the social and economic status quo, since it is those who already have the power to control resources and define institutional organizations that need to be housed and represented by architecture. It is for this reason that many architects are today pushing at the very envelope of either building or representation, hoping to shift the parameters of either side of the equation far enough to alter its normative reality. Ironically, the results are more often than not structures of great beauty and sophistication that only serve to represent the necessarily progressive role of the institutions they house. After all, the avant-garde even (or especially) in architecture is indeed only the research-and-development arm of the culture industry. The work of James Gamble Rogers, on the other hand, presents us with the pure seductive beauty of that representational activity known as architecture and shows us the strategy of affirmation in building. In placing itself in a vernacular, in monumentalizing its current situation, in realizing its functions to suit present needs, and in then projecting that reality out in a representational composition, Rogers's buildings seem today like a mirage of a fully functional architecture that seduces us with the siren call of pragmatic forms toward the representation of our own secure position.

NOTES

1. Donald Preziosi, *The Semiotics of the Built Environment: An Introduction to Architectonic Analysis* (Bloomington: Indiana University Press, 1979).

2. Beatriz Columina, "Introduction: On Architecture, Production, and Reproduction," in *Architectureproduction*, ed. Beatriz Columina (New York: Princeton Architectural Press, 1988), 6–23.

3. Mark Wigley, "Postmortem Architecture: The Taste of Derrida," *Perspecta* 23 (1987): 156–79.

4. For the best recent discussion of Hegel's difficulties with architecture, see John Whiteman, "On Hegel's Definition of Architecture," *Assemblage* 2 (February 1987): 5–17. See also John Ruskin, "The Nature of Gothic," in *The Stones of Venice* (London, 1853), 183–250.

5. Manfredo Tafuri, *Architecture and Utopia: Design and Capitalist Development*, trans. Barbara Luigi La Penta (Cambridge, Mass.: MIT Press, 1976).

6. T. J. Jackson Lears, *No Place of Grace: Antimodernism and the Transformation of American Culture, 1880–1920* (New York: Pantheon Books, 1981).

7. I do not claim that James Gamble Rogers was a conscious ideologue. An inarticulate, only semiliterate man, he was a representative of his class.

8. I have traced Rogers's life and career for my study *The Forms of Pragmatism: The Architecture of James Gamble Rogers* (New York: Architectural History Foundation/MIT Press, 1994).

9. Henry Cornelius Atkins, quoted in William Whitney Ames, *Yale Class Book, 1889* (New Haven, Conn.: Price, Lee & Adkins, 1889), 90.

10. George W. Pierson, *The Education of American Leaders: Comparative Contributions of U.S. Colleges and Universities* (New York: Praeger, 1969); David O. Levine, *The American College and the Culture of Aspiration, 1915–1940* (Ithaca, N.Y.: Cornell University Press, 1986).

11. Carl Condit, *The Chicago School of Architecture: A History of Commercial and Public Buildings in the Chicago Area, 1875–1925* (Chicago: University of Chicago Press, 1964).

12. David Van Zanten, "The Nineteenth Century: The Projection of Chicago as a Commercial City and the Rationalization of Design and Construction," in *Chicago and New York: Architectural Interactions*, ed. John Zukowski (Chicago: Art Institute of Chicago, 1984).

13. For the best discussion of the Columbian Exposition and its cultural significance, see Alan Trachtenberg, *The Incorporation of America: Culture and Society in the Gilded Age* (New York: Hill and Wang, 1983), 208–34.

14. The building in question was the Manhattan Building, finished in 1891, but the claim cannot be substantiated. This assertion and Rogers's reminiscences of the days of the Jenney office are contained in a letter to Charles Ulysses Gordon, which Gordon quoted on pp. 11–15 in his manuscript, "Buena Park & Graceland: A Choice Part of Chicago," 1940, Chicago Historical Society.

15. The building was jointly owned by Robert Waller, the brother of Rogers's childhood neighbor, friend, and benefactor J. B. Waller, and by Lucius Brodhead, a Kentuckian for whom Rogers later designed a home.

16. The drawings Rogers made for his diploma are located in the James Gamble Rogers Papers, Manuscripts and Archives Collections, Sterling Memorial Library, Yale University, New Haven, Conn.

17. "Mrs. H. S. Robbins' House at Lake Forest, Ill." *Architectural Record* 20, no. 2 (August 1906): 130–36; Ralph Mooney Root, "Country Place Types in the Middle West," *Architectural Record* 35, no. 1 (January 1914): 1–32, 18–21; "House of Lake Forest," *Architectural Review* 11, no. 3 (March 1904): 127–30; "House of Mr. C. Edward Pope, Lake Forest, Ill.," *Architectural Review* 11, no. 1 (January 1904): 80–81; photographs in the James Gamble Rogers Papers.

18. Gilbert A. Harrison, *A Timeless Affair: The Life of Anita McCormick Blaine* (Chicago: University of Chicago Press, 1979): Lawrence Arthur Cremin, *The Transformation of the School: Progressivism in American Education, 1876–1957* (New York: Vintage Books, 1964).

19. James Gamble Rogers, "The Architecture of the School of Education Building," *University Record of the University of Chicago* 7, no. 7 (November 1903): 183–86.

20. The Shelby County courthouse in Memphis, finished in 1910, was the result of a change in city government in which a professional manager was installed to replace corrupt and fractured political power. See N. C. Perkins, Levi Joy, John Colbert, John T. Walsh, and W. G. Allen, *The New Courthouse, Shelby County, Tennessee: Report of the Commission* (Memphis: private printing, 1910). The New Orleans courthouse and post office, finished in 1915, was designed to be a symbol of the renascent South, and its architecture was meant to recall not contextual prototypes, but civic buildings in the North. See Russell F. Whitehead, "The Old and the New South," *Architectural Record* 30, no. 1 (July 1911): 20. The New Haven post office and court (1914) was the result of a campaign for better government and sanitary conditions.

21. Trachtenberg, *Incorporation of America;* Francesco Dal Co, "From Parks to the Region: Progressive Ideology and the Reform of the American City," in *The American City from the Civil War to the New Deal,* ed. Giorgio Ciucci, Francesco Dal Co, Mario Manieri-Elia, and Manfredo Tafuri, trans. Barbara Luigia La Penta (London: Granada, 1980), 143–292; Kenneth Turney Gibbs, *Business Architectural Imagery: The Impact of Economic and Social Change on Tall Office Buildings, 1870–1930* (Ithaca, N.Y.: Cornell University Press, 1976).

22. A McCehee Harve and Susan L. Abrams, *"For the Welfare of Mankind": The Commonwealth Fund and American Medicine* (Baltimore: Johns Hopkins University Press, 1955), 13.

23. Rosemary Stevens, *In Sickness and in Wealth: American Hospitals in the Twentieth Century* (New York: Basic Books, 1989).

24. Paul Goldberger, *Harkness House* (New York: Commonwealth Fund, 1987); Montgomery Schuyler, "A Fifth Avenue Mansion," *Architectural Record* 27, no. 5 (May 1910): 383–99.

25. The history of James Gamble Rogers's involvement with Yale can be traced in the Papers of the President and Papers of the Secretary, Manuscripts and Archives Collections, Sterling Memorial Library, Yale University. Family friend and in-law John Farwell, golfing partner Edward Harkness, and Harkness adviser Sam Fisher formed a tight group that completely changed the physical form of Yale between 1916 and 1934.

26. James Gamble Rogers, undated and unidentified notecards, James Gamble Rogers Papers.

27. James Gamble Rogers, "Scrapbook Containing Postcards Collected and Used as Sources of Inspirations for Design of Yale Buildings," undated manuscript, James Gamble Rogers Papers.

28. James Gamble Rogers, "Notes on Impressions after Visiting Oxford," undated manuscript, Commonwealth Fund Archives, Rockefeller Archives Center, Pocantico Hills, N.Y. For a description of the campaign of the "college system" at Yale, which focused on the debate on the character of the Yale education and its relation to social values, see George W. Pierson, *Yale: The University College, 1921–1927* (New Haven, Conn.: Yale University Press, 1955).

29. Paul Frankl, *The Gothic: Literary Sources and Interpretations Through Eight Centuries* (Princeton, N.J.: Princeton University Press, 1963); Ralph Adams Cram, "The Beginnings of the Gothic: The Culmination of Gothic Art," in Ralph Adams Cram, Thomas Hastings, and Claude Bragdon, *Six Lectures on Architecture* (Chicago: University of Chicago Press, 1917).

30. James Gamble Rogers, "Notes by the Architect," *Yale University Library Gazette* 3, no. 1 (July 1928): 3.

31. James Gamble Rogers to Anson Phelps Stokes, 23 October 1919, Papers of the Secretary, Yale University.

32. The rector of St. Paul's School, for instance, had originally asked for a Georgian building because of its associations with the virtues of the Founding Fathers, while the donor, Edward Harkness, preferred the grandeur of the Gothic. See S. S. Drury, "The Annual Report of the Rector to the Corporation of the School—1933," St. Paul's School Archives, Sheldon Library, St. Paul's School, Concord, N.H., 7.

33. Rogers quickly concurred. See James Gamble Rogers to University Secretary William A. Dyche, 9 October 1930, in the Minutes of the Board of Trustees, Northwestern University, 28 October 1930, Northwestern University Archives, Evanston, Ill.

34. This connection was made explicit by University Librarian Theodore Koch, who thought the style more "appropriate" for a modern age because it spoke of "continual growth" and efficiency and would draw students toward aspiration. See Theodore W. Koch, "The Charles Deering Library: A Description of the New Building," *Charles Deering Library Bulletin* 1, no. 1 (January–March 1932): 3–7.

35. Reverend Albert William Beaven, "Address—The Divinity School and the Community," *Colgate-Rochester Divinity School Bulletin* 5, Nos. 1–2 (November 1932): 7–19; Howard Moise, "The New Buildings of the Colgate-Rochester Divinity School," *Colgate-Rochester Divinity School Bulletin* 5, nos. 1–2 (November 1932): 103, 113, 107.

36. Edgar Sheffield Brightman, "The Personality of God," *Colgate-Rochester Divinity School Bulletin* 5, nos. 1–2 (November 1932): 46–62.

37. The most succinct critique of Butler Library is to be found in Robert A. M. Stern, Gregory Gilmartin, and Thomas Mellins, *New York 1930: Architecture and Urbanism Between the Two World Wars* (New York: Rizzoli, 1987), 110.

38. C. Charles Burlingame, "The Medical Center in New York," *The Architect* 10, no. 4 (July 1928): 442–43; George Nichols, "The Development of the Medical Center," *The Architect* 10, no. 4 (July 1928): 447–551.

39. An enterprising paean to the Columbia-Presbyterian Medical Center is to be found in Eric Mendelsohn, *Russland Europa Amerika: ein architektonischer Querschnitt* (Berlin: Rudof Moser Buchverlag, 1929), 196, 216; says Mendelsohn, "Present-day New York, however, builds with the precise cunning of

technology. . . . This manner also evidences America's desire for the new, expressed in the disciplined power of its composition."

40. The successor firm, now called Burgun, Shahide and Deschler, is still in operation in New York, specializing in hospital design.

41. Richard Guy Wilson, *Public Buildings: Architecture under the Public Works Administration, 1933–1939* (New York: Da Capo Press, 1986).

III

ARCHITECTURE AND CONVENTIONS

INTRODUCTION

Critical and
Artistic Conventions

BARTON PHELPS

LONG AGO, when we set out the program for this symposium, it was entitled "Convention." At that time, we were to deal with what seemed to us very clear issues of convention in architectural practice. Things have changed a bit since then. Convention means the use of conventional elements in architectural composition—building forms, arrangements, materials—that carry with them some generally understood significance. To that, we need to add the idea of artistic convention—that is to say, ways of working, means of expression, how architects actually produce what they produce. Those means have remained beneath the surface of many discussions without ever having been really addressed. We should also include the idea of critical convention—that is, ways of responding to the things that we see.

Diane Ghirardo is a professor of architectural history at the University of Southern California. She is a native of Montana, but was raised with a deep immersion in the culture of Italy and has spent much of her life there since she was a child. That pattern continued in her education when she pursued her studies at the American Academy in Rome and when she was a Fulbright scholar in Italy. She received her doctorate from Stanford. She has been known for a rather expansive body of work dealing with Italian fascist architecture and for her translation of Aldo Rossi's work *The Architecture of the City*. We were particularly keen on having her contribute, because she has inserted herself in the postmodern discussion, in terms of both architecture and urban planning.

Frank Israel is the youngest of the architects included in this volume. Aaron Betsky has said he thought half the people involved had gone to Yale. I checked around, and I'm starting to think he is right. I find myself in the position of having been at the School of Architecture there about midway between Bob Stern and Aaron Betsky. That was in the late 1960s, when the Venturian position was newly established but still radical enough for people to get excited about things like rediscovering Henry Russel Hitchcock's famous old book *Modern Architecture: Romanticism & Reintegration,* which suggested that there might be more than one direction that modernism had taken and that the orthodoxy of the international style had eclipsed a fuller understanding of what had actually transpired. Now this is not a thought that I can imagine making incredibly sexy for my students today at UCLA. But what it does remind me of is that we are at this moment in a very dynamic situation. Frank Israel seems to have undergone a significant change in that same period of time that I'm talking about. He was born in 1945 and later appears to have bounced around the Ivy League from the University of Pennsylvania to Yale, finally receiving his degree in architecture from Columbia. He was a Prix de Rome winner at the American Academy in 1973 and has been a professor of architecture at UCLA since 1977. His built work has shown a rather remarkable development since his Snell House of 1971 on Long Island, which displays an early familiarity with what used to be called the Yale–Philadelphia axis. It is an essentially formalist approach developed by a succession of great teachers such as Paul Cret, Louis Kahn, and Robert Venturi. But the work he discusses, especially the Propaganda Film Studio of 1988, indicates an emphatic shift to an architecture of discrete collaged elements. This shift associates Israel much more clearly with emerging *artistic* conventions in Los Angeles.

Although the built output has been limited, it has been of significant quality and rigor to merit Israel's selection in 1988 as one of six young American architects exhibited at the Walker Art Center in Minneapolis in a program called "Architecture Tomorrow." The projects that Frank showed in that show differed significantly from one another, and it is my opinion that no consistent theoretical approach emerges from the work. What the work does seem to depend on is the repeated use of particular artistic conventions such as frontal projection, symmetry, processional development, and nonplumb elements.

Terragni, Conventions, and the Critics

DIANE GHIRARDO

THERE ARE TWO principal and related aspects of critical conventionalism that I plan to examine. One regarding the practice of architecture, and the second the practice of criticism. I understand convention as a customary practice or pattern of usage with its own rules and internal logic. In architecture, conventions very often derive from building types or combinations of building types, but they also engage most aspects of design and building, including fabrication, the deployment and treatment of materials, ornamentation, and the disposition of spaces. By contrast to this notion of conventions, Alois Riegl recognized the existence of a canon, or set of practices vested with a universal authority, that dominated architectural and artistic practice from the Renaissance until the nineteenth century.[1]

Adherence to the canon colored both the production of new work and the appreciation of old. Riegl noted that during the nineteenth century the canon's authority declined, giving way to a greater openness to many possible formal systems, one no more valid than another. This allowed formerly denigrated styles and attitudes toward design to be reevaluated—especially the late antique and the medieval—and opened the way for more variety in contemporary building and design. But, Riegl noted, though the canon no longer held undisputed sway, the belief that such a canon existed endured at least up until his time,

Casa del Fascio, Como, Italy. Façade (Giuseppe Terragni, 1932–1936). (Collection Diane Ghirardo)

even if everyone could not agree on its precise lineaments. Upholding the canon, a pursuit that required eternal vigilance, led to the condemnation of some works—for example, many of John Nash's projects in London—and marked others for praise—such as Inigo Jones's Banqueting House at Whitehall.

By contrast, architectural conventions oppose the notion of a canonic authority that supersedes all other claims to authority. Conventions are understood precisely as being embedded in social and historical reality, in other words, as being historically bounded. Hence, despite their internal rules, they often make no claims of transcendent and timeless authority but remain open to change.

Many factors prompt modification of building conventions, from new programs to new materials, not to mention new needs for variety and self-expression by the designer. The notion of critical conventionalism engages the designer in challenging the received conventions of the discipline. An ideal example of this strategy is the Casa del Fascio of Como, the provincial party headquarters of the Fascist Party (PNF) in interwar Italy, designed by Giuseppe Terragni and completed in 1936.[2] It is perhaps one of the best-known buildings from this period in Italy.

The building type, the Casa del Fascio, was one of several new institutional structures developed under fascism.[3] Others included the Casa del Balilla, a children's fascist organization more or less like the Girl or Boy Scouts; the Gioventù Italiano del Littorio for older children, which eventually embraced all youngsters up until about eighteen; and a variety of insurance and public assistance buildings, maternal and infant assistance agencies, and summer resorts. The notion of having a structure such as the Casa del Fascio developed from the Socialist Party's Casa del Popolo, or people's house. Under fascism, this building became the PNF's major institutional building, "the neurological center of a living organism," as Terragni's friend P. M. Bardi put it, the organ in which regional, political, and assistance activities were coordinated within the larger domain of the nation.[4] Although Case del Fascio were being built from about 1927 on, they took on definitive typological form only in 1932. And that typological form was borrowed from the northern Italian town-hall type of the late twelfth through fourteenth centuries.

Sound reasoning lay behind the choice of this particular typological configuration. It harked back to the self-governing communes of late medieval Italy, when the citizens gradually substituted communal authority for that of the bishop or lord. The assembled citizens typically chose a temporary *podestà,* or mayor, to serve as executive administrator for a specific period while they in turn established laws and rules for him to enforce. As communal government took on administrative form, so too did the typological configuration of its chief public building, the Palazzo del Commune or del Popolo. Its chief configurational elements include a rusticated, typically unfenestrated, corner tower like that of the Palazzo del Popolo of Piacenza. The tower was variously disposed symmetrically or asymmetrically and often, but not always, had a bell. It also included an assembly room, that was often raised above an open courtyard or loggia; an interior or external ceremonial staircase; an *arengario,* or balcony, from which to summon the populace; crenellation; and the office space in the palazzo itself. The ultimate model, of course, was the Senate with its tower on the Piazza del Campidoglio, which recalled the self-governing Senate of the Roman republic, but in particular the medieval administrative center of Rome.

When communal authority finally gave way to the authoritarian control of new strong men, condottieri as they were called, often one of the first acts of the new central authority was to revamp the town hall, the emblem of communal autonomy, emptying it of its real functions but preserving its heraldic ones. When the Visconti took over in Milan, they straightened the Torre de Commune in line with Renaissance notions of balance and order, and transformed it from the town hall to a training school for bureaucrats and city officials. That is, it retained the appearance rather than the substance of autonomy.

Another example of the same process is in Montepulciano. When Montepulciano lost its autonomy and was taken over by Florence, Florence sent the architect Michelozzo to Montepulciano, where he took a heterogeneous group of buildings on the main piazza and united them with a façade that gave the building the appearance of the Palazzo Vecchio in Florence, once again to accomplish the same end. Montepulciano was no longer an autonomous community, but retained the appearance of independence with the building.

The Fascist Party appealed especially to two periods in Italian history as putative models for the fascist state, the Roman and the medieval. Mussolini in fact often styled himself a condottiere. When PNF officials finally settled on a typology for the Casa del Fascio, they chose this reassuring and identifiable building type, which offered the deceptive promise of restoring a noble past, and sought to have the Casa del Fascio take its place among existing public buildings in the center of the city. At the same time, the PNF's administrative apparatus began to take on form, so that the appointed mayor of Italian towns was now called a *podestà*, a title that had long fallen into disuse but that was now recovered from the medieval past along with the building type. And the *podestà* would speak in loco parentis, so to speak, for Mussolini from the little balcony, the *arengario*.

The question one would pose, then, of Terragni's building is why it appears so different from the other Case del Fascio. The answer, I believe, lies in the critical stance Terragni adopted toward the conventional building type. In an early design, Terragni proposed to place a tower adjacent to his seven-bay façade, the party mandate clearly guiding this aspect of the design. When he eliminated the tower, he left the unfenestrated corner block as a virtual tower, and an interim drawing shows this corner block topped with an *altana,* a traditional crown on Italian towers, and an architectural element that immediately evokes an association with towers in Italy. And although Terragni ended up dropping the *altana,* the party engineers in Rome later recommended the addition of just such a structure in order to shore up the typological association—as Peter Eisenman has remarked, the PNF and other fascists always have wanted more and stronger typological associations.[5] The front elevation, with a recessed portico, likewise recalls the townhall type. Terragni reformulated it, however, with sixteen glass doors that could open simultaneously into a covered internal courtyard, effectively the loggia of the medieval town hall. In this case, the ceremonial staircase is internal on the diagonal axis leading from a covered interior courtyard. What we end up with is not the mindless repetition of a medieval town hall, as one so often found in other Case del Fascio, but a creative and critical elaboration of a contemporary convention.

Terragni obviously dropped the crenellation as unnecessary and an inappropriate addition to a modern building, and adopted a modern language as well as modern building practices. Like many other rationalists, Terragni believed fully and deeply in the fundamentally modern character of the fascist revolution. And he further held that only a modern architecture was appropriate for this new state. He and others, as his friend Bardi remarked in a 1936 publication dedicated to this particular building, believed that "the state and above all the fascist state must control architecture with scrupulous vigilance to give unity to this art that summarizes and expresses civilization."[6]

Instead of fence-sitting between the modern and the classical, as one scholar has recently charged, Terragni in fact deliberately sought that delicate point embracing both the security of a revered past and the challenge of the future, exactly as fascism claimed to do.[7] The Casa del Fascio was constructed with reinforced concrete, a new, modern material that was hotly debated in Italy, but with a marble revetment. He included the ceremonial staircase, but with a glass balustrade. He included a loggia, but one that could be simultaneously closed and opened by virtue of the glazing, as well as fully opened by means of the automatic doors. He framed the courtyard with columns, but some were sheathed with aluminum alloys. Although the town-hall type governed the typological configuration of the building, he claimed that the specific proportions, the location and height of windows, basement, parapet, smaller ventilation windows, and so forth, were all governed by the golden section and by regulating diagonals. Beyond this, Terragni also employed a variety of materials including glass, glass block, highly polished marble, and aluminum in a delicate tension exploring transparency, reflection, and opacity. And, of course, he did this in part because he himself said, "Fascism is a house of glass into which everyone should be able to look."[8] He tried to incorporate this belief into his design in the same way as he wrote in his publication on the building.

Terragni left further evidence about the typological origins of this building. The medieval core of Como, compressed and crowded with venerable buildings, afforded no space on the main square in town, the Piazza del Duomo, for the Casa del Fascio. The Torre del Comune, the Broletto, and the Duomo occupy the positions of honor. Terragni developed a plan and an image that allowed the Casa del Fascio to relate to the three historic buildings. The Casa del Fascio is in one corner; in a special issue of *Quadrante,* he illustrated the Casa del Fascio flanking the Duomo, just as the Broletto and the Torre del Comune did. Como was also scheduled to build a new *palazzo del governo,* or government office building, with a union office, militia barracks, and then the existing theater. And other existing buildings were destined to be torn out. In the same issue of *Quadrante,* Terragni diagrammed how crowds could be organized in the piazza in front of the building and how much space was needed to include larger and larger numbers in the audience. He remarked that the three monuments were three revolutionary artifacts flanking one another to form a superb ensemble on the western edge of the Piazza del Duomo.

His building and its political patron represent the fourth revolutionary period—the fourth revolutionary artifact, as he says.[9] The Casa, with its unfenestrated corner tower, open loggia, and internal courtyard, completes and balances the panoramic vista with the public build-

The Broletto, Duomo, and Casa del Fascio, Como, Italy. (*Quadrante* 35/36, no. 8 [1936]: 32)

ings flanking the central and most important one, the religious one. Of course, Terragni was also a devout Catholic, so the scheme was typologically, as well as symbolically, appropriate.

The building, then, is consistent with a contemporary typological invention, yet critical in its reinterpretation by means of a modern formal language. At the same time, as a committed fascist Terragni did not share the modern movement's expectation that architecture could reform anything. On the contrary, the process was already under way through the PNF's policies. The task of the architect was to reconcile architecture with politics. Terragni specifically affirmed this.[10]

Critics analyzing this structure in the last twenty years or so have proposed as the typological source the Renaissance palazzo (Cesare de' Seta), the Como courtyard house (Franco Purini), and the Venetian palace (Tom Schumacher).[11] This particular image offers telling evidence of a much more direct origin in the town-hall type.

While I'm not interested in taking issue with these interpretations, it is noteworthy, I believe, that none takes account of the public and political destination of the project or the quite explicitly political intentions of the designer. This brings us to the second part of my discussion, which concerns the conventions of criticism. The three typological interpretations just noted represent fairly conventional versions of the formalist genealogical approach, in which fundamental issues are brushed aside in order to propose an unbroken formal narrative in which things-as-things are related according to more or less obvious, more or less sophisticated similarities in appearance. Such an interpretive strategy skirts dangerously close to a formalist free association here in which anything can be related to anything. I have yet to figure out the precise point of such exercises, although they are the stock and trade of architects and architectural historians. Most such formalist criticisms seek to demonstrate how the building in question transcends history, how it finally defeats historical contingencies. Perhaps all one can say is that delimiting similarities, however strained the relationship, allows one to place the artifact in an orderly, dehistoricized, and, I suppose, ultimately reassuring progression of events and artifacts, just as the PNF, as noted earlier, chose the medieval town-hall type for similar reasons. But among the questions circumvented in these purely formal analyses are those concerning explanations. Why, for example, would Terragni, knowledgeable as he was about architectural history and typologies, want his Casa del Fascio to be based on the Venetian palace type?

On this point the historian is silent. No answer readily offers itself. Similar questions posed to other scholars also yield silence, a silence that has to be attended to. There is good reason for its presence, for it partakes of current conventions in criticism. As I noted earlier, the typological form had been set by the PNF, and thereafter was adapted by the many architects who designed hundreds of these buildings throughout Italy, including Terragni in the other PNF headquarters that he designed—for instance, the Casa del Fascio for Lissone, in this case with Antonio Carminati. To accept the style as the starting point for discussions signals the key problem at issue here.

The political matrix of this project presents a problem for conventional criticism of the Casa del Fascio, and it does so for two fundamental reasons. First, that political matrix is fascism. Second, a strategy that entails confrontation with the political institution here has implications for today's architectural and critical practice. Most historians and critics are now willing to acknowledge, albeit grudgingly, that Terragni and many other rationalist architects, along with others, of course, were dedicated fascists.[12] For example, Terragni's brother Attilio was the *podestà*, or mayor, of Como, appointed by the fascist state; it was Attilio who originally received the commission for the design but then passed it on to his brother. But we hear repeatedly that such information does not impinge on our assessment of a particular building. Most often, as with the scholars mentioned earlier, the political destination of individual buildings is simply ignored. In fact, one scholar even remarked that Terragni's work expressed sentiments antagonistic to those expressed by art more closely linked to the regime.[13] For the links to the regime, we need only listen to Terragni: "The concept which engaged me was that of reconciling two aspects of a new order: art and politics."[14] He proceeded to cite the party's statute as the logical source for the interior's spatial organization, for this is not simply a sequence of rooms but a sequence of purposes, functions, and relationships between people and party. I shall not here elaborate the body of evidence in Terragni's other buildings and writings, not to mention the testimony of contemporaries, that bears witness to the architect's attempt to give built form to the idea of the fascist revolution. But what he saw as the new order was the intimate link between the revolutionary fascist state and the revolutionary architecture of modernism, or rationalism as it was called in Italy.

A second type of critical discussion of Terragni's practice has emerged in recent years—for example, in the work of Manfredo Tafuri and José

Quetglas—and might be called paracritical.[15] In both their analyses, we encounter anthropomorphized forms that "do" things. In Tafuri, a wall "annuls or pushes to the margins the articulations of the organism." The stairs are "alien to the volumetric stability from which they issue. They have nothing to say concerning the purism of the volume of offices. They demonstrate the battle that takes place between the actors in turmoil."[16] And in Quetglas, the solid blocks "persist in their search, disconcerted." They seem to have "lost their capacity to turn toward one another, their capacity to attract and repel."[17] Both essays brim over with terms such as "fragment" "discontinuity," "fissure," "rupture," "interrogate the text," "affiliations," and so forth. And both insist on the textual nature of architecture. Tafuri tells us that "fragment and totality face one another"—in Terragni's work—"in silence, the mask given body, the subject placed in parenthesis."[18]

Although they do not seek a typological pedigree, no less formalism animates these essays than those to which I referred earlier; all are decontextualized and unsituated. But there is meaning to be found in Terragni anyway, and Tafuri specifically says that "to build houses that speak of the impossibility of offering shelter is the ultimate meaning of his act of composing." The problems raised by this approach are not trivial. Tafuri, for example, hinges most of his argument on the design for Solution A, for the Palazzo del Littorio competition of 1934, and in particular the massive wall, with isostatic lines and *arengario* for Mussolini that he then links up with other Terragni projects.

When I translated this article some twelve years ago, I warned of the danger of hinging an entire explanation of Terragni on a design produced by a team of architects and painters, and on one of two designs produced by the same team for the same competition. Tafuri's argument slips through our fingers like mercury, when we discover that Terragni served as chief architect for Solution B. And Luigi Vietti was chief designer for Solution A. Vietti specifically designed the wall, as Carol Rusche has lucidly and conclusively demonstrated.[19] Although an egregious example, Tafuri's sleight of hand is symptomatic of a formalist approach that chooses to ignore the highly ramified conditions in which Terragni's works were produced, and especially the many projects and designs that he undertook on behalf of the PNF. Along the same lines, Quetglas and others speak of Terragni's design for the O Room of the exhibit of the fascist revolution in 1932 and 1933, a profoundly political and pedagogical exhibit, by virtue of subject matter alone.[20]

In each of the chief rooms, exhibits and graphics recounted one year in the eight-year march of fascism to power. And for each room, a historian and a designer collaborated on organizing the material—everything from newspaper clippings to bloody shirts and bullets—and then the designer selected the organizing motifs for the decoration of the rest of the room. Using everything from photomontage to con-

Sala O, Mostra Della Rivoluzione Fascista (Giuseppe Terragni, 1932). (Archivio Centrale Dello Stato, Rome)

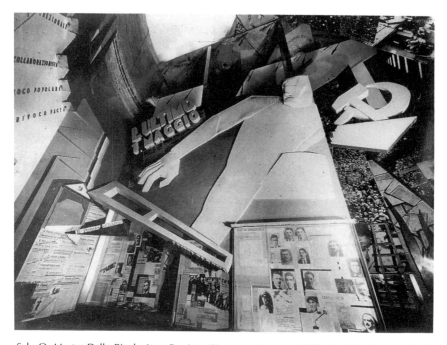

Sala O, Mostra Della Rivoluzione Fascista (Giuseppe Terragni, 1932). (Archivio Centrale Dello Stato, Rome)

structions of steel to breaking walls and exploding them into the space of the room, Terragni sought to create the atmosphere of 1922, the ten months leading up to the March on Rome and Mussolini's appointment as prime minister. His charge was to explicate the key themes of fascism, and he did so in a concatenation of materials and architectural volumes summarizing the force of the revolution. Terragni sliced through the room diagonally, rendering Mussolini's profile in metal, showing starving children under the caption "Bolshevik Paradise," and representing the strikes that paralyzed Italy after the World War I with a huge steel spider web. He also presented key phrases in oversized letters, such as "Absolute discipline," "To say hierarchy is to say discipline," and "To say hierarchy is to say scale of human values," hierarchy being a key principle of fascism. Terragni here expressed not only his political beliefs but his beliefs about the uses of art, specifically to work in harmony with the new state and to create the atmosphere in the proper setting and as a monument to fascism. Quetglas completely ignores the highly explicit political agenda and speaks of the frenetic, insistent fractures and the continuum of cuts, overlaps, and transparencies that link Terragni's design to the work of Piranesi.[21] This kind of discussion is akin to what Michael Sorkin refers to as the Stealth Bomber Syndrome, in which government officials, journalists, the military, and engineers speak about every aspect of the bomber from legislative history to technology to aesthetics without ever engaging the discussion of its single key purpose: to sneak under alien radar systems and kill millions of people undetected. However interesting, provocative, and informative all these conventional discussions about the bomber are, they exclude what is arguably its central point.

Such is the case with the conventional formalist analysis of the Casa del Fascio that erases *fascio* from its name. This robs it of its historical particularity, its expressed political agenda, its significance as a product of the designer's effort to wed a revolutionary aesthetic to a revolutionary political movement, to ground architecture in the new life praxis that he believed fascism provided. These conventional and fundamentally formalist critical practices with architecture spring from the problematic of architecture as set forth in contemporary practice, in which the boundaries of architecture, and hence the decisions about what is relevant to discuss, are set forth and maintained by an interlocking institutional web that includes architects but also the real-estate industry, developers, government officials, and of course educational institutions. Architecture, in this construction, appears to play but an abstract role in culture. It "relates to the city," "expresses discontinuity," "tampers with traditional relationships," "engages ornamental chaos," and, in the words of one commentator, "depowers structures."[22] But it has nothing to do with power and the wielding of power by the other elements in the institutional framework.

Proposed façade decoration (Giuseppe Terragni and Marcello Nizzoli, 1936). Mussolini's face looms over the piazza in this project for a photomontage to be placed on the Casa del Fascio in an undeniable demonstration of the political matrix of the building. (Archivio Centrale dello Stato, Rome)

Terragni did indeed challenge formal conventions, but he also challenged fundamental institutional conventions about architecture. For he insisted on his profound links with politics and fully acknowledged the primacy of this politics in his design. Today's confrontations with conventions, on the part of both the architect and the critic, remain exclusively within the domain of formalist issues, and therefore are but marginally critical, if at all, since the limited so-called critical moves take place within a highly circumscribed and frankly limited framework in which the only conflicts are formal and aesthetic ones.

I have been interested in the relationship of Terragni and his architecture to fascism in part because of more general interest in this particular period in history and in the relation of architecture to political structures, but also because the most cherished value of the recent architectural tradition has been precisely the political irrelevance of architecture, its autonomy as an art, and hence the autonomy of the architect. Italian scholars have refused to examine the significance of Terragni's fascism in part, I think, because of an unwillingness to confront the wide acceptance that fascism achieved in Italy; but the same cannot be said for American scholars. It is no accident that all the critics I mentioned earlier are architects. Their exclusive preoccupation with form in Terragni suggests more about their own culture than about Terragni's.

NOTES

1. Alois Riegl, "The Modern Cult of Monuments: Its Character and Its Origin," trans. Kurt Forster and Diane Ghirardo, *Oppositions* 25 (Spring 1982): 55–67.

2. The bibliography on Terragni and the Casa del Fascio is extensive. The most recent study, Alberto Artioli, *Guiseppe Terragni: La Casa del Fascio di Como* (Rome: Beta Gamma 1989), includes an updated bibliography. See also Diane Ghirardo, "Politics of a Masterpiece: The Vicenda of the Façade Decoration, the Casa del Fascio of Como, 1936–1939," *Art Bulletin* 62, no. 3 (September 1980): 466–78; and Thomas Schumacher, "Terragni and Classicism: Fence Sitting at the Barricades," *Journal of Architectural Education* 41, no. 4 (Summer 1988): 11–19.

3. Franco Biscossa examines the origins of the institution of the Casa del Fascio in "Dalla Casa del Popolo all Casa del Fascio," in *Case del Popolo*, ed. M. DiMichelis (Venice: Marsilio, 1986), 175–224.

4. P. M. Bardi, "Prima conclusione di una polemica," *Quadrante* 35/36, no. 8 (1936): 2.

5. Ghirardo, "Politics of a Masterpiece," 474.

6. Bardi, "Prima conclusione," 2.

7. Schumacher, "Terragni and Classicism," 11.

8. Giuseppe Terragni, "La costruzione della Casa del Fascio di Como," *Quadrante* 35/36, no. 8 (1936): 6.

9. Terragni, "La costruzione della Casa del Fascio," 16.

10. The special issue of *Quadrante* 35/36, no. 8 (1936), dedicated only to the Casa del Fascio, contains essays in which Terragni made these points especially clear.

11. Cesare de' Seta, *La cultura architettonica in Italia durante le due guerre* (Bari and Rome: Laterza, 1972, 1985), 230–50; Franco Purini, "L'architettura didattica," in *Giuseppe Terragni: Casa del Fascio*, ed. L. Ferrario and D. Pastore (Rome: Istituto Mides 1982), 11; Schumacher, "Terragni and Classicism."

12. Giorgio Ciucci, *Gli architetti e il fascismo* (Bari and Rome: Laterza, 1989), 146–51.

13. Giorgio Ciucci, "Italian Architecture During the Fascist Period: Classicism Between Neoclassicism and Rationalism: The Many Souls of the Classical," *Harvard Architecture Review* 6 (1987): 76–87; de' Seta, *La cultura architettonica*, 235.

14. Terragni, "La costruzione della Casa del Fascio," 21.

15. Manfredo Tafuri, "Giuseppe Terragni: The Subject and the Mask," *Oppositions* 11 (Winter 1977): 1–25; José Quetglas, "The Edge of Words: Prolegomena to Future Work on Terragni," *Assemblage* 5 (February 1988): 67–89.

16. Tafuri, "Giuseppe Terragni," 4, 9.

17. Quetglas, "Edge of Words," 76.

18. Tafuri, "Giuseppe Terragni," 22.

19. Carol Rusche, "The Palazzo del Littorio Competitions" (Paper presented at the International Symposium on Terragni, Villa Vigona, Menaggio, 11–13 July 1989).

20. Diane Ghirardo, ed., "Culture and Architecture in Fascist Italy," *Journal of Architectural Education* 45, no. 2 (February 1992): 66–106.

21. Quetglas, "Edge of Words," 82.

22. Such turgid and meaningless phrases can be found in most so-called deconstructivist discussions of architecture. These particular phrases are from Mark Zigley, "The Displacement of Structure and Ornament in the Frankfurt Project: An Interview," *Assemblage* 5 (February 1988): 51–58.

Montage, Collage, and Broken Narrative

FRANK ISRAEL

SOME WRITERS have described my work as quintessential southern California, although I have little idea of what that adjective implies. However, it is true that much of my work is influenced by the place where I work and where the particular work is located. Other factors of course influence the work, often to a greater extent. Before preparing this presentation, I anticipated discussing a series of projects that I had done prior to moving to California, in relation to the projects I have been working on since I moved here a dozen years ago. However, preparing for this seminar helped me clarify my thoughts on the various projects, and I decided in the end not to discuss my earlier work, which I now find inappropriate to this discussion. I now feel that while there can be important relationships between the place where one works and the projects themselves, often there are more underlying features that serve to unite different projects in different locations.

The most important feature is the nature of the project itself. All the examples I will discuss are modifications of original models, responses to existing contexts and buildings. Each project is an addition, a remodeling, or a renovation of something that existed prior to my coming into the picture. Once involved, I entered into a relationship with a client, a relationship on which I place great importance. I believe that the best overall results can be achieved when the client is involved in each stage of a project's development. Obviously, a client's involvement varies according to his or her interests. No architect would pretend that this client–architect relationship is an easy one, but I would like to think that in all my work a keen awareness of the needs and desires of my client is discernible.

Another factor that influences these works and ties them together is a series of formal conventions that are inserted into each—a readable and understandable language of composition. Formal conventions have always run through my work. When I tried to delineate the difference between what I was doing on the East Coast (which has a strong influence on me) and what I am doing here in L.A., I felt that there were easy differences. However, later I realized that the same language of composition ran through each project, east and west, and tied the site, the program, and the willful involvement of the client together. I have used these formal conventions to create a particular sense of the whole, which at times can be quite difficult to ascertain.

I have mentioned the importance of site. It is integral to development of any design. In several of the projects I will discuss, the problems of site and location have dictated the outcome. In one case, site difficulties resulted in the work's remaining unbuilt. In this case, the architect's job consisted of working with the physical limitations of a particular site as well as the restrictions imposed by local building authorities. The architect also has a responsibility to the urban context into which his work will be placed. Such contextual reference is vital to my work. I am always conscious of attempting to make a design unique and striking while at the same time anchoring it in its surroundings.

Two places in particular have exerted the greatest influence on my work: Rome, where I lived from 1973 to 1975, and Los Angeles, where I have lived for the last twelve years. It is fair to say that both of these places play an important part in the particular pieces that I have been working on. The two cities are obviously very different. Buildings are sited differently in Los Angeles than they are in Rome. In L.A., they crop up; in Rome, they are layered and embedded in the terrain. This can be partly explained by the geological and topographical differences between the two cities. In L.A., where the soil conditions are very poor and the risk of earthquakes is constantly high, buildings tend to have an ephemeral quality. The houses that are situated in the L.A. hills seem to hover above the ground like machines from another world, a constant reminder that Los Angeles, as a place, is not destined to exist without the mammoth willful exertion of man.

The two cities differ not only in regard to the physical landscape in which they are situated, but also in regard to the societies that spawned them. The needs, desires, and ideology of Rome, first an imperial seat of government, then the temporal capital of a spiritual power, and finally the center of a nineteenth-century nation-state, differ from the ambitions of a vibrant, commercially oriented conurbation on the

southern California coast. Rome is, and always was, a much more unified whole than L.A., which is made up of hundreds of distinct enclosed entities: shopping malls, cineplex centers, film studios, and urban villages. Each is separated from the others by the barrier of freeways
and garden streets. Elements like the freeways are an integral part of
the life force of Los Angeles. On one level, the freeway appears to
serve the same functions as the Roman street, being a way of moving
from one point to another. But unlike the unifying nature of the Italian street, the freeway can also be regarded as a vehicle of escape,
something that cannot be attributed to its Roman counterpart, unless
you consider the aqueduct an equivalent tributary.

It could be argued that L.A. possesses a more introspective atmosphere; its residents want a self-contained living and work space di-
vorced from the reality they see in the modern world around them.
Smog-filled air, traffic at a standstill, and an increasing perception of
horrifying violence have all served to reinforce the idea that the "real"
world is something to escape from. Architects must respond to these
fears and offer solutions that help all people's anxieties. Fear of the
modern world and how to conquer that fear is a theme that runs through
most of my work at times subtly, at other times more evidently. For
example, the project I did for Propaganda Films addressed these fears.
I have attempted, in that particular work, to create an urban environment, a safe, nonalienating place for its inhabitants, closed off from the
world outside.

Los Angeles proclaims itself an ultimate modern phenomenon: the
open, free, extroverted, modernist experiment brought to life. Fear,
anxiety, and introspection were not envisaged by the planners in the
first half of the century. They could foresee, however, the tremendous
eclectic building explosion of the postwar years. Once-separate towns
grew together into a great potpourri of urban villages. The nearest
equivalent to this phenomenon is New York of the early twentieth century, a city in which foreign styles and rituals were imported en masse
and used unashamedly in architecture. Similarly, L.A. exhibits a wonderful cornucopia of imported influences, some good, some bad, but
all helping to create a synergistic energy that infuses all pieces of work.
I am attracted by this process and its result, and have tried to incorporate the remnants or pieces that have been left over or broken up
from this creative energy. This can be seen in a simple and direct way
in one of the details of the Lamy House. Around the pool, we used
tiles and other bric-a-brac from the client's childhood home in France
that are a direct reference to the Watts Towers, themselves an amazing
mixture of influences and materials.

There is a garden near my house in L.A. that I pass every day when
I go to the gas station to fill up my automobile. For me it is an impor-
tant garden, reflecting an eclectic attitude and a mosaic of influences.
It is made of Astroturf, and in this little piece of vibrant artificiality can

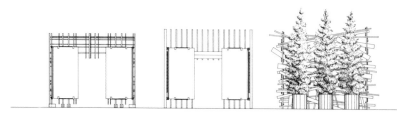

Installation at the Walker Art Center, Minneapolis. Section (Franklin D. Israel, 1988). (Courtesy Franklin D. Israel Design Associates, Inc.)

be found much of the underlying philosophy of L.A.: the blatant import of images, in this case green grass, has been a necessity in order to re-create the reality that the beholder wants to see. This architect, of course, was no mere stage magician or Hollywood illusionist. No matter how great his skills were, he had to find a way of creating this apparent reality while at the same time using real, native forms, governed by the true instability of the land, natural culture, and climate.

Before going on to discuss examples of my work that testify to the ideas I have discussed, I want to mention an installation of mine that was constructed for the Walker Art Center in Minneapolis in 1988. The exhibit neatly encompassed the themes of my work. The show consisted of six minimal wooden pieces, pavilions, arranged in a room: different places for showing work and displaying items. The display panels were of concrete; actually, they were made of a material called glaswal and were then hooked on to the wooden frames by a series of steel clips. In essence, the wooden pavilions became scaffolding on which to hang ideas. Each one represented a different form of structure and architectural pattern; these wooden grids announced a vitality of construction and a potential for different forms. They became a framework in which to locate fragments of industrial and mass-media vernacular that can, in turn, stand against the abstract background of sea, desert, mountain, and freeway of L.A. I used this technique of montage, collage, and broken narrative to emphasize a whole range of stylistic diversity, but I hope there are different themes to relate to in each pavilion. I also wanted to express a sensual handling of materials as well as a certain sense of theatricality. (When I first arrived in L.A., I did some work as a set designer before becoming, like so many before me, disillusioned with the film industry.) Lastly, I wanted to visualize these feelings of refuge and the need to escape what I have just been mentioning.

Five of the six pavilions allowed the viewer to enter and be surrounded by the installation. The sixth, however, did not. It consisted of six pine trees placed within the protection of one of the pavilions; the viewer could only touch the trees through some wooden slats. Here, I wished to express the idea of refuge. The trees were contained in a "safe oasis" that the spectator was prevented from fully entering by the barrier of the wooden grid. The viewer was kept at a distance; he could perceive the idealized world of trees but was prevented from fully being a part of it. As mentioned earlier, I adapted this idea of refuge and later expanded it in the project for Propaganda Films.

The first project I want to discuss is a renovation of a loft in New York City that I did while living in Los Angeles. I think it demonstrates each factor I have discussed, particularly the importance of the client—

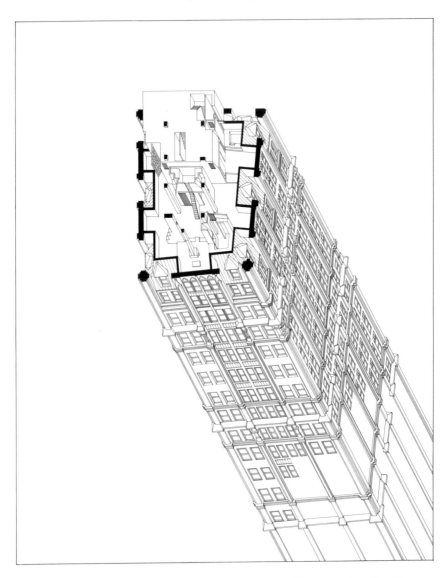

Gillette Studio, loft renovation, New York. Axonometric (Franklin D. Israel, 1982). (Courtesy Franklin D. Israel Design Associates, Inc.)

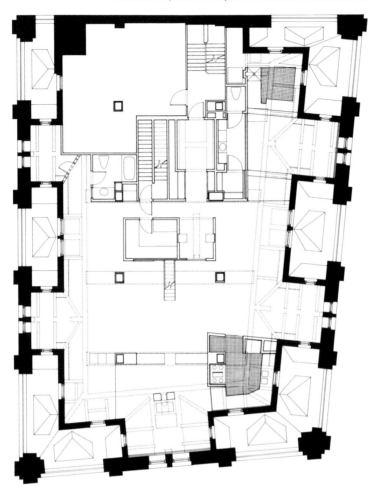

Gillette Studio, loft renovation, New York. Plan (Franklin D. Israel, 1982). (Courtesy Franklin D. Israel Design Associates, Inc.)

architect relationship. The site consisted of the boiler room at the top of the Liberty Tower, a building in lower Manhattan built in 1929. The space involved the top two floors of the building, which were demolished completely before I began the project. At that time, the client worked as a stylist in the fashion business (he is now a photographer). He wanted to create a place in which to both live and work. Once the space was demolished, we gave it a rigid formal structure uniting the project as a whole.

In this project, everywhere the visitor is guided by a strong axial symmetry; it draws one into this world apart and encourages one to move on through it. From the front door, a major axis follows, past the electrical and security systems, into a vestibule-like area where the client intended to place two major objets d'art. This axis continues into the major studio space beyond. As if in a ritualistic procession, the visitor is unconsciously propelled through a series of frames and gates. Visually, one may discern some references to the works of Louis Barragan. This was due to the interest my client had in Barragan's work after returning from a business trip to Mexico. He was in love with Barragan and demanded that we use particular pieces, which we did. You can see the references quite clearly, in the staircase without railings that does not really go anywhere (except to a closet), or in the shower spout and Jacuzzi pool where the water continually circulates from shower to Jacuzzi, overflowing, only to start its cycle again. I enjoyed the irony that this Barragan-inspired interior landscape is thirty-one stories up in the air. A disaster can happen when it leaks, as it has a couple of times. The juxtapositions in this project became a pastiche. The project as a whole does not depend on them. In fact, some of the materials and colors have since changed. Today the client no longer likes Barragan but prefers the Arts and Crafts movement. He has covered the concrete floor with wood, added upholstered walls, and painted the persimmon walls olive. It is a very strange place at the moment. Despite these superficial changes, the basic design and its formal organizational logic remain unchanged. I wanted to create a place where the original dark spaces were converted into a small village of closed forms, a space in which the visitor is saved from disorientation by strong axes and localized symmetry anchoring the rooms and interiors. The potential chaos of contemporary life has here been imposed with an order that comforts the visitor.

The second project reveals how the client–designer relationship and the physical limitations of the site can influence the outcome of a project. This project was never built. The original house was famous for being the first one in Los Angeles to use glass blocks; built in 1922, it is sited in the Hollywood Hills. After my client purchased it he decided that he did not like glass block and had all of it removed; he then asked me to design an addition. One of the main problems was that we had to fit a fairly complicated program into a small, steep site. Like the studio in New York, a strong sense of axiality underpins the workings of the program, making this addition and the original a coherent work. The completed building steps across the contours of the hills, giving way to a set of local axes shifting centers, leading the visitor from the rear entry through larger and more public space, and finally opening up to a view of the city below. The client also had a distinctive collection of furniture and other pieces from the *art moderne* movement. He presented me with a book of the work of Mallet-Stevens stating that this work represented what he wanted his building to look like. At the very least, he wanted his building to begin to reflect some of these stylistic motifs.

We worked with them. But we also had a series of very real and complex site relationships to grapple with. One of the solutions to the

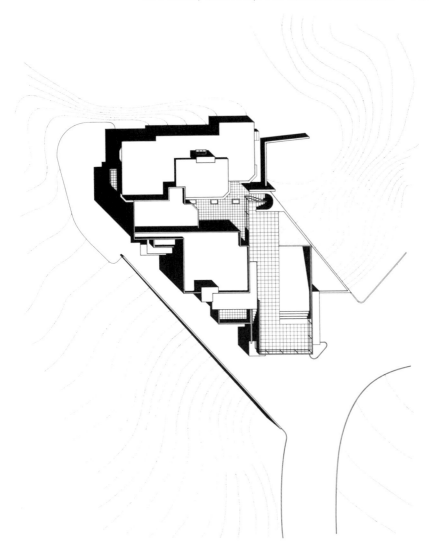

Bombyk residence, Los Angeles. Site plan (Franklin D. Israel, 1986). (Courtesy Franklin D. Israel Design Associates, Inc.)

lack of space on the hill was to position the pool over the garage, not an easy thing to do structurally, but one mixing two quintessential symbols of California: the automobile and the swimming pool. Here the pool is given porthole windows from which the swimmer can view the city. The automobile shuffles in underneath like some miniature submarine destined to float in the sky.

Problems of the site were similarly evident in a house in Malibu that I remodeled for the film director Robert Altman. Bob is an extremely creative and energetic man. When he came to me to discuss the project,

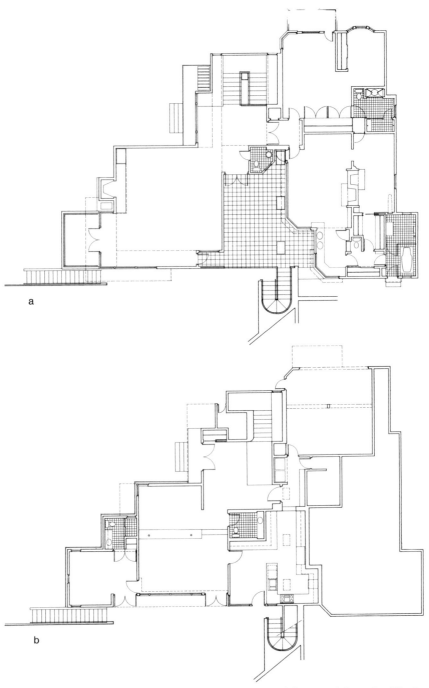

a

b

Bombyk residence, Los Angeles. Plans: (a) second floor and (b) ground floor (Franklin D. Israel, 1986). (Courtesy Franklin D. Israel Design Associates, Inc.)

Bombyk residence, Los Angeles. Section elevations (Franklin D. Israel, 1986). (Courtesy Franklin D. Israel Design Associates, Inc.)

he brought along a cardboard model that he and his son Matthew had built, showing what he wanted the new space to look like. He had bought a condominium out in Malibu, even though he knew it was sinking into the Pacific Ocean. He had been told, in fact, that the whole area would eventually slide into the sea. This did not bother Bob, who is a real trouper; in the meantime, he wanted to do something that would completely break up the existing plan. This was divided on two floors and broken up into little nondescript rooms. He and his wife, Katherine, wanted one very large loftlike space. To accomplish this, we gutted the entire lower floor, creating a series of different levels with no walls to separate the particular places. Creating a large vertical light well or interior court, we linked the first and second floors. We established a formal relationship between the façade that holds back the stairs, and the hallway that links the dining area to the living space. Formal elements here are set in the vertical plane; the horizontal floors remain free. For example, the fireplaces are set pieces that echo in the layout of the floor, but eventually extend into an informal overall pattern.

Bombyk residence, Los Angeles. Section elevations (Franklin D. Israel, 1986). (Courtesy Franklin D. Israel Design Associates, Inc.)

This project had the potential to be extremely difficult, given the willful model that Bob had given us and the parameters of what we had to deal with. Because of the nature of the slide area and the Coastal Commission's refusal to let us alter the exterior, we were very constricted as regards the exterior of the building. We couldn't add or change windows, for example. Certain items had to be omitted when they proved too expensive and impossible, such as the fireplace waterfall. We did salvage the deckside Jacuzzi, which links itself to the fireplace through a richly designed tile pattern. We retained the existing structure as much as possible. For example, the rafters in the bedroom were sandblasted and left exposed. Found objects and fossils from the beach were embedded into the concrete pieces so as to effect a unique texture and appearance.

An extension to a house in Hancock Park reveals a different form of client–designer relationship. Here the original house was in a "neocolonial" style with rather banal features. The client hated the house; he and his wife had moved there because of the proximity to their daugh-

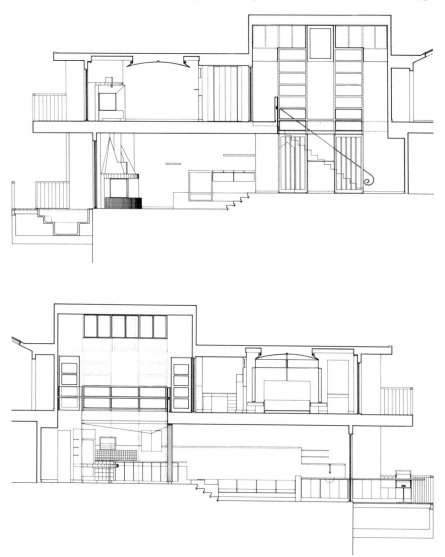

Altman residence, Malibu, California. Sections (Franklin D. Israel, 1987). (Courtesy Franklin D. Israel Design Associates, Inc.)

ter's school. The client liked to consider himself avant-garde. One day, he cut his front lawn in a severely expressionist way and, not surprisingly, upset the neighbors. When he added several pairs of sacrificial sculpture, they became outraged. We wanted to make this house a more livable place, or at least a place that could "work" for him, his designer wife, and his family. When we began, they had just come back from the Caribbean and wanted to add a Caribbean front to the house, but I refused. I felt that the front of the house was adequate and that it

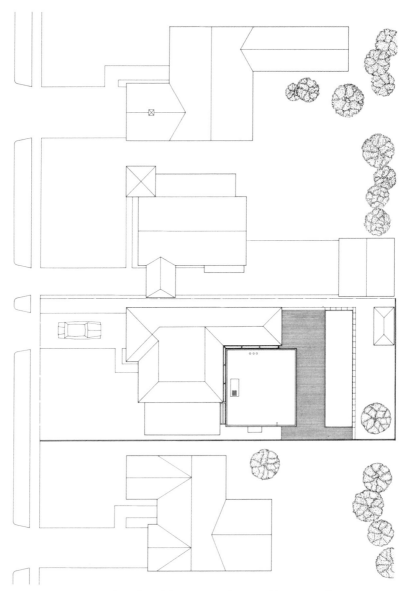

House extension, Hancock Park, California. Site plan (Franklin D. Israel, 1988). (Courtesy Franklin D. Israel Design Associates, Inc.)

related well to its neighbors. It grounded the project in the existing context. Instead, we concentrated our work on the back of the building, adding a 730-square-foot steel structure, a two-story pool house/ studio. In fact, the space can serve as an art studio, a gallery, a guest bedroom, a dining room, or just about anything. But this is mere addition. It is really a formal imposition on a nonformal house. House

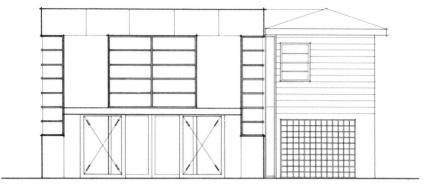

House extension, Hancock Park, California. Rear elevation (Franklin D. Israel, 1988). (Courtesy Franklin D. Israel Design Associates, Inc.)

and addition are linked together in a cubistic composition. Yet the studio maintains a self-contained aloofness from the original house.

Many of the elements used in this project are influenced by the work in California of Rudolf Schindler and Frank Lloyd Wright. The window details owe much to the work of these architects. In each case, they have been reinterpreted according to contemporary standards. The earlier details were fabricated in steel, which was less costly at the time. Today I have modified these in wood, which makes them thicker and creates a great sense of juxtaposition with the original columnar structure. Redwood siding that has been added has been left unpainted, an uncanny response to the white clapboard veneer of the original. Upstairs the master bedroom was enlarged by extending a deck that is accessed through double doors. The oak-clad balcony suspends over the entire space as a viewing platform for the client. It completes the axis that begins outside in the garden, ascending the pool steps onto the deck through symmetrically placed sliding doors. From this great porch, the client can survey the scene. At a recent event, it provided a place for a rap group to do their thing while an audience listened to them below.

All the ideas and strategies just outlined can also be found in a project we undertook in Hollywood. This project represents a process of understanding rather than a universal solution. The client was a small, young music-video and film-production company called Propaganda Films. They wanted me to turn a warehouse in Hollywood into their offices. The plan as it exists now is a series of conference rooms that are delineated as object pieces: a large central "boat" that floats in space, containing executive offices, a series of auxiliary facilities, a film vault, financial offices, editing rooms, and spaces for creative directors. Naturally there is a screening room as well. All these spaces are tied together by a major axis and subsidiary cross-axes.

At first, the client wanted an "office landscape," which is defined as a series of open partitioned spaces. I had just returned from a trip to

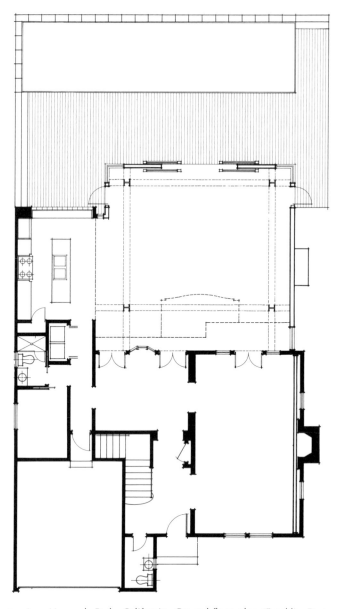

House extension, Hancock Park, California. Ground-floor plan (Franklin D. Israel, 1988). (Courtesy Franklin D. Israel Design Associates, Inc.)

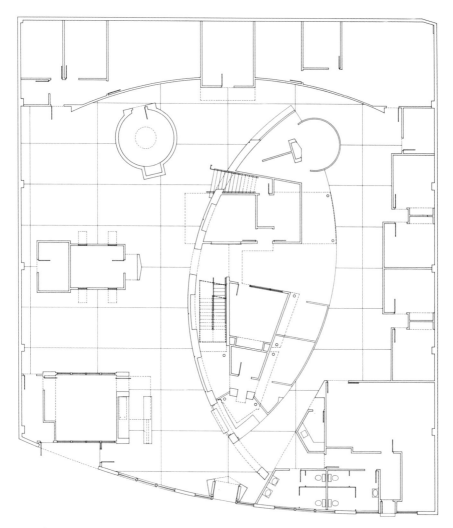

Warehouse-to-office conversion, Hollywood, California. Ground-floor plan (Franklin D. Israel, 1988). (Courtesy Franklin D. Israel Design Associates, Inc.)

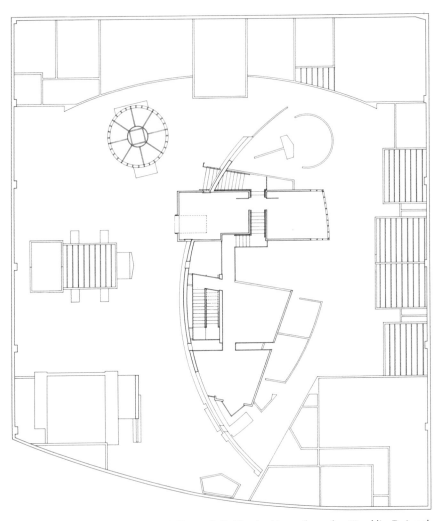

Warehouse-to-office conversion, Hollywood, California. Upper-floor plan (Franklin D. Israel, 1988). (Courtesy Franklin D. Israel Design Associates, Inc.)

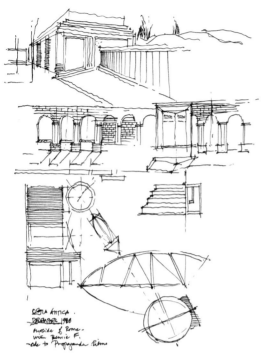

Ostia Antica, Italy. (Courtesy
Franklin D. Israel Design Associates, Inc.)

Rome, and during my visit I had spent a day at Ostia Antica. What
impressed me about this Roman town was its richly textured spaces and
carefully articulated edifices. There were object buildings and contextual pieces. The public spaces seemed to fall into these two categories
as well. Because Propaganda was composed of a group of persons with
distinctly different backgrounds and attitudes, I applied an urban village concept to unite them. The original is a vaulted shell organized by
a series of axes, to which the various components are aligned. The bow-
string trusses that restrain the vault were projected in plan; this image
was mirrored and the central office boat was made.

Experiencing Propaganda is akin to working in the film and video
business. The space is open but not open-ended. There is a front desk
that is the beginning destination, a large waiting area that can be the
entire residual space, and a somewhat obscured destination that is the
film vault. Formal relationships reinforce this experience without op-
pressing it. Tables and chairs and other freestanding pieces create an
urban scenography, one where the visitor, instead of being lost and
confused, is confronted by familiar pieces and guided through the chaos
by architecture.

Finally, I would like to turn briefly to the subject of what lies beyond
postmodernism. The way forward for architecture, I now believe, is in
recognizing some of the factors I have elaborated and in combining
them to produce works that achieve balance and harmony. Simply, there

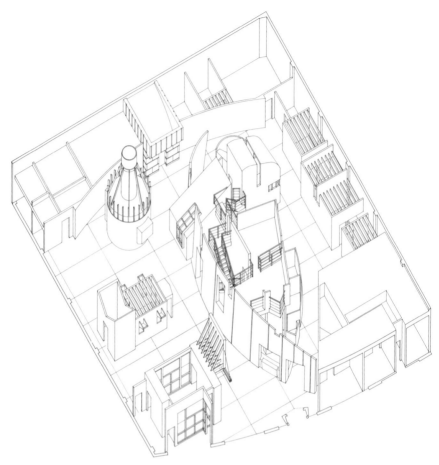

Warehouse-to-office conversion, Hollywood, California. Axonometric (Franklin D. Israel, 1988). (Courtesy Franklin D. Israel Design Associates, Inc.)

is the Site, the Model, and the Client. Within this triangle, the architect must be a planner, builder, illusionist, diplomat, manager, employee, juggler, and psychiatrist.

Architects do not offer ultimate solutions anymore. We no longer have the same kind of confidence that our predecessors had in the early part of the century to offer answers and lay down plans for the future. We now realize that control of the future is more difficult than we had presumed. But the past has always been able to provide us with directions. In our thought processes, we select from our memory in attempts to have more influence over the future. We can still be the creators of dreams and we can still bring images and desires to life. But we have to show a greater awareness of, and a sensitivity to, the realities of contemporary life. Only with this modesty, coupled with our technical knowledge, can we confront what is beyond and still to come.

IV

ARCHITECTURE AND SOCIETY

Socially Motivated Architecture

ANDREA DEAN

THE PREVAILING VIEW of architecture with a social or public mission is that it was buried by 1980s consumerism, self-involvement, and privatization, which elevated public greed over public need. As John Zeisel, a sociologist and advocate of social architecture during its heyday in the 1960s and 1970s says, "It's not what we praise, it's not what gets published, it's not what we teach."[1] Zeisel contends that social architecture has been abandoned by architects and by academia, and that neither took it seriously enough to begin with.

More surprising is a diametrically opposite assessment by, among others, Robert Sommer, an environmental psychologist at the University of California at Davis. Sommer's influence during the halcyon days of social concern in architecture was rivaled only by Zeisel's, but unlike Zeisel, Sommer concludes that the battle for social architecture has been won. Oddly, both claims are true, though each obscures the real story. Zeisel's cynicism about architects is bolstered by the fact that most designers, like most other Americans, spent most of the decade in a muffled state of detachment from social and political problems. Out of feelings of impotence or indifference, and because image was everything, many architects took refuge in nostalgic fritterings with form.

How, then, to explain Sommer's conviction that the battle for social architecture has been won? And what was the battle about, to begin with? Attitudes and ideas about social architecture during this century have been defined by modern architecture and by reactions against it. So for our purposes, the battle took form with the early modernists' struggle to come to grips with a massive housing shortage during the 1920s and 1930s and to erect a belief system opposed to prevailing totalitarian ideas.

To fight fire with fire, perhaps, the convictions developed by modern architecture's founding fathers often had the same exclusive and tyrannically paternalistic qualities as the ideas they opposed. Both Wright and Le Corbusier, for example, while agreeing on little else, were convinced that a revolution in architecture that swept aside the past and traditional culture would spearhead a utopian new social order. Enlightened buildings, they believed, would reform the world and human nature. As Lewis Mumford wrote in 1968, recalling modernism's early heroic days, "We identified the new with the good and hailed the New Man, the New Woman, the New Politics, the New History, the New Science: in short, the new world. History, we thought, began and ended with ourselves and we expected the new to last forever."[2]

By the late 1940s, modern idealism governed urban renewal and reform programs. Harvard's dean, Joseph Hudnut, confidently wrote in 1946, "When the slums are cleared, when the people live in cleanliness and space, when good schools and recreational areas are available to every citizen . . . we shall have established the basic conditions for social and political health."[3] Today, such tidings of a brave new world sound like messages from the planet Krypton.

By the late 1960s, credence in modern architecture's brightest hopes began to unravel. Ironically, the faith was shattered by a widespread perception that modernism was indifferent to human needs, that its look-alike, sterile-seeming boxes were socially inept and irresponsible. Architectural historian Joseph Rykwert only half-jestingly noted that modern buildings hate people.

Reflecting a broad disillusionment with modern architecture's agenda, Ada Louise Huxtable wrote in the *New York Times* in 1971, "The naive faith that a certain kind of design would result in a certain kind of human response is simplistic nonsense."[4] The 1972 decision to dynamite the unmanageable and dangerous Pruitt-Igoe housing complex in St. Louis seemed proof of modernism's failure as an instrument for social betterment.

Belief in architectural determinism was replaced by a new confidence in what was hailed as "socially responsive architecture." In addition to being a reaction against modern architecture, the new attitude was a reflection of the antiauthoritarian climate of the late 1960s and early 1970s, which grew out of the civil rights and antiwar movements. During President Johnson's war on poverty and the early years of Nixon's presidency, construction of low-income housing was at its height, and advocacy for the rights of the poor and minority groups was supported by a host of federal programs. In the spirit of egalitarianism, architects forswore their roles as social engineers and aesthetic pooh-bahs, and tried to demystify their craft and make it more accessible to ordinary citizens. "User participation" and "advocacy planning" became the call to arms in a series of battles in the war for social architecture.

It is these skirmishes that psychologist Robert Sommer had in mind when declaring the battle won. Because behavioral scientists like Sommer and Zeisel were trained and skilled in ferreting out the design needs and wishes of ordinary people, they often served as commanding officers in these maneuvers. In fact, social scientists were often asked to play a larger role than they were prepared for by schooling or inclination. As Princeton sociologist Robert Gutman wrote in 1968, "Architects, having become ethical relativists confused about what is good or bad for man, for the community, and for society . . . turn to the sociologist in the hope that his discipline has somehow been spared this form of demoralization."[5] By the early 1970s, the social aspect of architecture had become so important that the value of design itself came under fire. Those who entered the profession were highly idealistic but often lacked basic design skills; architects ended up doing far more organizing and planning than designing of social architecture. Many of the early attempts at advocacy and community design were, in fact, hostile to architecture. Always fearful of losing control over the design process and being elbowed out by specialists, architects now had ample reason for anxiety. The profession seemed to be losing its grip even while admitting that its hold—its elitism and know-it-all-ism—had been spurious.

The late 1960s and early 1970s were, nonetheless, an exciting time of intense social involvement. Community groups and community action flourished with some eighty community design centers nationwide providing technical assistance for neighborhood plans, day-care centers, health clinics, housing, rehab, and other projects. Only about thirty community design centers survive today.

To repeat the question: Why, then, does Robert Sommer think the battle has been won? Sommer, who now directs a consumer-interest research center at the University of California, Davis, and does consulting work for architects, believes that the values, beliefs, and methods developed by social architecture in the 1960s have unalterably changed the practice of architecture and planning.

Among the legacies, for instance, are today's widespread design procedures, which originated in the community design review boards set up in the 1960s. They institutionalized participation in urban planning and design decisions by all kinds of citizen groups. As a result of such procedures, the following scenario would seem inconceivable today. In 1962 Philip Johnson, Aline Saarinen, Uhlrich Franzen, and other design notables led a protest against the demolition of New York's venerable Pennsylvania Station. Nonetheless, it succumbed to the wrecking ball and was replaced by the new Madison Square Garden, a thoroughly nasty-looking building of no redeeming cultural value.

A related bequest of the social architecture movement of the late 1960s is a heightened urban concern and sensitivity. As Romaldo Giurgola said in a 1980 speech about the 1968 protest movement at Columbia, "The whole question was about the emergence of an urban consciousness. The legacy of 1968 calls on us as architects to become aware of different cultures, of different ways of life."[6] Issues of context and appropriate scale have gained prominence and improved our cities. A direct result is that the 1980s have produced some of the most humane works of urban design of the last half century. As Robert Geddes of Princeton said, "Ideas of the public realm have been absorbed into architects' and developers' vocabulary while the resurgence of the city street is a very hopeful sign."[7]

Community design centers, meanwhile, though diminished in numbers since their heyday, are far more effective, professional, and knowledgeable about finance, management, and related disciplines. Robert Shibley, former chairman of the Architecture Department at the University of Buffalo, asserts that "social architecture has grown up." He says,

> It doesn't make the outrageous claims of the 1960s. It doesn't feel it has to attack the aesthetic conceits of the profession to work, and it no longer calls for false choices between aesthetics and social, political, economic and ecological values. It is quietly, perhaps too quietly, working on several contexts.[8]

Rather than looking to government for funding and guidance, most community design centers today work as self-sufficient organizations and encourage corporate input and participation. Mary Camerio, who teaches community development at the University of California, Berkeley, explains: "People who want to work in low-income housing today understand that they have to know about the development game. The deals are the deals whether they are made for profit or not."[9]

Often unnoticed, the methodologies developed by social architecture in the 1960s have become an integral part of the design process, much like energy-conscious design. Market research is just another name for user studies and sensitive programming. Design management, postoccupancy evaluation, and other contributions of the behavioral sciences have been folded into the design process. There is far more awareness today of the needs of special populations—the old, the disabled, the abused, the dying—and most reputable schools of architecture and landscape architecture now employ social scientists on their faculties, while several schools of psychology have active research and teaching programs in environmental psychology. But sociologist Robert Gutman sounds a couple of warning notes:

Behavioral science approaches are being used less frequently by architects than by major developers, housing administrators and the new client group of facilities managers, the people who determine how much space is needed, how it should be configured and furnished, and how various arrangements can affect morale, behavior, and productivity.[10]

Gutman says this is integrally connected with the most important movement in architecture of the last twenty years. It is the increasing power and control of the design process by clients.

As clients have gained control over the design process, architects have lost out. One reason is that projects have become so vast and complex that most designers have neither sufficient skills nor knowledge to assert control. Many architects have narrowed their role to the business side of architecture or to the fashioning of façades. One result, according to Gutman, is that many behavioral scientists have given up on architects.

Among them is John Zeisel, the environmental psychologist whom I quoted at the outset as saying of social architecture, "It's not what we praise, it's not what gets published, it's not what we teach." He left academia some years ago to form a private consulting firm that provides market research, programming, and other services not for architects, but for building clients. Though many of the objectives of 1960s social architecture have been embedded in our culture and in building and development procedures, the optimism and idealism that produced them were as good as dead during the 1980s. Gutman places at least partial responsibility for "the lack of a prominent sense of social mission in architecture" on Robert Venturi's call for a narrowing of the field to exclude social and political issues in his book *Complexity and Contradiction in Architecture.*[11]

But there are other reasons for architects' disillusionment and retreat. As former USC dean Robert Harris says,

> In the 1960s, as socially motivated architects, we expected to be hugely welcome into poor neighborhoods and exactly aligned with the expectations of the people. Today our expectation is that the local neighborhood is not going to be that thrilled with the arrival of an architectural team. The people have twelve voices rather than two. Often, it is not even sure what the social good is.[12]

Moreover, Harris and many like him are increasingly stymied by new sets of problems that resist known solutions. They are all too familiar: homelessness, the scourge of drugs, violence, intractable poverty, and illiteracy among a new American underclass; the imperilment of the planet's ozone; and so on and so on. There is anger at the pervasive greed that drives up land and housing costs, that devours the countryside and replaces it with soulless commercial malls and strips, office parks, and traffic jams. There is a widespread feeling of being overwhelmed, victimized, at a loss for what to do, especially as the costs of construction and social programs far outstrip the cost of goods and other services that are affected by increased technological productivity.

In the face of huge, seemingly insoluble problems, our tendency has been to distance and to distract ourselves from perceptions of inequity, from our feelings about that inequity, and from government. Michael Brill, president of BOSTI (Buffalo Organization for Social and Technological Innovation), points out that architecture itself has become part of the distraction and entertainment industry. He says it has a fraudulently soothing and sentimental quality. Yet many architects are choosing tactics more constructive than distancing and despair. For the most part, they concentrate on modest acts of responsible design and resource preservation. Designers are staffing review boards and participating in other community groups that influence planning and architectural decisions, and in RUDATS, the American Institute of Architects' regional urban design assistance teams. Furthermore, the organization called Architects, Designers, and Planners for Social Responsibility has grown in numbers and influence in recent years.

But in most of the country, no response commensurate in scale to the size of our problems has emerged, nor are most educators yet encouraged by student attitudes. For some time now, students have been concerned with careers and personal achievement at the expense of social commitment. Bernard Spring, dean of the Boston Architectural Center, described to me how "students at Harvard take you through mythical axes of design. That is all they are interested in. If you ask what is the room going to be used for? they don't know what you are talking about. Architecture is being remystified."[13] Dana Cuff, who teaches at the University of Southern California, told me that her students are "interested in real context, real clients," which is also a way to raise social interest. But she adds, "it hasn't happened yet and there are very few role models. Few professors are working on socially motivated projects and students don't see much socially motivated architecture published in magazines."[14]

There is some evidence, frail as yet, of increased interest in social issues. Among the hopeful signs was a symposium at the University of California, San Diego, at which Richard Meier, Ricardo Legeretto, Fumihiko Maki, and Richard Rogers each talked with some passion about the importance of social concerns to their work. Another positive indication is a new interest in landscaping, which is architecture working with issues of environment and ecology. Historicism, with its stress on surface and a sentimental past, is on the wane. Also encouraging are some of the results of AIA's Vision 2000 program, an ongoing study of architectural needs at the turn of the century. Participants at a recent Vision 2000 conference placed community design and planning at the top of their list of important roles for architects at the beginning of the new century. The conference report concluded that "the public is slowly beginning to face economic challenges and assume responsibility for untended social problems."

Social problems are again making headlines and being addressed with a new urgency, though we are not beyond the talking stage. For instance, the *Washington Post* ran an essay by Robert Borasage of the Institute for Policy Studies headlined "Are We On the Brink of the Progressive Comeback?" His thesis is that we are entering an era of populism far different from so-called bleeding-heart liberalism. He argues that the changing global context is transforming national priorities and rights. It is no longer guns versus butter, economic competition versus environmental degradation. The flow of drugs into our country poses dangers far more clear and present than a Soviet leadership suing for peace. Borasage contends that "more and more business leaders endorse the vital need for new public investment if the economy is to prosper, hundreds of billions to modernize the infrastructure, to clean up the environment, to educate the work force of the future." He adds that because such public programs are vital to the growth of the economy and the health and welfare of the entire nation, they cannot be attacked as taxing the middle class to subsidize the poor.[15]

Historian Arthur Schlesinger, Jr., who regards the late 1980s as comparable to 1928 or 1958, has suggested that the 1990s, like the 1930s and the 1960s, will be a decade marked by idealism. Let's hope that 1990s social activism is different from that of the 1930s, with its noxious drum-tight totalitarian ideologies of Right and Left. Let's also hope that it is more inclusive than 1960s attitudes, that it is not us against them, and that it is more clearheaded and realistic, skillful and informed.

NOTES

1. John Zeisel, telephone conversation with author, May 1989.

2. Lewis Mumford, *Architecture as a Home for Man: Essays for Architectural Record* (New York: Architectural Record Books, 1975), 151.

3. Joseph Hudnut, "The Political Art of Architecture," *AIA Journal,* June 1946, 295.

4. Ada Louise Huxtable, *New York Times,* 4 July 1971, sec. 2, 20.

5. Robert Gutman, *AIA Journal,* March 1968, 74.

6. Quoted in Paul Goldberger, *Architecture on the Rise: Architecture and Design in a Postmodern Age* (New York: Times Books, 1983), 14.

7. Robert Geddes, telephone conversation with author, May 1989.

8. Robert Shibley, telephone conversation with author, May 1989.

9. Mary Camerio, telephone conversation with author, May 1989.

10. Robert Gutman, telephone conversation with author, May 1989.

11. Gutman, referring to Robert Venturi, *Complexity and Contradiction in Architecture* (New York: Museum of Modern Art, 1988).

12. Robert Harris, conversation with author, September 1989.

13. Bernard Spring, telephone conversation with author, September 1989.

14. Dana Cuff, telephone conversation with author, September 1989.

15. Robert Borasage, "Are We on the Brink of the Progressive Comeback?" *Washington Post*, 22 October 1989, C1, C2.

N I N E

User-Oriented Architecture

PAUL ZAJFEN AND MICHAEL WILFORD

THE UCI SCIENCE LIBRARY: PROGRAMMING

One of the legacies of the social movement is the influence that non-architects have on building, especially public building. One of the first major decisions made by public user groups is the selection of the architect, which will clearly have the biggest impact on the form of the building. The IBI Group, my firm, together with James Stirling Michael Wilford & Associates, were selected as architects for the Science Library at the University of California, Irvine. The program had not yet been completed by the university. It is very often the case with university facilities that the university will select different firms to do the program and ultimately design the building. We were fortunate in being selected as both programmers and architects; this allowed us to build on the rapport and the enthusiasm of the user committee, including the campus architect, David Neuman.

The program was extremely important in the design of the facility, as it sets out a budget and square footage for the building. Those numbers could not be changed throughout the design process, and therefore the degree of latitude inherent in the program determined the

The first section of chapter 9 is by Paul Zajfen.

ease with which we, the architects, could manipulate the space and create interesting public places.

Our team felt that the building design should flow from the unique requirements of the site and the special characteristics of the building as delineated by the program. We were determined that the programming phase should draw out the wishes of the users in a manner clear enough to give direction to the subsequent design phases.

A facility like the Science Library is a public facility—for the community at large as well as the university. It serves faculty and students, primarily in this case graduate students, but also undergraduates. This Science Library will house various disciplines: physical sciences, sociological sciences, medicine, engineering, and computer sciences. Presently each of these disciplines has its own library in its own building, with its own librarians. We knew it would be easy for us to get information about the facility from the librarians, but we wanted to have input from faculty and students as well.

We designed a questionnaire that we mailed out to all the staff and faculty; students had them available at various points throughout the library. We scheduled a series of half-day meetings with the faculty of the various schools, at which only a few attended except for the Department of Computer Sciences, where fifty people appeared. At the School of Medicine, the dean showed up; finding that a good friend of mine was on the faculty, I brought him to the meeting, coercing him to tell us his thoughts about the future library.

Three or four vocal people told us that they really did not want a unified Science Library. They wanted their own particular building, and enjoyed their personal relationships with each of the librarians. However, planning decisions such as these are made several years in advance, and it became one of our priorities to create a unified library acceptable, even desirable, to those originally against it.

To create the intimacy of a small library, a special reading room was incorporated into the program with access limited to the faculty. This will allow faculty to develop this one-to-one relationship with the librarians. They insisted that the periodicals and books (monographs) be in separate areas of the library, to conform to the arrangements familiar from their existing libraries. This had direct implications for the building, as Michael Wilford will illustrate.

Disciplines would automatically be grouped together so that, for example, biologists need only go to "their" area of the library. The questionnaire we sent out to faculty asked about the kinds of information that people would use and how they would use the books and resources. We also tried to get an image of certain spaces from the people responding to the survey. For example, did they think the lobby should be grand or intimate; should the reading room have good views or no windows; should these spaces be active or quiet? In the questionnaires, we allowed for comments.

We sent out about 480 questionnaires to the faculty and 1,800 questionnaires to graduate students; 28 percent responded. What they told us was no surprise: 90 percent would be using the library for specialized research, which meant that they would come in quickly, look for an article and a periodical, copy it, and then run out. Some faculty responded that they usually sent someone out to do this for them. Most of the information would be from periodicals.

We asked users about work space preferences for either carrels, work tables, or study rooms; ultimately the results of that questionnaire, and the percentages given, were reflected in the building presently designed. The questionnaire responses told us that the lobby could be noisy, that one should be able to see people there, that the reading room should be private and quiet, and that exhibition spaces should be related to the outdoors with good views.

Some of the comments we received included: "I want large reading rooms to be elegant," "Don't use orange anywhere," "Are the people who wrote and will analyze this questionnaire qualified?"

As part of the programming effort, we then had a series of day-long meetings with the library staff. We developed a rapport and devised a strategic game whereby the participants gave us information about how the building worked. We constructed a three-dimensional Plexiglas scale model. Most of the programming work was already done by this point, so we cut coded pieces of foam core to scale, to represent the programmed spaces; the librarians then worked with the pieces, placing them on the model, telling us how the spaces related to one another and how the adjacencies worked, how the building worked. We tried to assure the librarians that this model didn't represent a building, and that they shouldn't think of it as such. Unfortunately, because a lot of them work in the present library, where there is a real dearth of light, they were desperate to have exterior light: they kept pushing their own spaces to the perimeter of the building. It was difficult to get people to start playing with the model, but once they started, it was really hard to stop them. All we did was back away; two hours later, they were still playing with the model. We then photographed the results of their play, and they ultimately formed part and parcel of the program; the building disposition had begun.

To augment this information, we sketched relationships on a blackboard and got user ratification of the program, which is, in a way, the written manifestation of the building. It was ready to be dismembered and reconstructed in steel, as it were, on a new plane, a task about which Alberti in 1450 cautioned:

> In my opinion, the labor and expense of building should not be undertaken lightly. From everything else that may be at stake, one's esteem and good name may suffer. A well-constructed building may enhance the renown of anyone who has invested understanding, attention, and enthusiasm in the matter. Yet, equally, should the wisdom of the designer or the competence of the workmen be found wanting anywhere, it will greatly detract from his reputation and good name. Merits and defects are par-

ticularly obvious and striking in public buildings, though for some reason I do not understand, criticism of impropriety is more readily given than approval for work elegantly constructed with no imperfections.[1]

THE UCI SCIENCE LIBRARY: DESIGN

First, I'd like to discuss our design for the new UCI Science Library, and then a selection of projects produced in our office around the same time. I cannot offer development sketches of our project, but I have comprehensive examples of the presentation materials.

As Paul Zajfen has explained, James Stirling and I were hovering in the background during programming activity for the Science Library. When the program was finalized, we began work with the Library Building Committtee, sharing ideas stimulated by the programming exercise. It is our custom, particularly with this kind of building, to involve the clients and users throughout the development of the building design.

When complete, the program forms the basis of a thorough and wide-ranging diagrammatic exercise to establish all possible ways of configuring the building. For us, design is an explicit and reiterative process involving research, conceptual design, and consideration of alternatives and their evaluation and reevaluation. Initially we analyze the program and reduce it to the minimum basic graphic representation. This gives us a visual appreciation of the relative sizes and relationship of the constituent parts of the program and allows a direct-scale comparison with the site.

We then explore in outline as many ways as possible to satisfy the challenges and opportunities of program, site, and context. Over a two-month period, we produced approximately twenty potential architectural solutions. Working with the Building Committee, we progressively edited these to a concept that we knew from discussions with the librarians would function well as a science library, and that we were satisfied could be developed architecturally into a significant building.

The concept diagram, agreed on with the Building Committee and the campus architect David Neuman, was then systematically developed into the schematic design through response to further inputs and considerations. After a thorough review of the schematic design by the various client constituencies, including the regents of the University of California, all aspects, including materials, were comprehensively investigated in the course of the design development stage in order to provide a firm basis for the construction drawing and specification work currently in hand.

The site for the building is in the Biological Sciences Quadrangle,

This and the following sections of chapter 9 are by Michael Wilford.

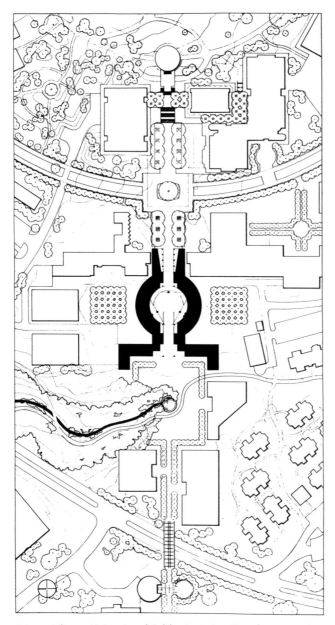

Science Library, University of California, Irvine. Site plan (James Stirling Michael Wilford & Associates, 1988). (Courtesy James Stirling Michael Wilford & Associates)

the future development of which is planned along a "spoke" mall radiating from the hub of the campus and terminating in the College of Medicine.

It became apparent, as the program developed, that this would be a special type of library unlike the traditional form of city or university library, with neither a strong civic image nor a grand reading room. However, it was clear that it would be an important and symbolic building in the Bio Sci Quad. Future development is envisaged as primarily laboratories; the library will be the focus of the quad containing essentially written and electronic information for rapid reference by faculty and students.

To establish a presence and ensure maximum contribution to the developing Bio Sci Quad, we suggested that the new Science Library be moved from the site originally proposed to a more central location astride the axis linking the Bio Sci and Medical School Quads. The library will be a campus landmark. It responds to the desire of the UCI Campus Design Objectives, established by the campus architect, to evolve urbanity and place identity, and increase the variety of pedestrian experiences. It will be highly visible from all directions and approached equally from the existing Ring Mall, Bio Sci Quad, and College of Medicine. Its gateway form defines a plaza at the Ring Mall and creates a portal to the Bio Sci Quad.

The building form not only satisfies the library's programmatic requirements, but also suggests ways in which the Bio Sci Quad could be developed in the future. An extension of the diagram generates a spatial sequence from the Ring Mall to the College of Medicine. To the west, for example, the sequence could include a square enclosed by laboratory buildings in subsequent stages of expansion. This square would be penetrated by an arroyo, one of the few features of the original Irvine Ranch topography that still exists on campus and that would constitute a central figural incursion of the natural landscape into the formality of the proposed quad plan.

The extended passageways and courtyard create a spatial sequence for visitors entering or leaving the library and for those walking along this campus axis. Twenty-four-hour activity in the library will enliven the pedestrian axis and make it a safe route across the campus, day and night.

The entrance colonnade is first in a sequence of contracting and expanding spaces. Splayed walls focus toward the courtyard, encouraging entry into and passage through the building. The open central courtyard enables the entrance to the library to be located at the heart of the building and provides daylight to the interior of the levels above. The circular form centers the composition and allows the building to face in two directions, forming a gateway to the Ring Mall and a wide, expansive façade toward the developing Bio Sci Quad and College of Medicine.

Science Library, University of California, Irvine. Model: view from the entrance side (James Stirling Michael Wilford & Associates, 1988). (John Donat Photography)

The building form was derived from three basic premises. As Paul Zajfen has explained, strong on the librarians' list of priorities for a building in which staff and visitors were going to spend considerable time was access for everyone to natural light and views. This was a reaction against the existing library and deep buildings that remove people from the external experience. They were also concerned that the building should be coherent, so as to enable visitors to understand their way around, and flexible in the disposition of books and periodicals.

Accommodation is planned on six floors. Entry is at grade with the

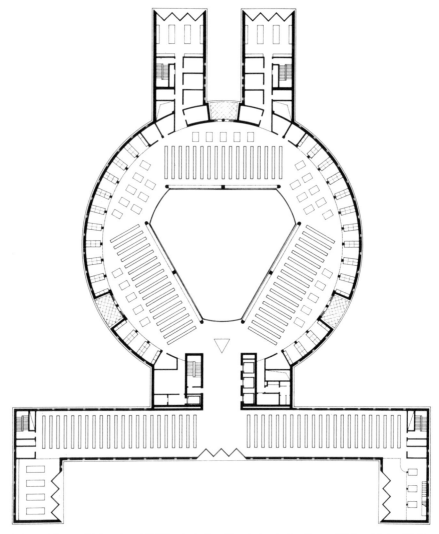

Science Library, University of California, Irvine. Fourth-level plan (James Stirling Michael Wilford & Associates, 1988). (Courtesy James Stirling Michael Wilford & Associates)

majority of public services on level 2. Reference and periodicals are also situated on level 2, and the general reader and stack areas on levels 4, 5, and 6.

Visitors enter and leave the building through an entrance/exhibition lobby. An information desk also supervises the adjacent on-line catalogue area and twenty-four-hour study room. A dramatic stair and three elevators rise to the second-level loan desk counter. Primary staff–reader contact and visitor access to all parts of the library emanate from here. Reference and periodicals are combined in a double-height reading room that encircles the lower part of the courtyard. This provides flexibility in layout and enables readers to move conveniently from one section to another. The faculty reading room is situated midway in this space with a view to the Ring Mall. A variety of individual and group reader spaces are distributed throughout this building, ranging in location and ambience from centers of activity to absolute seclusion. The general reader and stack areas on the fourth, fifth, and sixth floors occupy the center of the building, and each floor has three stack zones at right angles to the sides of the triangular upper courtyard plan. The triangle-in-circle arrangement enables users to quickly perceive the layout of the stacks and allows easy use by providing all-round circulation with no dead ends. Study carrels line the outer wall in groups of six interspersed with outdoor reading terraces. Reading tables with views into the courtyard, or informal seating adjacent to group study rooms, occupy areas between stacks and carrels.

Double-height reading rooms and group study rooms terminate the long wing and overlook the quad. The two short wings contain group study rooms with reading rooms overlooking the Ring Mall.

Public services and administration are lodged in the long wing of the building. Enclosed offices along the outer edge have adjacent work areas with windows to the gardens. Level 3 accommodates the technical services section of the library, where books are catalogued, indexed, and repaired. Education and learning resources are at ground level, entered separately from the courtyard opposite the library entrance to allow use outside library hours.

The narrow width of the building is necessary to provide good natural light and its highly articulated form, which generates the sequence of exterior spaces.

The courtyard faces are a combination of clear and translucent glass, in contrast to the outer faces of the building, which are expressed as a solid mass. These outer faces are penetrated by individual carrel and office windows forming a "crust" protecting the interior from the rigors of the climate. This building will be surfaced in colored stucco with a red-brown sandstone base and intermediate string course. As visitors pass under the building and into the courtyard, the transparent façades welcome them "inside" the building. The main axis of the Bio Sci Quad is clearly visible throughout the building. People who have no business in the library can pass through the courtyard and catch glimpses into the upper floors, particularly at night, as part of their normal route across the campus.

An elaborated cornice at roof level visually terminates the vertical "extruded" form of the building and screens rooftop air-conditioning equipment.

We are still working closely with the Building Committee and will continue to do so through to completion of the building. In addition to designing reference and information desks, carrels and other built-in furniture, and agreeing on interior colors, we are also consulting with the committee in regard to loose furniture.

Construction of the building started in 1991 and will be completed in 1993.

OTHER STIRLING/WILFORD DESIGNS: PROCESS

Number 1 Poultry, London

Number 1 Poultry, in the heart of the City of London and bounded by Poultry, Queen Victoria Street, and Sise Lane, is presently occupied by Victorian buildings and shops, some of which are listed as buildings of grade 2 historic interest. Our design is the second attempt by an enlightened patron (Peter Palumbo) to build a major office building on the site. His first attempt involved a glass tower designed by Mies van der Rohe (denigrated by Prince Charles as a "glass stump") that was denied planning permission after a public inquiry.

We were commissioned to design an alternative building containing shops, offices, and public spaces occupying a smaller site than that of the Mies van de Rohe project.

Our design relates to existing street patterns and the Bank Junction, which is surrounded by several historic buildings—for example, the Bank of England (Soane), the Midland Bank (Lutyens), and the Church of St. Mary Woolnoth (Hawksmoor). All the historic buildings are symmetrical in plan, although they face onto an informal street pattern. To relate to these historic examples, Number 1 Poultry is planned about a central axis with similar façades to Queen Victoria Street and Poultry. The parapet height and vertical façade divisions correspond to surrounding buildings.

The new building contains shops at basement and ground-floor levels, and offices at first- to fifth-floor levels, with a garden and restaurant at roof level. At street level, a pedestrian passage across the site links the shopping colonnades on Poultry and Queen Victoria Street. This passage passes through a circular court open to the sky and connected to the basement shops and the Bank underground station below. The court, circular at ground and first-floor levels, interlocks with a triangular plan for the upper office floors, allowing daylight to reach the center of the building at each level.

Public access to the offices is from the lobby; there is also a VIP entrance at the apex of the building. From the entrance lobby, a grand stair leads to the central court at a level above the pedestrian passage. Lifts connect public and private levels of the court and all office floors with the rooftop garden and restaurant. The roof garden, enclosed by a circular pergola wall, forms a sanctuary from the hustle and bustle of

Number 1 Poultry, London. Model: relation of Number 1 Poultry and surroundings (James Stirling Michael Wilford & Associates, 1986). (John Donat Photography)

the City. The building will be faced in sandstone with bronze metal windows.

The City of London planners rejected the scheme, and it followed the Mies tower through the public inquiry process. During this time Prince Charles chose to pronounce again, describing the building as a "1930s wireless set." The public inquiry in this case supported the design, and planning permission was granted. The conservationists, however, being anxious to protect the existing Victorian buildings on the

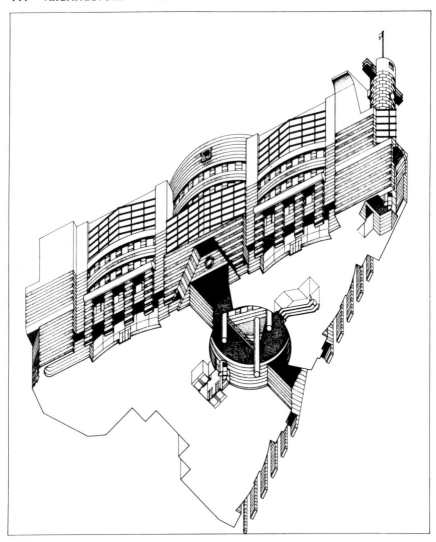

Number 1 Poultry, London. View of the façade to Queen Victoria Street and the central court as pass-through (James Stirling Michael Wilford & Associates, 1986). (Courtesy James Stirling Michael Wilford & Associates)

site, appealed to the High Court against the planning decision. As a result, the project is now embroiled in protracted legal argument, and we do not know if and when it will proceed.

As a footnote to my description of this project, it may be of interest if I briefly explain the significance of the listing process. Nine buildings on the site are registered by the state as of historic interest. They are listed as grade 2 and are therefore considered to be of secondary interest. There is conflicting opinion over the value of these buildings. We believe they are rather poor examples of speculative Victorian buildings, with better examples elsewhere in London.

Listing recognizes that a building has historic significance and value. It does not mean that it must be preserved forever. The review process set in motion when an application is made to demolish a listed building enables appropriate debate to take place on the merits of the existing building and the proposed substitute. If it is considered that the new building has merit superior to that of an existing building, then demolition consent is granted by the state. I think it is a fair and democratic process that has been diligently followed in this case.

Canary Wharf, London

Another project completed recently was a limited-competition submission for the redesign of the west end of Canary Wharf on the Isle of Dogs in London's docklands, east of the city center.

In response to Olympia and York's land-use reappraisal, our alternative design proposed a large riverside park with terraces stepping down to the Thames. This park contains a series of freestanding apartment towers ranged informally along the river frontage and is semienclosed on the island sides by linear buildings accommodating offices, retail spaces, and a hotel.

The park surrounds West Ferry Circus, a large road intersection at the entrance to Canary Wharf. Together with its approach roads, the circus is incised into the stepped terraces. The airy spaciousness of the

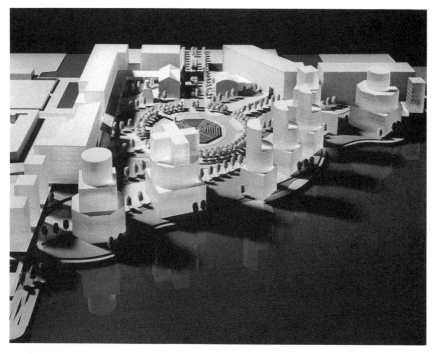

Residential development, Canary Wharf, London. Model: general view (James Stirling Michael Wilford & Associates, 1988). (John Donat Photography)

park will provide an arcadian contrast to the "downtown" commercial core of Canary Wharf. It combines public and private open spaces accessible as appropriate to residents, office workers, and adjacent communities. The new park creates an interesting gateway to Canary Wharf, and the varied building forms with their reflective glass surfaces would create a dramatic riverfront on the Thames. The garden terraces are surfaced alternately with gravel and grass. Adjoining terraces are connected by short ramps and have stone retaining walls, trees, and low planting. Residents, office workers, and visitors could enjoy garden walks, picnics, and impromptu events on these terraces. An esplanade along the Thames is proposed as an informal public promenade, connecting Limehouse to the Isle of Dogs.

The residential towers would enjoy views toward the Thames, the

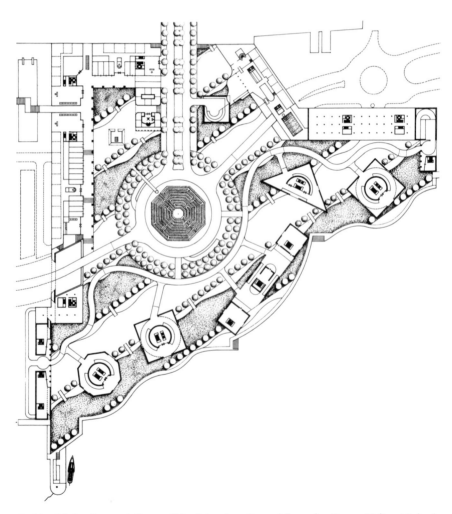

Residential development, Canary Wharf, London. Ground-floor plan (James Stirling Michael Wilford & Associates, 1988). (Courtesy James Stirling Michael Wilford & Associates)

City of London, and West India Dock. Their varied forms provide each building with a distinctive appearance. Each tower has a private approach road to an entrance foyer at the base of the building. Car ramps lead to private parking garages below. Loggias in the linear building enclosing the park contain pubs, restaurants, and shopping, and provide covered access to the offices. A river-bus pier extends into the river, and a covered promenade provides a weather-protected route to Canary Wharf for river commuters. A hotel occupies the diagonal building on the eastern edge and forms a portal to West Ferry Road. A cinema complex is sited below the northeast corner of the park, entered through a pyramidal advertising pavilion.

The residential buildings are designed as a series of minitowers. This strategy is radically different from the solid massing of the earlier project inherited by the developer, yet it produces the same residential density. The towers are stepped vertically with three differing plan forms to provide a variety of apartment types. In fine weather, restaurant and health facilities could open onto the roof terraces, which are wind-protected by high-level glazed screens.

The site planning of individual buildings provides flexibility in investment and implementation. Each building has its own parking for each tower, allowing phase development and construction.

We understand from Olympia and York that a final decision has yet to be reached on the future of this important site. We are awaiting the outcome with great interest.

The Walt Disney Concert Hall, Los Angeles

Along with Frank Gehry, Hans Hollein, and Gottfried Bohm, we made a submission in the Disney Hall competition for a site at the Music Center in downtown Los Angeles.

With our project, we set out to achieve a civic identity for the concert hall. It was immediately apparent that it should form a focal point in Los Angeles, symbolic of the importance of music in the cultural life of the city and a highly accessible public place encouraging community involvement with the arts.

Our design is an ensemble of architectural forms related to the functional elements of the program. The disposition and design of those elements is informal and yet geometrically related to the north–south axis of the Music Center. They are unified at ground level by a grand concourse representing a microcosm of the city.

The circular and stepped concert hall is the centerpiece of the composition. Its diagonal orientation toward the corner of Grand Avenue and First Street reinforces Grand Avenue as the primary boulevard for the whole of the Music Center. A smaller group of three pavilions containing the gift shop, box office and cinema, and grand stair and club lounge are arranged along First Street. These pavilions define the northern entrances to the building and are a visual foil to the large form of the Chandler Pavilion. A rotating electronic billboard above

Walt Disney Concert Hall, Los Angeles. Model: general view (James Stirling Michael Wilford & Associates, 1988). (John Donat Photography)

the gift shop would announce current events at the Disney Concert Hall.

The glazed concourse is transparent, highly visible, and accessible. It opens out toward the city, embracing the surrounding city and inviting entry from all sides. Daytime and evening views into this concourse should attract pedestrians to the entrances on Grand Avenue, First Street, and Hope Street.

The informality of the concourse, with its performance and intermission activities, contrasts with the calm ambience of the concert hall and chamber music hall. There are floor-level changes to articulate various activities, provide views, and allow people-watching. An illuminated floor beneath the crystalline soffit of the concert hall is flanked by the adjoining vertical circulation towers and defines the center. From here, escalators and elevators rise to all levels of the concert hall.

During the day, the concourse would be flooded with natural light from all sides, making it a friendly place to meet, purchase tickets and gifts, listen to recitals or lectures, see exhibitions, and visit the garden.

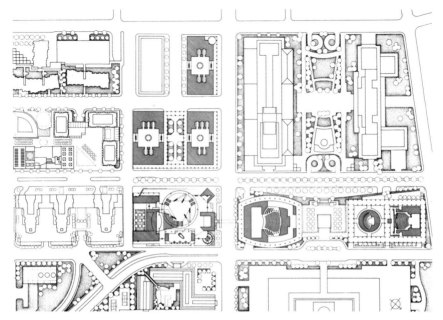

Walt Disney Concert Hall, Los Angeles. Site plan (James Stirling Michael Wilford & Associates, 1988). (Courtesy James Stirling Michael Wilford & Associates)

It would be a bustling center encouraging visitors to explore the world of music.

The concourse is animated by flying escalators gliding the audience upward to the ring galleries around the concert hall. Dramatic lighting would contribute to the excitement and anticipation of patrons attending evening performances. In the evening, the building would be ablaze with light evocative of a beacon or magic lantern.

Bars and lounges overlook Hope Street and downtown through bay windows. Shallow stepped seating levels and a platform for preconcert lectures, recitals, and happenings are recessed in the concourse floor to form an informal open "theatre." A spacious double-height grand reception hall is raised slightly above the concourse level, overlooking the garden. A café and a gift shop are accessible from both the concourse and the Grand Avenue sidewalk. Café tables could spill onto the sidewalk terraces and into the villa garden.

The concert hall and chamber music hall have separate vertical circulation to avoid congestion. Escalators, elevators, and staircases would convey the audience quickly from the concourse to the upper-ring galleries encircling the concert hall. The circular pavilion on the corner of Hope and First Streets encloses a grand staircase that spirals around two glass-enclosed elevators, providing a traditional approach to the chamber music hall. Over the concert hall are a rooftop restaurant and a garden with views across the Civic Center into the Hollywood Hills.

The concert hall is designed as a series of tiered, interlocking seating

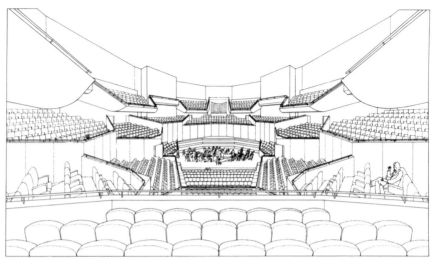

Walt Disney Concert Hall, Los Angeles. Interior view of concert hall (James Stirling Michael
Wilford & Associates, 1988). (Courtesy James Stirling Michael Wilford & Associates)

balconies clustering three-dimensionally around the stage. This arrangement places the conductor and orchestra centrally in the room,
uniting audience and orchestra and intensifying the impact of a live
performance. The balconies range in seating from 70 to 150 people on
three levels. All 2,470 seats would have complete views of the largest
orchestra. Seating platforms enable the stage size to be adjusted to accommodate orchestras ranging from 45 to 150 musicians, thereby
maintaining the intimacy of the audience–performer relationship.

High-quality natural materials (timber, fabric, plaster, brass, plush,
etc.) would provide warm tactile surfaces. The ceiling would be cof-
fered and have adjustable soffits to provide good sound diffusion.

The traditional chamber music hall design as a "shoebox" would have
good acoustics and an appropriately dignified environment for small
ensembles, recitalists, and soloists. It could have 800 seats on the main
floor and 300 in the balcony around three sides of the room. A flexible
floor allows variations in stage–audience relationships for chamber music, chamber opera, experimental music, and dance. Straightening Grand
Avenue between First and Temple Streets would provide a wide promenade adjacent to the Music Center, allowing the introduction of outdoor cafés, restaurants, and arts-related retail shops. These improve-
ments would provide a lively pedestrian link between the Music Center
and the Walt Disney Concert Hall, consolidating the area as the cultural focus of downtown Los Angeles. External materials of the concert
hall would be glass and red sandstone, similar to the Museum of Contemporary Art. Stone would be applied to the faceted surfaces of the
concert hall within the concourse. Similarly, the concourse floor, adjoining terraces, and podium walls would be of stone. The wall surface

of the villa and the First Street pavilions would be of beige-colored stucco. Metalwork for glazing and fascias is envisioned as bronze.

The competition was won by Frank Gehry, and we understand he is currently developing the project in preparation for construction.

The Bibliothèque Nationale de France, Paris

Another competition entry that we finished more recently was for the new Bibliothèque Nationale de France situated on the Seine, east of the center of Paris. It will be a huge building of nearly 2 million square feet, containing four major libraries.

Our proposal is conceived as a group of buildings around a new public park rising in stepped terraces from the Seine to the main entrance. This concept allows each of the four libraries its own separate identity and avoids the unpleasant "Kafkaesque" experience that such a large building could produce, if planned as a single volume. A new footbridge crossing the Seine will relate to the park and provide panoramic views of the new buildings. Three elements of the library—the dome, the vault, and the tower—rise above a general level to enliven the skyline of the Tolbiac quarter.

Internally, the library is planned around a U-shaped concourse. From this entrance, at the heart of the plan, the concourse flows westward through the domed Recent Acquisitions Library and passes the Café Europe en route to the Sound and Moving Image Library on the edge of the Seine. To the east, the concourse incorporates exhibition galleries leading to the entrances of the vaulted Reference Library and then extends to the Catalogue Room and to the Research Library, which overlooks the Seine. This open concourse encourages a sense of exploration and discovery. It has transitions in scale and changes in ambi-

Bibliothèque de France, Paris. Model: view from the River Seine (James Stirling Michael Wilford & Associates, 1989). (John Donat Photography)

Bibliothèque de France, Paris. Roof shadow drawing (James Stirling Michael Wilford & Associates, 1989). (Courtesy James Stirling Michael Wilford & Associates)

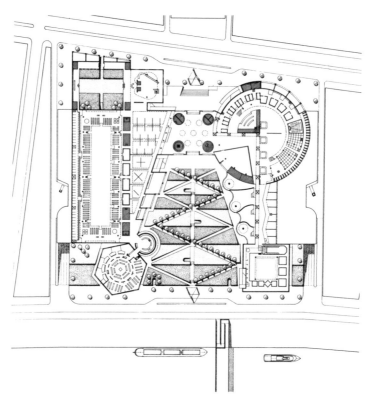

Bibliothèque de France, Paris. Garden and entrance level (James Stirling Michael Wilford & Associates, 1989). (Courtesy James Stirling Michael Wilford & Associates)

ence, from the transparent public activities surrounding the park, which includes shops and restaurants, to the private study areas of the libraries.

The four libraries and the Catalogue Room each have a unique architectural expression. A large translucent dome identifies the Recent Acquisitions Library. Auditoriums, information banks, and video screens are planned in radiating patterns, with book stacks, viewing booths, and reading carrels on three curved terraces all linked by escalators, stairs, and elevators.

The Sound and Moving Image Library is a long, vaulted, top-lit room with large circular windows at both ends providing views across the city. The circular Catalogue Room services the Reference and Research Libraries with catalogues, computer terminals, and microfilm readers arranged concentrically on four levels.

The Research Library is a hexagonal building, and the central reading room has a glass-domed ceiling. A researchers' lounge and café opens to a terrace with views across the Seine.

The conference center is beneath the administration tower, with an adjacent courtyard garden for delegates and library staff. Shops and restaurants are distributed throughout the public areas of the building and around the park. Café Europe, which overlooks the park, is a large informal restaurant and meeting place.

Public footpaths pass over and through the library, allowing twenty-four-hour connections between the Tolbiac quarter and the quayside. The more direct route is a pergola footway that passes over the reception area and links the avenue Nouvelle entrance court with the park terraces. Windows allow views into the reception areas and exhibition galleries below. The second public route is an elevated glazed promenade passing inside the building with overviews of the Recent Acquisitions and the Sound and Moving Image Libraries.

The combined library complex would become a familiar landmark in Paris and a major contribution to the eastern part of the city. Throughout the history of architecture, libraries have been among the most persistent of archetypes to combine the monumental and informal with the traditional and modern.

Our design placed second in the competition, which was won by Dominique Perrault of Paris.

Tokyo International Forum

The final competition entry carried out during this intense period of activity was for the Tokyo International Forum in Japan, a large convention, conference, and information center. The site is in the center of Tokyo, close to the central railway station and on an axis with the Imperial Palace.

Our proposal emphasized the symbolic importance of the complex by placing a tall building in the center related to an outdoor plaza with

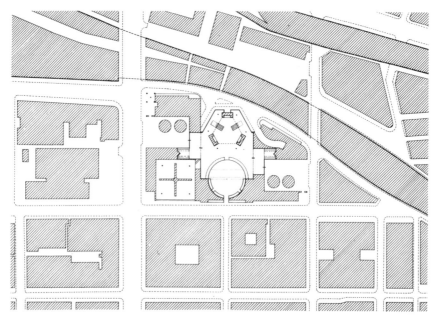

Tokyo International Forum, Tokyo. Site plan (James Stirling Michael Wilford & Associates, 1989). (Courtesy James Stirling Michael Wilford & Associates)

lower, equally monumental buildings situated on each side. A towering centerpiece surrounded by identifiable elements is in the twentieth-century tradition of *Stadtkrone* (city crown). This allusion can be extended to include the transparency of the buildings, which is both a sophisticated interpretation of *Glasarchitektur* and an expression of new building and servicing technologies in an age when energy conservation is critical. Searchlights, lasers, and other "fantastic" components contribute to this association.

The transparent buildings are placed on a sandstone base that encloses the most publicly accessible areas of the complex and provides a strong façade to the primary street edges. The base can be considered as either a traditional counterpart to the "technological" structures above or a hill with approach paths to the "city crown." The circular courtyard plaza forms part of the base and is enclosed by a stone wall. This wall has large "window" openings allowing views from the upper terraces to the activity below.

In addition to these symbolic considerations, the building organization has been determined by the functional requirements for clear visitor and delegate movement patterns, earthquake-resistant structure, and emergency evacuation procedures arising from high-density occupancy. To satisfy these requirements, the major volumes are designed as separate forms connected by a base that contains the information exchange, gallery, and central common lobby. The tower contains smaller

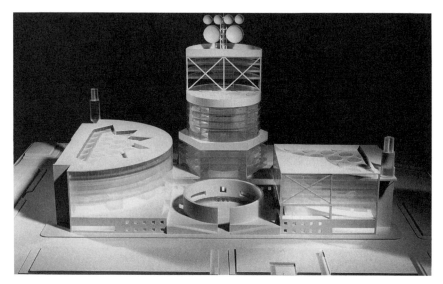

Tokyo International Forum, Tokyo. Model: general view from the west (James Stirling Michael Wilford & Associates, 1989). (John Donat Photography)

Tokyo International Forum, Tokyo. Roof shadow drawing (James Stirling Michael Wilford & Associates, 1989). (Courtesy James Stirling Michael Wilford & Associates)

conference facilities, and the buildings at the northern and southern ends of the site contain respectively the primary conference hall (5,000 people) and secondary and tertiary halls (2,000 people each). The exhibition halls are located below street level, parallel with a travelator link between subway stations at each end of the site.

The conference tower comprises three volumes in a sequence of hexagonal, circular, and semicircular forms. At street level, the entrance common lobby is the major gathering place and forms a literal exchange of people and activities. Visitors from the subway stations below and the surrounding streets converge in a central triple-height space. The VIP entrance is on the central axis. Connection beneath the railway tracks (leading to the central station) can be made between the common lobby and the Ginza to the east. Escalators and elevators lead from the common lobby to the upper delegate and ticket-holder concourse, which in turn gives access to the major halls.

Moving up through the tower, a core of large double-story rooms surrounded by smaller reception and conference rooms responds to the requirements of congress or assembly meetings with intense discussion, and provides darkened rooms for presentations, grand rooms for formal events, and open rooms for informal use, more intimate discussion, or recreation. The banqueting hall and conference halls are enclosed and located in the center of the plan. Waiting rooms, tea ceremony rooms, and small rooms for discussion and group meetings, open and transparent, are arranged on the periphery.

The upper semicircular portion of the tower contains a luxury restaurant and administrative offices with a reception suit for VIPs. The restaurant opens onto a roof terrace with a garden of gravel and shaped hedges.

The distinction between the common lobby at street level and the upper delegate and ticket-holder concourse is central to our proposal. Ticket desks, information counters, and all publicly accessible areas are at street level. The upper concourse is accessible only to delegates and performance ticket holders.

Once again, our design placed second, this time to Rafael Vignoli of New York.

The Performing Arts Center, Cornell University

Finally I am going to talk about a building that we have just finished at Cornell University in Ithaca, New York. It is the Performing Arts Center, a teaching and performance facility for the theater arts, dance, and film. Prominently sited on College Avenue close to the bridge over Cascadilla Gorge, the new building stands as a gateway to the campus. A cluster of theater volumes is configured by a loggia, relating to the small-town character of Collegetown and the picturesque aspect of the gorge. The location, which is just off campus, is well situated to draw audiences from both Town and Gown.

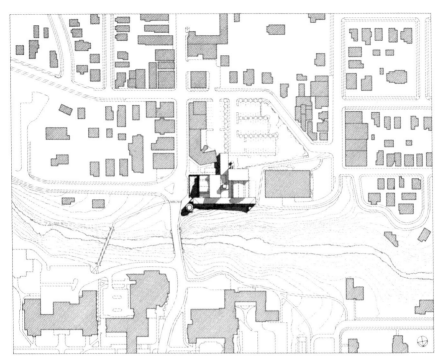

Performing Arts Center, Cornell University, Ithaca, New York. Site plan (James Stirling Michael Wilford & Associates, 1983–1988). (Courtesy James Stirling Michael Wilford & Associates)

The building had to be planned in two phases, since the university was not sure it could raise funds to construct the entire building at one time. Despite some difficulties with the budget, we were eventually asked to complete the whole building. Occupancy in stages commenced in September 1988 and was completed by the spring of 1989.

The octagonal pavilion that signals the approach to the Performing Arts Center is a campus information post and a shelter for the adjacent bus stop. Its upper floor has offices for the Theater Arts Department and for touring companies such as the National Theatre of Britain. A new plaza containing a pergola and seats is entered from the sidewalk and is a place for students to meet and give informal performances.

Entry to the building is from the plaza and along the loggia, providing a promenade approach with views across the gorge toward the campus and Lake Cayuga. Part of the loggia is enclosed as an alternative bad-weather route from the plaza to the central entrance hall. A spiral staircase at the far end of the loggia connects to ground level, allowing access to adjoining footpaths and the nearby multilevel parking garage.

The three-story-high entrance hall is also the main foyer for the Proscenium and Flexible Theaters. Located in the center of the building, it connects with all major spaces, encouraging interaction between

Performing Arts Center, Cornell University, Ithaca, New York. View from College Avenue to east elevation (James Stirling Michael Wilford & Associates, 1983–1988). (Richard Bryant)

theater, dance, and film groups and bringing guèst artists and public into contact with students and faculty. The foyer opens to the loggia, enabling audiences to stroll in and out and take the view during intermission. Upper balconies are connected to the entrance level by a staircase and an elevator that together extend upward as a campanile, floodlit at night, announcing the presence of the Performing Arts Center to downtown Ithaca.

The 456-seat horseshoe-shaped Proscenium Theater has two entrances from the foyer. Fixed seating on the main floor has parallel aisles. Loose seating on two levels of balcony and boxes above extends around the room, bringing audiences and performers together in the intimate atmosphere of a small-scale theater. Sound and light booths are at second-balcony level, with technical ledge and follow-spot rooms above. The forestage of the proscenium is adaptable as either a thrust stage or an orchestra pit with an electrically operated lift.

The Flexible Theater is also approached from the foyer and has multiple entrances that allow arena, thrust, alley, or proscenium seating. The audience is seated on adjustable platforms with capacity varying from 140 to 175 people.

Visitors descend from the entrance hall to the Dance Performance Studio located beneath the Proscenium Theater. This studio accommodates an audience of up to 132 on bleacher seating, allowing the floor to be cleared for teaching. At the same level beneath the Flexible Theater is the Laboratory/Black Box Studio, which accommodates 50

Performing Arts Center, Cornell University, Ithaca, New York. View of the entrance hall through the loggia (James Stirling Michael Wilford & Associates, 1983–1988). (Richard Bryant)

to 100 people on adjustable seating platforms in a variety of configurations. Both the Laboratory and the Dance Performance Studio have multiple entrances and overviewing control booths.

Public audiences enter the Film Forum from a lobby below the entrance hall. This raked multipurpose auditorium has 103 fixed seats and a small stage. Additional studios and classrooms for the Theater, Dance, and Film departments are interspersed between the performance spaces. In all, ten auditoriums or studios are accommodated within the building.

The main Dance Studio has outdoor terraces on two sides overlooking the plaza and the gorge. A triangular bay window projecting over the plaza is a resting place for dancers with views of passersby on College Avenue. Upper floors rise above surrounding roofs and trees, allowing faculty offices extensive views in all directions.

Performance and studio support areas are arranged vertically around the elevator core. Student changing rooms are on the third floor, with

Performing Arts Center, Cornell University, Ithaca, New York. View
of the seats of three levels in the Proscenium Theater (James Stirling
Michael Wilford & Associates, 1983–1988). (Richard Bryant)

showers, lockers, and dressing rooms connecting via backstage stairs to
all performance areas. Scenery and props production is at the rear of
the building, with truck access into a high bay area. The scenery shop
opens through sound-isolating doors on to the Proscenium and Flexible Theater stages. Costume shop areas are beneath the proscenium
stage, linked by backstage stairs to all performance and production
spaces.

The Proscenium Theater has painted plaster finishes combined with
oak paneling. Balcony fronts are perforated metal with oak caps and
polished brass rails. Floors are carpeted, and the seats have a plush
finish. The Flexible and Laboratory Theaters and dance studios have
wood-paneled walls, sprung wood floors, and suspended lighting grids.

The entrance hall and loggia are paved in marble. The pavilion, loggia, and College Avenue façade are clad in open-jointed Vermont marble. Stucco is used on other elevations, sometimes in combination with
a horizontal course of marble. Pitched roofs are lead-coated copper

with Vermont slates on the loggia. The steel trusses carrying the loggia roof are painted French green, matching the windows. The soffit of the loggia is stained redwood, as are the plaza benches and the pergola.

The building was dedicated in April 1988, and we have had excellent response from audience, faculty, and students using it.

CONCLUSION

In conclusion, I would like to stress that we practice architecture as an art. We constantly seek to produce buildings of the highest architectural quality that satisfy the requirements of the client's program and respond to the opportunities of site and context. We are fully involved in all phases and aspects of the work from concept to completion of construction.

We are striving toward a richer, more inclusive architectural language based on the integration of modernity and tradition, using the multiple layers of historic precedent and the abstract styles of modern design. We are also concerned with producing a fusion between the monumental tradition of public building and the informal, populist image of today's places of public entertainment.

NOTE

1. Leon Battista Alberti, *On the Art of Building in Ten Books*, trans. Joseph Rykwert, Neil Leach, and Robert Tavernor (Cambridge, Mass.: MIT Press, 1988), 33.

V

AFTER POSTMODERNISM

Keynote Address

FRANK GEHRY

I FOUND OUT EARLIER [from David Neuman] that this was to be a key-note address, and I thought, God, I would be the last guy in the world who anybody would pick to give a keynote address, especially one on linguistic architecture: I dropped out of linguistics back with "language-in-action." Anyway, my wife studies it, and so we talk. I was at Peter Eisenman's office in New York a few years ago, and he and Jacques Derrida were in intense conversation for three or four hours. I sat very obediently and listened to both of them, and then Derrida and I walked out together and got in the elevator. I said, "Mr. Derrida, do you un-derstand what Peter Eisenman was talking about?" He said, "Not really." And I said, "God, that makes me feel good, 'cause I didn't either."

Peter is for me the respected father of linguistic architecture, and he seems to know what it is. One thing that held us together in the "De-constructivist Architecture" show at the Museum of Modern Art was the sense that we are all intentionally working in the present, with some hopes that our stuff has some lasting value for the future. I think that is the thread that binds us together.

Now I'm going to tell you a few fish stories.

The fish was a reaction to all my friends looking backward for mean-ing in architecture in the so-called postmodern period. I was reacting to the regurgitation of the past in that sort of flimsy way in which I saw

165

Kobe Fishdance Restaurant, Kobe, Japan (Frank Gehry, 1987). (C. Gregory Walsh)

it being brought back. I am not against history; I think that all of us, in our way, do start with history. I always start with some kind of reference. But my intent has always been to move it somewhere—transform it in some way into some other, maybe more personal or more present, form.

So I got angry and said, "Well, if they're going to go that far, I'll go back further. I'll go back to the beginning. Fish are 300 million years older than man." So I started drawing fish as a symbol of that anger and frustration. Then I became fascinated with the form of it and I made a few fish and a few snakes. They were kindred spirits.

And then fish crept into the architecture, and I was commissioned to do a restaurant in Japan.

FISH WITH HEADS and tails are very difficult to represent in architecture, but I tried. I then did "fillet of fish" and took the head and tail off for the fish room in the show at the Walker Art Center. I think to this day that this is the best fish I've ever made. You can imagine the next move has to be gefilte fish.

I STARTED using metal in my early work (i.e., the Davis House) because it was the only material I could use with which you could make both

Fish sculpture, Frank C. Gehry Retrospective, Walker Art Center, Minneapolis. (Daniel Sachs)

roof and walls. I had a lot of trouble getting metalworkers to work with me because most of those guys work behind the ceilings, and they are not too interested in the craft. I think this is happening in all areas of construction in this country. In order to make contact with them personally, to get to know how to achieve a level of craft, I did an exhibit for the metalworkers' union at the National Building Museum in Washington. We made a deal that if I did this, they would help me from here on with my work. And they have. They came through. I've got all the metalworkers' unions in Canada and the United States on my side now.

I DESIGNED a building for Herman Miller International. It is a factory in Sacramento. It is out in no-man's-land with no trees. Herman Miller had an interest in creating "a people's space," as they said, and so this courtyard with this big pergola is an attempt to give some kind of sym-

Sheet-metal exhibition, National Building Museum, Washington, D.C. (Frank Gehry, 1988). (Walter Smalling)

bolic center to the complex, which is essentially a factory. But the way Herman Miller orchestrates its employees and its relationships is very much a family kind of operation in which the goodies are distributed through the building in some way.

I was recommended for this job by my friend Stanley Tigerman and his wife, Margaret McCurry. When I got the job, I suggested to Herman Miller that Stanley do a cameo piece on the property for the project. So he did the little dome with the pink stuff. That's Stanley. We did it on the fax machine. I sent him the plan and said, "Stanley, I

Herman Miller International, western regional facility, Sacramento, California (Frank Gehry, 1989). (Hedrich Blessing)

Herman Miller International, western regional facility, Sacramento, California (Frank Gehry, 1989). (Hedrich Blessing)

want you to go there." Stanley sent back a drawing that was very complex. He had a tower and the whole thing. I said, "No, no, you can't do that. Just one move." So he did this little dome building. I cut the ground out from under it and instead of putting it on a pedestal, I sloped the grass down so people can sit on the grass and look at it. He read that as me trying to bury him. So he faxed back the bridges, the pink bridges. And I faxed back this big billboard behind him. I call it "David and Goliath."

From the distance sometimes, the siding on the factory buildings looks like stone. Everybody works hard to get metal panels straight and flat, and that costs money. Oil canning is generic, so I used it.

THE METALWORKERS helped me in Boston on the building at 360 Newbury Street in Back Bay. We added a floor. Obviously, it is a highly visible building. This is the first time we used lead-coated copper.

360 Newbury Street, Boston (Frank Gehry, 1988). (Jeff Goldberg)

Laser laboratory, University of Iowa, Iowa City. Model (Frank Gehry, 1990). (David Pakshong)

I DESIGNED a laser laboratory on the banks of the Iowa River for the University of Iowa in Iowa City. The program is represented in the plans. The copper piece in the back is the support labs. The long, bar-like block next to it contains the laser laboratories and the wide band at the top of that piece is a pipe canyon. The next bar, which has a sloped roof on it, is kind of an entry with elevators and stairs. The box and the more animated buildings are the offices. They are positioned to get views of the river. The little copper building is the conference center.

People ask me about my process, so I'll explain the way the project developed. It started with this model. The offices are the three boxes in some kind of atrium. I didn't like the idea of an atrium. I started to enclose it.

The laser scientists talked a lot about crystals. I looked at a lot of crystalline shapes. The shape at the top that has become boatlike or fishlike (whichever you like) is the support lab, and because it is next to the pipe canyon and has all mechanical equipment in it and by pro-gram requires no light, I was able to have a clean form with no pene-trations for vents and things like that. So I took advantage of it and started to mold the shape. There are more crystals. You can see the beginning of the separation of forms. This was too expensive, so we cut back the lab's form and made a box out of it. We simplified some of the pieces. And because the pipe canyon had a solid wall, I was able to make this kind of sculptural form, which I wanted to put on the street to animate it. You enter the building between the student union and a bridge that goes across the campus, so there is a space at the entry that is a point of arrival. You can see the patterning for the cop-per and the joint patterns.

Edgemar development, Santa Monica, California (Frank Gehry, 1988). (Tom Bonner)

A CLIENT for a small strip center in Santa Monica, California, asked for a courtyard. There are offices on the top, and there is a museum, an old building on the back that is being converted into the Santa Monica Museum of Art. I just fixed the outside, and one of the young architects who used to work for me, Paul Lubowicki, is doing the interiors. The green part of the building was an Art Deco façade that we left standing as part of the approval process for the city. When construction started, it fell down. The city made us build it back, and the only concession they made, so that I could signify that it was new, was to let me cover it in tile. The Art Deco copper work is all copied from what was there originally. The sign wasn't there; that is by a graphic designer who was hired independently of me.

WE BEGAN work on a high-security psychiatric clinic at Yale University, with sixty-six beds for schizophrenic adolescents, with Bart Giammatti, the former baseball commissioner and former Yale president. The budget was really tight. There are three boxes, essentially. The one on the right is the high-security section. The one on the left is for the offices. It has a bookstore and a coffee shop on the ground floor. The one in the middle is the open unit, as they call it, for patients returning to normalcy.

It is rare these days to build a facility like this in the city; usually it goes in the suburbs. But because this is a part of the Yale Medical School, it had to be built next to the school on a piece of land that is in a somewhat run-down section of town, a transitional area that is called "The Hill." We used brick because it was cheap and all the buildings

Yale Psychiatric Institute, Yale University, New Haven, Connecticut (Frank Gehry, 1989). (Olivier Boissiere)

around there are brick. It was almost mandated to use brick, to hold the edges as kind of bookends. The centerpiece was intended to be more sculptural. On the roof of the centerpiece is the recreation building or gymnasium. The intent is that the patients look out into a garden and see places they can go to as they improve. They can see buildings like the Work Adjustment, or the cafeteria, or arts and crafts buildings that are part of the program and that the patients are introduced to as they get better. The whole intent is to show them their way back to normalcy.

The form of the site plan follows the Yale college format. The little building we placed next to the bookstore and the coffee shop is called Work Adjustment. That is where the kids will go to serve coffee to medical students and start to deal with the real world again. The original idea was to have some housing here also. In China, schizophrenics return to normalcy much more rapidly because they force the families to live in the clinics with the kids. They are in and out in three months because of that. At Yale, it takes two years. We wanted to build some housing, and there wasn't money in the budget. It would have made it a much better facility if we could have had a couple of apartments where kids could start to live more normally and have parents and siblings come stay with them.

It is a very basic building. The back side gets a little bit more interesting. It faces a small street that originally was supposed to be closed off. It will be the point of entry; the little bottle-shaped thing is the entry pavilion. You come in here and can go on into the bookstore or the coffee shop and look out into the gardens. It makes the entrance into this building a little bit more ambiguous and may help relieve the stigma of going to the clinic.

A NUMBER of years ago, after I started working on that notorious house of mine, I decided I really wanted to build a different kind of house. I explored this idea of having separate pavilions forming a courtyard. A young lady worked in my office at that time and came back years later as a client. She asked me if I would build that house for her. We started to do it. The program was a bit too big for the lot when it was all laid out on one floor. It is a 100- × 250-foot lot, and so from this we segued into a different scheme. But it grows from this idea of creating separate pavilions that in turn define a series of courtyard spaces.

I used the slope and the site. I cut into it and took the master bathroom, closets—all that stuff that is getting so big in fancy houses now—and made that program into a retaining wall, buried it underground, and created a small lake at the back of the site that became a private space relating to the master bedroom. The piece in the middle is the living room.

In the final design, the master bedroom became more boatlike and the living room/dining room building became more churchlike. The master bedroom has a row of closets and a work-out room behind it as

Schnabel residence, Brentwood, California (Frank Gehry, 1989). (Grant Mudford)

Schnabel residence, Brentwood, California (Frank Gehry, 1989). (David Pakshong)

a retaining wall. On the upper part of the bar building are two bedrooms. The living room/dining room is a cross, touching the big family room. The guest house with the dome is in the front yard, and the little bedroom out on the point in back is kind of a studio.

The client asked for the dome. She didn't care where it went. It could have gone anywhere, so I made it the guest house.

As you enter the master bedroom area you come down toward what looks like a boat, just kind of moored there, and again it is sheathed in lead copper. The bathrooms face out. In the morning, all the doors are open. It is a nice place to be. The bedroom turned out great. I told my client I would marry her so I could sleep in the bedroom.

I don't do a lot about furniture with my clients. I'm sort of voyeuristic about it. I like to see what they do. I say things about what I don't like, but usually I'm pretty open. When you're sitting on the bed in the master bedroom, you can see the water and you feel like you're on a boat, and it's very private and very peaceful and very comfortable.

The guest room became the man of the house's office. It sits in a garden of olive trees.

PETER EISENMAN started a project in Cleveland for the Progressive Corporation. It is adjacent to the railroad tracks near the stadium in Cleveland along the lake, and it fronts onto the Daniel Burnham–designed mall, which was never completed. There was supposed to be a big railroad station on axis. A parking lot and a railroad station are on the site now.

Peter did a horizontal building. I did a vertical building. I wanted to make two goalposts that sort of completed the mall. There are high buildings going on around it by Pelli and Kohn Pederson Fox, so that

Progressive Corporation, Cleveland. Model (Frank Gehry, 1987). (Tom Bonner)

the language and the scale of this whole place is going to change very rapidly to these kind of big sticks facing in on the old mall. Our client wanted an art museum as part of his lobby. He wanted a health club as part of his lobby. He wanted a scholar's library as part of his lobby. He wants to live in the top of the building. He wanted me to work with all kinds of artists like Richard Serra and Claes Oldenberg, who suggested the C-clamp that clamps the health club to the parking deck. He also folded the *New York Times* [proposed Oldenberg sculpture] up there. All that stuff at the bottom has to do with the museum and the lobby being used for all those wonderful uses. I think that the justification for putting a commercial office building (a headquarters for an insurance company) on this kind of site is that, if all that nice public space for a museum could be incorporated into it and become part of the given, it would make a more civic kind of gesture to the Burnham mall. The building to the left, the other part of the goalpost, would be a hotel.

WE WON the competition for the Walt Disney Concert Hall in Los Angeles. The models are those that were submitted and became the winning design. The program called for a commercial building on the same site, but because a hotel or an office building design was a big load of complexity for a competition, and the clients were interested in picking only an architect and not a design particularly, the commercial building was left out of the equation. As in all competitions, when somebody wins, the images that you win with get buried in people's minds. Every-

Walt Disney Concert Hall, Los Angeles. Exterior model (Frank Gehry, 1988). (Tom Bonner)

thing you do after that is compared with the original image; that is not exactly fair, but everybody always says, "Well, the original was better."

I'm just going to explain where we were and then some of the issues that we're exploring. I agreed with the premise that the building should be a populist building, not an elitist building; that it be welcoming to a great number of people, not just to a few music aficionados; that it be a place where people from all parts of L.A. would feel comfortable entering.

So the body language of the building, as I call it, had to be welcoming, accessible. And that led me to the idea of making the foyer into a garden court with a trellislike structure that had big doors so you could leave them open during the day. Part of the program asked for a lot of gardens. Gardens in sort of a downtown urban setting seemed a little bit strange, but in our climate we can do it year round. And it seemed appropriate, too, that the back side facing Hope Street toward the west could be used for that kind of space. You could create an interior space in a sense. So the foyer/garden structure is backed up by a garden that you walk out into for intermissions.

The other part of the building to have priority is the facilities for the orchestra. In most of these kinds of buildings, by the time the orchestra gets there they are put into a little closet in the back where they change their clothes in practice rooms with no windows. That tends to be the rule because no budget is left over for it. In our scheme, the orchestra facilities—the orchestra rehearsal rooms and dressing rooms—all open to a garden and are accessible to the orchestra café, which is also part of the garden. These wonderful humanistic issues were incorporated and will find their way into the final project.

The relationship to the Dorothy Chandler Pavilion was an important piece of the equation. While Mrs. Chandler is getting on in years, many of the people who helped build the Chandler Pavilion are still around, and although architects tend to knock it as not a very good building, really a lot of blood, sweat, and tears went into building it. Since it is there and it is real, I took the optimistic view that it could be incorporated sculpturally and positively as part of the composition.

That is the way I approach all my buildings everywhere. I don't exclude. I try to be part of, in some way, what is around me. Even the little Norton house on the beach, in Venice, California, with the lifeguard tower that looks weird if you see it in a picture separated from its context, really belongs to that context.

You can see what I mean by sculpturally connecting and composing with the existing building and the connection to the Chandler. A big piece of this is Grand Avenue, an avenue that, just by its location, links the Museum of Contemporary Art to the Disney Concert Hall, the chandler, the Taper, the Ahmanson, and the Civic Center. A group of us have gotten together and are agonized about this street. What could it be? It should be something that grows out of L.A. and a collaborative process.

Some of us working several years back on the original Grand Avenue project, California Plaza, proposed a kind of *grand* Grand Avenue with sculpture and trees. It was to be very special. Now, as part of my project, I am pushing that idea further because there will be a new development across the street and that developer can be enlisted, since his development project will face the Disney Concert Hall and will benefit from the hall in a kind of urban relationship. At the same time, the city and county have gone out to various consultants and are making proposals for the design of the rest of the street from First Street to Temple, and for redoing the plaza of the Chandler to make it more accessible from the street. If that happens, we have only one more block to go to get a really Grand Avenue.

The concert hall was designed with the acoustician from France who gave us criteria that led us to this kind of configuration. When we won the competition, I was told that this acoustician was not going to be the final acoustician, that we were getting a new one. And, of course, the three new ones whom we interviewed all wanted to do shoe boxes. My clients do not want to do a shoe box. They want to do a surround hall more like Berlin. You get into this whole issue of how you listen to music, who listens to music, what kind of music. It may be easy to solve it all electroacoustically and that could be the answer, because you can take any room and very easily transform it electronically. Boulez uses electronics, but still some people want to hear it purely and they are part of the equation. I'm not sure they are wrong. I think you should be able to do both. If you want to hear it purely, then how do you know how it sounded in the seventeenth century with those instruments? There were smaller halls then, they are not 2,500-seat halls, and so on. So there is a whole agony and Angst going into how many seats you put in, how people listen to music and the purity of it, and the issue of the shoe box, the Boston Philharmonic being the best in the

Walt Disney Concert Hall, Los Angeles. Interior model (Frank Gehry, 1988). (Tom Bonner)

world, and so forth. Many people like going to Berlin. Berlin is sold out every night. You can't get a ticket to a concert in Berlin. People sit behind the orchestra. They are not hearing the music exactly as it was intended, but they love this experience.

I remember the rug concerts in New York where we sat on a stage on a rug and I felt very much as if Boulez were conducting me, even though I am not a musician. There is a variety of experiences possible. Anyway, the hall shows the form. It shows you these rooms. I had an opportunity to put a column at the corner, and it let me use that for light. The lamp and the acoustical ensemble reflectors and the organ could be a way of dealing with the decoration. These were just early beginnings of it.

The new acoustician said either choose this or that box, none of this extravagant stuff. My clients love the energy of free-flow seating and asked me to try to incorporate that into the concert hall. I tried every shape. We sent them all to Japan. Our acoustician is in Japan and we are getting close, but it keeps coming back a box. He says, "Yes, yes, Mr. Gehry, we are happy to try this." He is very polite, as Japanese gentlemen are.

But it keeps coming back—the box—so this is where we are going. We decided to try to capture some of that old flair of the seating by making the seating shape into a kind of boat that would be like a free-standing object sitting in the room and that would be made out of wood and upholstery and separate itself from the plaster walls. The columns are structural. We still were able to retain those points and get some of that energy that we had from the columns. There is a kind of energy and a sense of intimacy. The columns make a kind of proscenium, a peripheral proscenium, if you will. The organ is in front. Our intent is to make it like the Concertgebow organ, where it is a freestanding object. It's not plastered or papered onto walls.

We are at a point where we are starting to understand what we can do acoustically. Every few days, the acoustician sends me a fax in which he lowers the ceiling a foot or two, so we are fighting back at the corners. He is letting us open up the corners. It is our intent to get skylights in the corners so that, for the few matinée concerts a week, there will be natural light coming in and it will be a different experience. Maybe it will create a constituency of people who would like that.

So now, how do you take that box and crank it on the site? It is a lot harder than the other, froglike shape, which was easy to rotate. And how to you get all the same spaces with a thirty-or forty-story hotel on the site?

I particularly like having the hotel there because it makes for a more interesting project. It also gives us a backdrop that will be architecturally part of the same material as the concert hall—a very powerful backdrop, as you approach the site from the city.

ON THE SEINE near the rue Bercy, near the Gare de Lyon, near the new opera house in Paris, is a site to the right of the Palais OmniSports, a big park with full-grown trees. In it we were given a site for the American Center that is a kind of entrance to the park from the land side. They gave us a fairly square site, but the French cut the corner off. They call it a *pan coupé*. They seem to like doing that. It works in Barcelona; every corner is like that. But to just all of a sudden come along and have a corner cut out is one of the more difficult problems to solve architecturally.

The program is for theater, housing, restaurants, art museums, dance schools, language schools, bookstores, and God knows what. It is a very intense and compact project. We arrived at a scheme in which we separated the building with a crack, and the housing is separated on the corner. A movie theater and a restaurant face the plaza. There is a foyer: a big public space like a lobby in the middle, and the theater is to the right and the top two floors, which hold the museum and the dance school.

These were my study models. I sketched in the models trying to get an idea of how to deal with this *pan coupé*, what materials to use, how to deal with the crack, how to move around this building. I did sketches and made awkward and terrible-looking models. When the model was built, I went into a deep depression for two weeks. Then the lights started to dawn. I started to get a little bit more excited. A lot of drawings started to kick away. This whole process was about a three-month

American Center, Paris. Model (Frank Gehry, 1989). (J. Scott Smith)

continual process. The building will be in stone. The wood in the model represents stone, and the curved roof is metal.

You enter from the park through the *pan coupé*. You may also enter on the other corner. The housing has a sculpted form facing the park that we call the pineapple. The mansard has slipped a little purposefully. The commercial ground floor contains the restaurant, theater, and lobby. This is an American center, a place where Americans come to get tickets to events in France, where they are taught how to speak French, if they want. It is also where the French come to see American avant-garde art and music and dance performances. They traditionally had John Cage and Lucinda Childs, and shows by Stella.

The main street side is a very kind of traditional street-front façade. The schools and the offices are behind a grille, and the housing is separated by the crack. The corner is the other entrance from the street with the shops and the restaurants.

The loading for the theater is under the crack. There is another building about thirty feet down the street, so you won't see much of the east façade. There will be a row of trees in the side street, and there is a long housing building that goes easterly for many meters and was to have been done by a French architect. Lately, the newest trick in Paris is to get thirty architects to build buildings next to one another, so the French decided to cut up that long sausage building into thirty-foot-wide pieces and give them to twenty or so young architects to each do a piece.

I DESIGNED a project in Germany just across from Basel; a furniture factory. These people make Herman Miller furniture. They were old

Vitra factory and museum, Weil am Rhein, Germany (Frank Gehry, 1989). (Richard Bryant)

friends of the Eames family. Several years ago, they hired Claes Old-enberg and Coosje van Bruggen, who made a "tool gate" sculpture. They will display furniture in this museum, just chairs. They have a most incredible collection of Eames, Begoia, Aalto—all the molds and all the maquettes, models, and drawings. It is an extraordinary collection.

There is an existing factory by Nick Grimshaw. We built a new factory here, and in the same location in front we did our furniture museum. The client asked that our furniture museum be a very sculptural piece. We added a couple of ears to the factory building. Grimshaw had the bathrooms and stairways expressed. So we did the same with entry points for the factory. We made them more sculptural: they are ramps, bicycle sheds, and toilets. The point of entry is under them. This factory goes way back on the site. The museum is three fairly simple rooms with three skylights, stairs, elevators, and all that stuff expressed very sculpturally. So as you drive by, there is always a relationship of the pieces. It is an urban idea.

I'm not given to do white buildings, but Switzerland felt white to me. All the plaster will be white. You arrive under the canopy, which is zinc, and when you enter, you find the stair and the skylights. This building reminds me of a washing machine with the laundry tumbling. It is sort of all swishing. The roof is zinc. We just followed the logic of plaster and metal: wherever the wall was vertical or inclined in, we used plaster; wherever the wall was tilted toward the horizontal, we added metal.

From the highway that runs along the site, those ears are always talking to each other. The factory area in the back will be filled eventually with a bunch of white trucks. These are the ramps, which are also white, but as you walk you always see these pieces together.

We worked with a German firm, Gunter Pfeifer & Associates. They were incredibly attentive and helpful; it was a wonderful experience.

There are ramps at the factory building leading up to the offices overlooking the museum. There is a nice skylight at the rear of the space, and from there you can look at this sort of ship passing by.

There are three exhibition spaces. They are fairly simple; two are very Zenlike, but the upstairs has a little more animation. The action on the outside doesn't come on that heavy on the inside. There are cutouts in the corners, and then the central skylight, so the daylight inside the gallery is quite nice. You can see the organization. Upstairs in the upper gallery you can look down into the others.

I'M DOING a little house in New York State. It is a small house for an advertising client of mine, Jay Chiat. I have been working on it for three years. There will be a fish living room. He asked me what the elongated form was for, and I said, "So you can always know there is light at the end of the tunnel." I told him I put it there so we could really go over budget, to make sure we go over budget. So we had something we could take away, if we had to.

BACK TO fish and snakes. In downtown L.A., we are doing a sculpture at the top of Larry Halprin's Spanish steps. I was asked to do a fish,

Chiat residence, Sagaponacy, New York. Model (Frank Gehry, 1986). (Brian Yoo)

Latticed sculpture, Library Square,
Los Angeles. Model (Frank Gehry,
1989). (Brian Yoo)

but like the Spanish steps, the top needed a building. In this case a
building that was a sculpture. We proposed a latticed public space you
can go in. It is a kind of latticed kiva—a shaded, comfortable public
space.

THIS IS the fish that got away in New York. I was all excited that I was
going to do this high building. I made lots of fish shapes, but it fell by
the wayside.

MY GRANDMOTHER did have a bathtub like this when I was a kid. She
used to have carp in it. This is in Toronto, where I come from. They
were going to put a sculpture here and they procrastinated, so I went
out and bought this bathtub that looked like my grandmother's and I
put a fish in it, in lead.

I TEND to work intuitively. I have ideas that I formulate verbally and
ideas—principles—that I live and work by. And I have a bunch of heavy-
duty rules that I make, that I judge my work with as I do it. I always
start with some kind of reference. Then my intent has always been to
move it somewhere—to transform it in some way into some other, maybe

Madison Square Garden, New
York. Model (Frank Gehry, 1987).
(Kevin Daly)

more personal or more present, form. For instance, chain-link material
doesn't have popular connotations (prison and barbed-wire camps), but
it is liberally used in the culture. A lawyer friend of mine who always
kids me about chain link asked me to come to his house. He is not
interested in architecture very much. He bought a $6 million house in
Brentwood, California. He was having trouble with his kitchen, and he
was having trouble with his architect. He begged me to come look. So
I went and walked in the front door, and the foyer looked out at the
garden. There was a tennis court, and it was covered with chain link.
It was right in front of his entry. I went in the kitchen, and you can
see chain link. I went in the dining room, and you can see chain link.
I went in the living room; you can see it. I went in his bedroom; you
can see it. And I said, "Mickey, I see I've converted you to chain link.
You have spent 6 million bucks for a house with a centerpiece chain-
link court." He looked at me kind of crazy and said, "No, that is a
tennis court." It is that kind of denial that I am interested in. The

Sculpture, Chiat Day Toronto, Toronto (Frank Gehry, 1988). (Steve Evans)

material itself inherently is a fabric. When you get rid of all those posts and things, you hang it swaying in the breeze. It is one of the only materials I know that you can do that with and get a kind of softness. Bob Erwin did some scrim pieces that look quite beautiful. Chain link is like a scrim. It was a dialogue with Erwin as much as anything.

A Postmodern
Fable on Postmodernity, or:
In the Megalopolis

JEAN-FRANÇOIS LYOTARD

1. I HAVE BEEN kindly invited by William Lillyman and David Neuman to conclude this conference by taking the bearing of postmodernity ten years after the publication of my text *The Postmodern Condition.*[1] With this invitation, I understand that I have been asked to answer the question: What is post-postmodernity? The trap doesn't lie where it seems to; the mind is able to double the *post* as many times as it wants to. According to the basic property of time and number series that mathematics calls "the successor of," every number n, considered as an ordinal number, implies that it is followed by a number $n + 1$, whatever the one may be. The trap lies rather in the request for a conclusive bearing of post-postmodernity; for what I would underline first and foremost is the relativity in which thinking is obliged to operate under postmodern conditions. With relativity, such a conclusion is excluded and a bearing may only be taken arbitrarily.

In order to take the bearing of your positions, a system of reference such as a set of cardinal points, a map, clock, or calendar is needed first of all. It is only in space and time, let us say, in the crisscrossing of space-time, that a position may be pointed out and an account of a change or shift affecting this position given.

But the mapping itself is always controversial, because it depends on the space-time units chosen for the building of the reference system.

Here we encounter the problem of scale with regard to the perception of changes. Whereas changes may appear imperceptible in relation to the space-time units of a particular scale of measure, those same changes would appear dramatic and even drastic on a smaller scale. Clearly the impression one has at the end of something—for instance, modernity—depends on the scale of the units used to measure the changes affecting it. I think the diagnosis of the end of modernity stems from the way we measure extension and duration. We use the visual units employed by historians and anthropologists to clarify and dispatch human facts onto maps and calendars. In this way, the employment of these units operates as a filter that is unable to apprehend changes according to other scales, because the units employed are either too big or too small. Our eyes give us an example of such filtering: having only the capacity to capture a change marked by this *post* is relative to the assumption that *modernity* was and still is concerned with "Grand Narratives," and that *postmodernity* conveys the global feeling that they no longer "work."

A few remarks about this. Modernity is a state of mind, rather than a period or an epoch. The modern turn is ancient. We can take a bearing on it from the classical world's viewpoint. Modernity started with an extension of the Christian vision in which there was general purposiveness or finality polarizing the course of the world. A horizon was proposed: redemption, as in Augustine's *City of God*. Even if many secularizations would subsequently occur and have occurred, with the result of changing the nature and the name of the horizon and inducing more and more new readings of reality, the general frame of history, be it human or not, would remain, and has remained still unchanged. History was a story relating the account of a long episodic journey toward the accomplishment of freedom. Although redemption may have turned into emancipation as a result of the Enlightenment's and Marxism's development of the epistemological, philosophical, social, economic, political, and cultural prerequisites for liberty, the fact remains that the principle of narration was never brought into question. Communities were still viewed as being intensely eager to know that what was coming on would be better than what was given. And the "best" and the "better" were always understood as having the closest proximity to freedom possible.

Of course, it is possible to oppose a lot of counterfactual evidence against this reading. Once again, it's a question of scale and the zero point. Nonetheless, compared with the spirit of the classical age, this reading of modernity is unquestionable. It is the same with postmodernity. It's not as epoch any more; it's a state of mind. Clearly the postmodern mind is implicated in modernity itself every time the modern narrative and/or the goal that is its aim are submitted to criticism, skepticism, foreshortening, or anticipation. Furthermore, inasmuch as questioning the state of things is implied in these attitudes, and modernity is inseparable from its self-questioning, the postmodern gestures are part of the modern mind. This means that the Grand Narratives have almost never been assumed without doubt, criticism, or a desire to hasten their closure through the immediate actualization of their goal—as is the case with most revolts and revolutions, for instance. On the contrary, most of the forms taken by the severest criticisms of modernity have subsequently appeared useful to modernity itself by enabling it to continue in its progress toward emancipation. Finally, there is a dialectical relationship between modernity and postmodernity that inscribes itself within the way the Grand Narratives have had to change in order to be realized.

In this context, we should consider postmodernity as either an increase of skepticism or, at least, a greater reservation with regard to the Grand Narratives and their goals, rather than a new period in human history. What is called the crisis of the fundamentals in the hard sciences and epistemology; the avant-garde in the arts and literature; the often disastrous efforts to create right- or left-wing alternatives to the liberal communities as well as the failure of such attempts; the social and economic crisis of 1920 to 1950, followed by the reorganization of communities on the international level after World War II—all this may be ascribed to postmodernity, but only to the extent that it posts in the foreground a lot of implicit or latent questions already present in modernity. As was previously said, it is a question of systems of reference, scale of measure, and determination of a zero point of observation.

2. Now, THIS being assumed, I don't deny that something is changing, has changed, or is going to change in the contemporary world. But, being quite receptive to this change, as most of us are, I find it amazing to consider how far the interpretations, which are supposed to provide an account for this change, are from dealing with the wide range of facts implied by it. I think that the shift in circumstances, if any, requires a respective shift in the point of view and approach. The question is: What kind of shift are we capable of envisaging?

As to circumstances, it seems possible to come to an agreement on some of the characteristics of contemporary times, such as the following:

1. There is an increased capacity to apprehend events, whatever their nature (micro as well as macro, mental as well as physical).
2. Along with this greater capacity to apprehend, there is also an increased ability to translate events into data very quickly. Data are events that have been rendered significant by and for a reading code. Once turned into data, events are stored inside memory banks and, as such, are made easily accessible at all times. Here I am referring to data processing.
3. Linked to these developments in such technologies, there is a huge

increase in the competence available to every system processing data in this way; therefore, an additional increase in performance is expected from them.

4. In addition, there is a tendency to mobilize and direct energies of all kinds, human or nonhuman, toward the formation of even more differentiated systems. To be differentiated means that a system has an ever greater capacity to apprehend, translate, store, and make usable those data that were previously out of our perception and reach.

5. As a result of this increase in competence, competition is going to become the general rule and regulator of systems, be they human or not.

6. As competition becomes the rule, there is a tendency to deal with every issue, be it human or not, in terms of performativity and "feasibility." The slogan "nothing is impossible" positively means that whatever is possible should be attempted in any field that one can imagine: science, technics, arts, commodities, communities, and communication.

7. Finally, something that is noteworthy: there is no mode of thinking capable of giving an account of this process with which we are now confronted. Of course, we use the old terminology of democracy in order to legitimate this stubbornness to compete. At the same time, everybody knows that inasmuch as democracy means the voluntary consent of the majority on problematic issues, it cannot serve as the basis for assessing a scientific, an artistic, or an ethical proposition. Unlike Richard Rorty, I assume that truth, beauty, and justice are not matters of consensus, and that objectivity is not exchangeable with solidarity. It seems better to leave these issues pending than to pretend to resolve them under the idea or ideology of democracy.

Before ending with this last point, I would like to observe that far from the modern mode of thinking, which tried to give numerous philosophical reasons for modernity under the aegis of the idea of progress—that is, a founding by way of the future—postmodernity doesn't seem committed to the same issue of founding in general. The job of establishing a foundation—that of philosophy—is first of all considered to be useless and secondly hopeless, that is, neither competitive nor performative.

Professionals and executives continue to call on philosophers to consult them (the reason I am here), but I wonder whether it is because of tradition—that is, because of a sincere and deferent nostalgia for the old days—or because philosophers may render a performance, a conference for instance, more performative in terms of a "cultural industry" success. (This last case appears hopeless.) Anyway, one of the main characteristics of postmodernity is, as I just described it, to be totally unconcerned with regard to its own legitimation. As Engels ingeniously said, the proof of the pudding is in the eating.

3. Now THE POINT is actually about eating. We intake less and less "natural" food. The body is maintained by industrially produced farm products. To the extent that a whole range of environmental conditions, and not only the composition of food, causes imbalances and disorders in the human body's natural metabolism, all kinds of prostheses are used to make up for these disturbances. Consequently, the maintenance of the body turns into a sophisticated set of procedures, while the human body itself increasingly becomes the artificial result of the competent and competitive technologies of birth, death, health, and especially food production. Thus the fact of eating is no longer sufficient proof that the pudding is real. The notions of reality, proving, body, and showing are put into question with no hope of being resolved. Unlike Jean Baudrillard, I don't think that this shift results in a wide range of simulation (or simulacra), a term still too close to the belief that reality exists in itself. Rather, I guess that this development entails a move away from traditionally modern values such as truth, justice, long-term finality, and the hope of legitimation.

Please allow me to make a modest remark on architecture. It seems to me that the same problem can be likewise traced in terms of the ancient "art of building." From time immemorial, the building of a dwelling place had been regulated by the idea that dwelling itself— having a home and occupying it, be it common or private—was a kind of favor, and therefore the building was supposed to be dedicated to the someone (or something) who was considered to be the addressor of such a favor. It was as if human beings were merely tenants of such grounds. Thus, far from being conceived and realized in terms of function and performativity, the idea of building was guided by one's duty of paying homage to the donor.

When modernity began, the mode of dwelling that I would designate by the ancient Latin noun *domus* (in which the connotations I just mentioned are implied) started to vanish. I think that what was called modernism in architecture was directly linked to the disappearance. While the *metropolis* was coming about and finally replacing the traditional settlement with the establishment of villages and cities, a new type of human beings, the "lonely crowds" of workers and employees, had to find accommodations. Through diverse and even contradictory ways, modernism was the attempt to provide answers to this unexpected challenge by means of the home dedicated to the donor; *domus* was still haunting modern architects and buildings. The only dispute had to do with the nature of the donor, the donee, and the dedication.

We are presently at a moment when *metropolises* themselves have to yield to a new form of settlement, the *megalopolis*. It is a response to the end of the predominantly (mechanical) industrial era and the disappearance of the workers associated with it. Along with the technological electronic developments that allow people to speak, see, listen, work, and communicate far away from one another, the requirements of "being together" are submitted to a great change, a consequence of which consists in what we call *conurbation*. An outstanding example of this manner of dwelling and building is found here on the southern California coast, where still undeveloped rural spaces between metropolises like Los Angeles and San Diego are gradually being occupied by new communities. Urbanism and architecture are confronted with new data.

Indeed, it is arguable that the *ghost* of *domus* still remains vivid in those conditions. In other words, besides having to make accommodations in which individual humans feel comfortable, architects are still asked to give an answer to the question of dwelling—that is, to whom or what their art is dedicated.

Nonetheless, insofar as this change implies the separation between country and city, or nature and culture, or better, the incorporation of the former into the latter as part of the human communication network, one can observe the same type of result as previously mentioned—an increase of artificiality and a loss of legitimacy, that is to say, the impossibility of determining the nature of the donor. But, as already said, this "loss" or fall, as it were, is hardly experienced as such. It is concealed by the conviction that mankind is going to overcome the "natural" challenges with which it is confronted. In short, it is the evidence of progress conceived as emancipation. Insofar as this is still a representation issued forth from the modern Enlightenment, I think that it is an ideology rather than just an idea, in comparison with the postmodern features just briefly described.

4. PERHAPS THE WHOLE point is the following paradox: in the course of its development, modernity also develops the ability to question every datum or reality; but at the same time that this incredulity is developing, a sense of self-reliance comes about, accompanied by cynicism and arrogance. Further advancement of this paradox turns into the unique value of living one's life. Other considerations don't matter. Now if one thinks along these lines, one will arrive at a conclusion or picture that hardly allows mankind to congratulate itself on this development. I would like to tell a story that illustrates the motives of such a disappointment. It is a fiction or fable that doesn't pretend to have a scientific or even a cognitive status. Furthermore, neither the audience nor the narrator is expected to believe that what the fable relates is the truth. It is exemplary only because it is, or could be, told with regard to any place: scientific and technical laboratories, artists' studios, university and community conference rooms, corporate and executive offices, and so on. Nobody would actually dare assume it, but everybody allows it to circulate as a rumor. I'll tell it as a probable version of postmodernity narrated by itself—that is, when it obeys its own mode of understanding.

First of all, let us recall postmodernity's characteristic features, which I previously cited: increased capacity to apprehend and process data, the growing up (complexification, proliferation, expansion) of system performances (whatever those systems may be), the predominance of the efficiency value, the "total mobilization" of all types of energy, the urgency to compete, and the disregard of legitimacy.

All these features seem to be relevant to systems regulated by the "optimization" principle. To optimize the performance or efficiency of a system, the ratio between the output and the input must be increased in relation to what it previously was. If its consumption of energy remains constant, the system's production of transformed energy (work) must nevertheless increase. Development entails the optimization of a system's performance.

A system regulated in this way should be understood as being continuously submitted to a process of additional internal differentiation. This additional differentiation is achieved by introducing a third element between at least two elements that were previously linked together by themselves. The former link is commonly said to be natural, whereas the additional one is mediated.

According to the second principle of thermodynamics, when a system is left isolated, its internal differentiation tends to decrease and disappear. This is the system's "death," as is the case with stars and, in particular, the sun. We call this process entropy. Development implies, then, that systems are never isolated.

The "story" relates that a process of development, or negative entropy, has contingently taken place over the surface of the small planet Earth. The synthesis of life provided the first monocellular organisms (algae) from molecular components, thanks to the causal conjunction of elements such as sunlight, temperature, water, and their respective chemical components. It is from this very beginning that the process develops, that is the erstwhile story of living beings, mankind, human languages, communities, writings, and technical devices of all sorts. Knowledge and sciences should be taken as the results of it.

The "story" also indicates that under the name of liberal democracies and capitalist economics, a way to promote, apprehend, store, and use energies has triumphed over all the other systems because of its superior efficiency. This success has required a lot of time to be spent in trials, errors, and selections. Thus human history is nothing but a developing process based on mankind's proportions and conceived in terms of Grand Narratives. Actually, mankind is the ultimate and most differentiated conveyor of the developing process. Its advantage lies in the fact that the human brain represents the most open system we know. It is capable of accepting and integrating events at a tremendous rate and creating new forms of response.

The "story" merely says that development develops. Mankind is required to accommodate itself to the ever more differentiated conditions in which development fashions its way to life. Development had no need for mankind except as its conveyor. Parts of mankind can be, have been, and will be its victims. Development isn't progress in the sense of the Enlightenment. The notions of emancipation, freedom, good, and evil are irrelevant in the last analysis.

Megalopolis is the response to development as it affects the ways of "being together" and dwelling of the most developed parts of mankind.

The only actual change that development is likely to meet in the future is represented by the death of the sun. The research carried out in various scientific, technological, and social fields should be understood as focused on the target that will render human brains capable of escaping the disaster that the explosion of the sun will be. There is still a little time to respond to the challenge: more than 4 billion years—not a long time by the cosmic clock.

5. Now A FEW remarks by way of conclusion.

The story implies that alternatives are merely possibilities issued by a developing system when it is scanning a theoretical or an empirical field in order to "read" it differently than normal. An alternative is at best a "misreading," as Harold Bloom says. Criticisms, critical breaks, and revolutionary programs are part of the system's very development. They are useful for maintaining its openness. The appeals to humanism, consensus, the Third World, and the rights of man and woman must be understood as ways for the system to make itself more complete, flexible, and bearable for mankind, and therefore more able to mobilize all forms of human energy.

Is the story itself a Grand Narrative? At first glance, it seems to be. As a story, it tells the adventure of a mysterious character, Development, who has, and who has to have, both partaken in and created these adventures. The character is confronted by one and the same enemy, Entropy, who challenges Development throughout the episodes. The stage is the cosmos.

In addition, the story is unquestionably a metaphysical fable, as all Grand Narratives have been and must be. Indeed, the metaphysics implied by the story of development belongs to the metaphysics of energy rather than to that of subjectivity. Nonetheless, it is a metaphysics insofar as there is no evidence that attests to the existence of energy any more than of a subject. By "metaphysics" I understand a way of thinking that fails to criticize the presuppositions implied by the terms of its own argument.

Now what distinguishes the story of development from a Grand Narrative is that it isn't anthropocentric at all. With the change of scale and measures, mankind appears as nothing more than a transitory form taken by development over a small observatory, the Earth.

Accordingly, time implied in the story no longer takes a human shape. Even if the universe is kept open, as it were, by the story, it's only to the extent that development operates at random, trying to apprehend and digest the events as they occur. And yet, through the contingent occurrence of unexpected events, development necessarily develops. (Here I understand necessity in a special sense linked with the relativity I mentioned in the very beginning. The contrary development, entropy, isn't impossible; it is the impossibility itself to develop the story. Either development develops, including its story, or development fails and then everything ends; for there will not even be anyone to tell the end.)

With such a necessity, the major ideas we find as aims for the Grand Narratives—redemption, emancipation, the end of historical sufferings, all of which have the sense of opening another age, the freedom era for instance—must be given up. We'll never be emancipated from the process.

In this context, the story of development doesn't imply—as it usually does with stories, be they short stories or Grand Narratives—that there must be a moral, and that the audience should change its mind and behavior in order to put into practice what has been fictionally told on the stage. Necessity excludes ethics and politics. Values are valuable only insofar as they can contribute to the systems' optimization. Consequently, the multiplication of experiences and values—that is, what we call permissivity—is good for the system, regardless whether they imply identification with or resistance to it.

I confess that the scenery of postmodernity represented in this way is not very pleasant. It maximizes the strength of the enemy. It is a good strategy. By using terms like "enemy" and "strategy," I suggest that I am tempted to resist development. As you know, such resistance can easily be reactionary. If it wishes not to be, resistance may be but a manner to contribute to the system's optimization. The margin is quite narrow, if there is any at all. We can only grope our way. Where the idea of resistance comes from, and how it might be actualized, could be the object of another story.

NOTE

1. Jean-François Lyotard, *The Postmodern Condition: A Report on Knowledge*, trans. Geoffrey Bennington and Brian Massumi (Minneapolis: University of Minnesota Press, 1984).

The Ground Is No Longer Flat: Postmodernity from Architecture to Philosophy

STEVEN TAUBENECK

Being slippery by the way is the trait of a postmodernist.
Peter Eisenman

AT FIRST GLANCE, it may appear as though the several speakers heard at the Irvine conference had very little in common. How, for example, could the blunt intellectualism of Peter Eisenman, who spoke casually of the distinction between repetition and iteration, be related to the more folksy, "aw shucks" manner of Frank Gehry, who acted as if his models simply flow from his hands without any hesitation or anxiety? How could these, in turn, be related to the serene coolness of Michael Wilford, who insisted on clarity above all in his drawings?

Admittedly, it is possible to see many of the recent developments in architecture as completely unrelated to one another, but also as unrelated to other developments in literature, philosophy, and politics. The buildings of Peter Eisenman, Frank Gehry, Zaha Hadid, Frank Israel, Robert Stern, James Stirling, Bernard Tschumi, and Michael Wilford may seem entirely different both from one another and from the stories, plays, and films of Donald Barthelme, Heiner Mueller, Christa Wolf, Peter Handke, and Wim Wenders, from the philosophies of Jacques Derrida, Jean-François Lyotard, Jean Baudrillard, and Richard Rorty, or from the politics of Mikhail Gorbachev, George Bush, Saddam Hussein, and Nelson Mandela.[1] Like the patchwork of styles in Berlin, Paris, Tokyo, or Los Angeles, the field of international contemporary culture seems to have dispersed into an incoherent collection of

197

random and arbitrary instances. From this perspective, the concept of "postmodernity," when applied to contemporary culture, is so vague, diffuse, and general that it loses all specific shape and definition. Indeed, it could well appear that the concept of postmodernity is so porous that it should be dismissed altogether as the nightmare of some hyperactive critics. Perhaps we should view contemporary culture as Charles Jencks, one of the most prominent disseminators of the term, has done in his recent version of *Architecture Today*—as a wildly disparate collection of individual styles.[2] Or we could simply pronounce, as the critic Andy Grunberg wrote in the *New York Times*, that postmodernism is dead: "Ten years after it created a sensation in the art world, the tendentious, media-conscious movement known as post-modernism has lost its momentum.[3]

But postmodernity, as Irving Howe and Harry Levin recognized as far back as the late 1950s, was always already "dead on arrival."[4] For even in those days it seemed an ersatz successor to the high modernist energies of Brecht, Eliot, Joyce, and Pound; Gropius, Le Corbusier, Mies van der Rohe, and Frank Lloyd Wright; Picasso, Schoenberg, and Stravinsky; Adorno, Freud, and Wittgenstein. The grand seriousness of their works, the heroic efforts by many of those people to visualize a new, more rational design for cultural and social modernization, make the impossibly heterogeneous pop experiments of the Beats and Andy Warhol, the comics and Westerns celebrated by Leslie Fiedler, the rock and roll culture of the 1960s and 1970s, and the "decorated sheds" of Robert Venturi look corrupt and pale in comparison.[5] In contrast to the massive renovation of the Western cultural tradition desired by the modernists in general, the emphasis on pop and non-Western culture, pastiche, ornamentation, and mauve and turquoise walls could seem to be weak, pretentious symptoms of cultural exhaustion.

For all its alleged triviality and apparent weaknesses, however, it is remarkable how epidemic postmodernist culture has become. From architecture to philosophy since the 1950s, a situation has developed globally that can be described, as Andreas Huyssen sees it, as "an ever wider dispersal and dissemination of artistic practices all working out of the ruins of the modernist edifice, raiding it for ideas, plundering its vocabulary and supplementing it with randomly chosen images and motifs form pre-modern and non-modern cultures as well as from contemporary mass culture."[6] Especially in contrast to the modernists just named, the particular efforts of the several architects and theorists featured at the Irvine conference share a considerable number of these specific features. Indeed, it may be that the only substantial issue is not whether postmodernity exists, or even what it might be, but how one's beliefs and sense of humor will deal with the lumpiness and the contradictions of, as Peter Eisenman has described it, a "ground that is no longer flat."

From the many affinities of form and content shared by recent cultural innovations, seven are among the most significant: (1) a general antifoundationalism, the awareness that "God is dead" in Nietzsche's terms; (2) the ensuing inflation of language as ground, the reconceptualization of any ground as a rhetorical construct; (3) simultaneously, but in the opposite direction, the dissolution of language itself into a conflicted field of borrowings or quotations; (4) the parallel globalization, on the one hand, of certain tendencies: the relentless internationalization of pollution, technology, and multinational corporations; (5) the separation, on the other hand, of large political blocs in general into smaller, more regional zones; (6) the increasing recognition of accident, chance, or contingency as a factor shaping language, the self, and the community; and (7) the awareness that moments governed by contingency are eminently ironic and potentially reversible at any time.

A book by Richard Rorty entitled *Contingency, Irony, and Solidarity*[7] addresses many of these concerns. In this book, Rorty shows how philosophy has been moving against various concepts of a foundation or ground since the time of the French Revolution and Hegel. Antifoundationalism within philosophy primarily involves the notion that truth is "made rather than found" (*CIS*, 3). Previously, and especially for Kant, truth had meant Higher Truth, the Truth about Mind, an area seen as the special domain for Philosophy. With the French Revolution, however, and its demonstration that social relations could be changed overnight, writers sensed that truth was a matter of description and not something "out there," apart from language. Truth—indeed, all the foundational concepts that had been the basis of Enlightenment optimism, whether God, Man, Nature, or the World—became "de-divinized," lost their capitalizations, and were seen as the products of imperfect human activity.

The dislocation of the idea of truth drained it of foundational importance, and led to an inversely proportional inflation in the role of language: "To say that truth is not out there is simply to say that where there are no sentences there is no truth, that sentences are elements of human languages, and that human languages are human creations" (*CIS*, 5). The concept of truth was displaced into the realm of language, of metaphoric description (*CIS*, 16).[8]

According to Rorty, a number of eminent philosophical writers following Hegel have recognized the importance of language: "The phenomenon Hegel describes is that of more people offering more radical redescriptions of more things than ever before, of young people going through half a dozen spiritual gestalt-switches before reaching adulthood" (*CIS*, 7). Rather than claiming the absolute truth for themselves and their systems, philosophers like Nietzsche, Wittgenstein, Heidegger, Derrida, and Lyotard have seen that what they produce is first of all language, scripted in the forms of written narration. These writers share a belief in the primacy of language, what might be called the "rhetoricity of ground"; the privileging of language is what joins many architects, philosophers, poets, and politicians today.

Both cultural observers and professional architects, in other words, now refer to buildings in terms of communication, narrative, metaphor, signs, and symbols.[9] These people share the realization of philosophers that language is a central problem. Derrida has dramatized the point:

> However the topic is considered, the *problem of language* has never been simply one problem among others. But never as much as at present has it invaded, *as such,* the global horizon of the most diverse researches and the most heterogeneous discourses, diverse and heterogeneous in their intention, method, and ideology. . . . This inflation of the sign "language" is the inflation of the sign itself, absolute inflation, inflation itself. It indicates, as if in spite of itself, that a historico-metaphysical epoch *must* finally determine as language the totality of its problematic horizon.[10]

The "absolute inflation" of language as the central concern of our time suggests that, in Rorty's terms, the "world is well lost."[11] An inflated language replaces the notion of a hard, unyielding world "out there" with the notion of the "world" as a metaphor in a language game, a linguistic practice within a certain vocabulary: "The world does not speak. Only we do. The world can, once we have programmed ourselves with a language, cause us to hold beliefs. But it cannot propose a language for us to speak. Only other human beings can do that" (*CIS,* 6).

From the speakers at the Irvine conference, at any rate, it is evident that architects have become centrally concerned with language. Among the terms most often used by Frank Gehry, Robert Stern, Peter Eisenman, Michael Wilford, and Frank Israel were the interrelated concepts of language or narrative to describe their designs. Not only the concept of language itself, but many of the specific terms of philosophers have been transposed into the vocabulary of architects. Charles Jencks, while describing Eisenman's work since 1987, emphasizes the close relationship to Derrida: "Eisenman's rhetoric machine seems to have dominated Derrida's programme—'excavation,' 'palimpsest,' 'quarry,' 'self-similarity,' 'superposition,' 'scaling,' 'textual figuration,' 'dissimulation,' 'point grid,' and 'ghost representations'—these are the tropes from his armory which are evident in the garden."[12] Paolo Portoghesi describes the view from the architectural world: "The crisis of theoretical legitimation has unhinged the fundamental principles of architectural modernity"; he notes that architects can no longer talk of any kind of architectural "truth," any stable foundation on which to base their drawings, designs, and completed projects.[13] Without a level ground to stand on, the intuitive belief in the solidity of buildings has melted into the thin air of metaphor.[14]

At this point, of course, it can be charged that the statement that there is no such thing as truth "out there," only "language games," amounts to an inconsistency or self-contradiction. It sounds as if Nietzsche, Wittgenstein, or Derrida, for example, is "claiming to know what they themselves claim cannot be known" (*CIS*, 8). But Rorty argues that such statements should be taken pragmatically as recommendations that the concept of "truth" should be dropped as an unprofitable topic. Instead of a firm "this is how it is," Rorty recommends that we say, "Try thinking of it this way" (*CIS*, 9). A more pragmatic, contingent, self-ironic, and imaginative use of language would be the result.

A second objection to the expansion of language is also possible, however, if it amounts to a new apotheosis, the assumption that *language* will now afford a real foundation upon which to build. It might seem that "language," "our language," now represents an underlying unity that would bring together the self and reality. "Language" would be enshrined as the new synthesis, an ahistorical medium that, if understood as in linguistics, would enable us to solve the problems of culture and society. But Rorty's account of linguistic communication, following the work of Donald Davidson, asserts that there "*is no such thing as a language,* not if a language is anything like what philosophers, at least, have supposed. There is therefore no such thing to be learned or mastered. We must give up the idea of a clearly defined shared structure which language users master and then apply to cases" (*CIS*, 15). Once Language has undergone an "absolute inflation," then the idea that *it* has an intrinsic nature can be dropped as well. Hyperinflation in this case leads to dispersal, and the concept of Language itself, following those of God, Man, Nature, and the World, becomes the product of contingency:

> [T]hink of the history of language, and thus of culture, as Darwin taught us to think of the history of a coral reef. . . . . This analogy lets us think of "our language"—that is, of the science and culture of twentieth-century Europe—as something that took shape as a result of a great number of sheer contingencies. Our language and our culture are as much a contingency, as much a result of thousands of small mutations finding niches (and millions of others finding no niches), as are the orchids and the anthropoids. (*CIS*, 16)

The expansion of language into an all-pervasive medium leads to the realization that it, too, cannot stand as a stable foundation for our experience. Language comes to appear as a collection of "thousands of small mutations," or a "mobile army of metaphors," as Nietzsche put it. In Rorty's view, Language loses its quasi-divine status and becomes just one more metaphor created by particular users in particular situations for particular purposes.

To see language this way, as central yet contingent, is not to dismiss historical progress altogether, to reject innovation or the "shock of the new." For Rorty, changing the way we talk will amount to "changing what we want to do and what we think we are" (*CIS*, 20). It amounts to giving priority to the poet over the philosopher, and especially those poets who can provide new vocabularies: "A sense of human history as the history of successive metaphors would let us see the poet, in the generic sense of the maker of new words, the shaper of new languages, as the vanguard of the species" (*CIS*, 20). For Rorty, post-Nietzschean philosophers like Wittgenstein and Heidegger "became caught up in the quarrel between philosophy and poetry which Plato began, and both ended by trying to work out honorable terms on which philosophy might surrender to poetry" (*CIS*, 26).

But the poet does not create a new language out of a vacuum. On the contrary, "the terms used by the founders of a new form of cultural life will consist largely in borrowings from the vocabulary of the culture which they are hoping to replace" (*CIS*, 56). Rorty's emphasis on the largely *borrowed* phase of "a new form of cultural life" coincides with Derrida's practices. In a famous definition of "deconstruction" from *Grammatology*, Derrida highlights the importance of "borrowing." The movements of deconstruction do not

> destroy structures from the outside. They are not possible and effective, nor can they take accurate aim, except by inhabiting those structures. Inhabiting them *in a certain way*, because one always inhabits, and all the more when one does not suspect it. Operating necessarily from the inside, borrowing all the strategic and economic resources of subversion from the old structure, borrowing them structurally, that is to say without being able to isolate their elements and atoms, the enterprise of deconstruction always in a certain way falls prey to its own work.[15]

What Derrida and Rorty share at this point is part of the widespread obsession with the gesture of citation. "Borrowing," in their vocabulary, refers to the citation or quotation of conceptual frameworks, terms, metaphors, imagery. Beyond "straight" citation, however, quotations will often be coupled with pseudoquotations, imitations of form and style, and persiflage.[16] Evidently, the persistent interest in the uses of citation does not involve a mere problem of details, but issues of worldview and their formulation. The "law of quotation marks," as Derrida describes it in his recent study of Heidegger, produces a ghostly, suspended drama, a hallucinatory and unsettling kind of hyperreality:

> It's the law of quotation marks. Two by two they stand guard: at the frontier or before the door, assigned to the threshold in any case, and these places are always dramatic. The apparatus lends itself to theatricalization, and also to the hallucination of the stage and its machinery: two pairs of pegs hold in suspension a sort of drape, a veil or a curtain. Not closed, just slightly open.[17]

In architecture such suspensions appear in what Jencks calls "the ghost buildings of Venturi, and Jim Stirling at Stuttgart."[18] As became apparent during the conference, the inflation of language, its eventual dispersal into a collection of contingent adaptations, and the importance of borrowing or citation, all play decisive roles in philosophy and architecture today.

Perhaps the most visible embodiment of contingency in architecture is the very lack of a postmodernist style, particularly if "style" is understood in the singular. Each site addressed by the architects had a strong influence on the plans for the building, and each design emerged as a series of adaptations—"mutations" in Rorty's terminology—that were developed to meet the perceived demands of the site. There was, for example, Frank Gehry's Disney Concert Hall, which is designed to interact with the Chandler Pavilion across the street in Los Angeles. The hall was given particular features in response to the particulars of the Chandler Pavilion. There was also Robert Stern's building for Disney, which adapts many of the local icons to the cathedral framework. While it suggests that the Disney Corporation has become a nearly religious institution in our time, the basic cathedral shape also allows Stern to incorporate local architectural and landscape features as well. And there was Peter Eisenman's Wexner Center at Ohio State, which seeks to intercept and interrupt students on their way to football games. The pronounced interest on the Ohio State campus for football is parodied and disrupted in the dislocations of the center. Each of these buildings responds to the particular requirements of the particular site, and in various ways makes use of these sites within their designs. This particularization is the result not of a search for an underlying authenticity hidden within each site, but of the contingent responses by a particular architect to the contingent demands of a particular location. The search for depth in these instances has given way to the play of surfaces, a lyrical chorus of partially visible, partially hidden allusions and interventions. If one wanted to imagine such a trend as the "International Postmodernist Style," it would be plural, multiple, complex, and contradictory.[19] It would also include, as in the cases of Eisenman, Gehry, Hadid, Tschumi, and others, the effort to produce an antiarchitectural architecture, a series of constructions organized to deconstruct architecture itself.

Related to the contingencies of site are the techniques of dislocation, segmentation, and citation. Each of these gives an architect greater flexibility in the use of a particular site. Consider Frank Gehry's house for the Finnish ambassador. On a tiny 100- × 200-foot lot, Gehry has adapted numerous different forms in the assemblage of a particular dwelling. Dislocation and segmentation are also quite evident in the works of Michael Wilford and James Stirling. From the Stuttgart Staatsgalerie to the Cornell University Performing Arts Center, the designs of Wilford and Stirling tend to break down and segment massive conglomerations of form. Such segmentation is particularly visible in the Cornell project. Hence the complaint of monumentality often directed against Wilford and Stirling does not actually apply, for they consistently break down larger shapes in their designs and reassemble them into discrete elements within montage or pastiche constructions. Insofar as segmentation and pastiche join such differing architects as Eisenman, Gehry, Wilford, and Stern, these techniques appear among the most characteristic of recent production. Wilford's and Stirling's buildings especially make use of the technique of citation. Wilford and Stirling frequently employ distinctive features from Schinkel, Luytens, Le Corbusier, and Aalto in their works, while also responding to elements from the particular surroundings of the particular buildings. Hence it is also not the case that their work is antihistorical, as was briefly suggested in the Irvine discussion. It seems rather that Wilford's and Stirling's buildings rely heavily on historical models, selectively borrow the forms they like, and apply them pragmatically to the particular sites.

In fact, the varieties of citation are widespread and contribute substantially to the vitality of contemporary architecture. Robert Stern's designs, like Wilford's and Stirling's, often rely on the citation of particular instances from particular contexts. It is important to reflect, however, on just what kind of "authenticity" the uses of citation create. If it is indeed the creation of an authentic design, then it is at most an authenticity entirely composed of borrowed materials, what could be called a type of "synthetic authenticity."[20]

Citation as the manipulation of historical materials extends to the designs of Frank Gehry. At first it may look as though these designs have nothing to do with history, but attempt to escape or to move back before history altogether. The fish shape, however, the snake or the boat, all important shapes in Gehry's projects, can also be seen as attempts to outhistoricize the historicists. As he suggests in his essay, Gehry evidently became so disturbed by the historicism of recent architecture that he went back 300 million years to a nonhuman history, a time of primordial shapes, for his models. On the one hand, this primordialism undoubtedly seeks to escape history, but, on the other hand, it also enlarges the scope of historical references to a prehuman time. From this perspective, it appears that the richly archaic sense of modeling in Gehry's designs is what creates the "shock of the new": the shock of the newest art lies precisely in its revisioning of the old.[21]

With the many intersections among recent architects and theorists, it is of course necessary to distinguish the crucial differences among them as well. For some of the deconstructionist architects, particularly Frank Gehry, Peter Eisenman, Bernard Tschumi, and Zaha Hadid, the classical typology of architecture such as windows, doors, rectangles, columns, and colonnades is to be radically criticized or subverted. In Gehry's Wosk House additions, for example, "one fractured language" is set in "contrast with a second, conventional one."[22] This critique of the classical is also found in many of Eisenman's recent urban projects, such as his design for social housing in Berlin. Or, in the Wexner Arts Center, Eisenman fractures and collides the red masonry towers with a series of jumbled rectangles, creating the "fiction" of a "ghost tower."[23] While using the rhetoric of postmodernity, such as "fiction," "antimemory," "representation," and "figuration," Eisenman and Gehry nevertheless seem to bend architecture against itself, to move against "the natural language of architecture."[24] In Eisenman's view his interventions into architecture's classical typology are more of a dislocation than the projects of Robert Stern and James Stirling.[25] As he describes it: "The difference between what I'm doing and the other people in the show is that my work is about textual multivalence or *betweenness*."[26] Deconstruction as antiarchitectural architecture would from this perspective function differently from the plural field of postmodernist constructions, while nevertheless overlapping in the usage of citation, contingency, and dislocation as part of a general response to modernity.[27] It is precisely at those points of overlap that Stern and Stirling, Eisenman and Gehry, for all their manifest differences, share in the operations of postmodernity. Their strategies can be summarized in terms relating to the postmodernity of philosophy and critical theory:

> Postmodernity therefore reveals itself as an ironic notion communicating indirectly, by way of circumlocution, configuration, and bafflement, the necessity and impossibility of discussing the status of modernity in a straightforward and meaningful manner. Postmodernity, in its twisted posture, seems to be the awareness of this paradox, and consequently of the status of modernity, in a somersaulting fashion.[28]

Together with the manifest differences, in other words, it is characteristic that the techniques of segmentation, dislocation, and citation are brought together with a frequent recourse to self-irony and contradiction. The example of the T-shirt worn by Peter Eisenman during his lecture at the conference clarifies the point. On one side the T-shirt read "Eisenman," but on the other side it inverted the name into forgetfulness: "Amnesie." At one moment he advertised his own name, but at the next he indicated that we should forget it. This ironic and openly contradictory suggestion, coupled with the fact that Eisenman used a T-shirt to make his statement in the first place, thus breaking the convention of formal attire for an official conference, enacted a characteristically self-ironic performance.

Several examples lend support to the claim that irony and self-contradiction are among the most widespread elements within postmodern production. There was, for instance, Eisenman's pronouncement that he was moving toward a "weak form" that stood in ironic contradiction to the evident forcefulness of his Wexner Center at Ohio State. Another highly ironic use of contradiction appears in Robert Stern's Disney building. On the one hand, the Disney building borrows the style of the Gothic cathedral, while on the other hand, the building is filled with the well-known, kitschy artifacts of Disney's culture. As the French social theorist Jean Baudrillard suggests, the increasing "Disneyfication" of the American landscape has fostered considerable uncertainty over the reality or the hyperreality, the actual problems or the simulatedness of everyday life; Robert Stern's building provides a significant example of this process.[29] But perhaps the most striking use of ironic contradiction is Frank Gehry's fish restaurant in Japan, a form that returns to the primordial shape of the upturned fish in the midst of a harshly industrial freeway landscape. Throughout the conference, both the concept of language and the configuration of ironic contradiction repeatedly linked the architects' production and the theorists' positions. To be sure, each speaker used these elements in different ways to describe different kinds of effects, but their reiteration can nevertheless be taken as a shared constellation.

In Rorty's terminology, people who make such ironic and contradictory utterances are "ironists." Ironists are people who realize that anything can be made to

> look good or bad by being redescribed, and their renunciation of the attempt to formulate criteria of choice between final vocabularies puts them in the position which Sartre called "meta-stable"; never quite able to take themselves seriously because always aware that the terms in which they describe themselves are subject to change, always aware of the contingency and fragility of their final vocabularies, and thus of their selves. (*CIS*, 73–74)

Just as Rorty's argument emphasizes the importance of language, contingency, and irony, these elements play important roles among the designs of contemporary architects.

As Rorty points out, however, and as Andrea Dean emphasized, the intensification of ironic contradiction and the awareness of contingencies have led to a crucial problem in the relations between the private and the public realms, in both architecture and American society in general. On the one hand, architecture, the most public of the arts, seems perfectly suited to the demands for the creation of a public sphere in this country. One could imagine the proliferation of public projects such as university buildings, as at the University of California, Irvine, under David Neuman's direction, museums, and concert halls in postmodern styles. On the other hand, however, it seems clear from the discussion at Irvine that the bulk of production over the past ten years has involved the creation of private housing. Particularly in Los Angeles, energy seems devoted to private projects. More than ever, Americans and American architects are intent on the process of self-creation.

Andrea Dean suggested that the absorption in projects of self-creation, no matter how ironic, has led to considerable and sometimes disastrous uncertainty in contemporary society over how the public and private realms should be articulated together. The effects of this confusion emerge most clearly for architecture in the uncertainty shown by local, state, and federal governments with regard to the crisis of the homeless. Thus the vital epidemic of postmodernity, as it has spread across the United States and into Europe and Asia, also has a virulent side, evident in its sharpening of the gulf between the public and the private realms. But by sharpening the divide between the public and the private, while it is certainly possible that architects and philosophers will focus on their own private vocabularies at the expense of the public, it is also possible that they will see more clearly how to deal with both together.

And this is a central irony in terms of the impact of postmodernity on the community: it may, through the potentially reversible effects of contingency, and through the enlargement of the gap between the public and the private, enable the articulation of both realms pragmatically together, the kind of moral progress that Rorty sees "in the direction of greater human solidarity" (*CIS*, 192).

In sum, then, it is indeed possible to derive a picture of recent architecture and philosophy together through the notion of postmodernity. The pivotal elements are the concepts of rhetoricity, ironic contradiction, contingency, segmentation, citation, and the problematic relations of the public and the private spheres. Of course, the notion of postmodernity might still be rejected in favor, for example, of a proliferation of -isms. Then we would find instances simply of Gehryism, Sternism, Eisenmanism, Wilfordism, Israelism, and so on. Yet the more proliferation of -isms would obscure the many shared features of contemporary architecture and philosophy. And my point is that we can improve the general conditions of our lives today only if we try to look for what these might be.

NOTES

1. The literature on postmodernity is voluminous and expanding rapidly. Some of the more significant discussions include Jonathan Arac, ed., *Postmodernism and Politics* (Minneapolis: University of Minnesota Press, 1986); Ernst Behler, *Irony and the Discourse of Modernity* (Seattle: University of Washington Press, 1990); Hal Foster, ed., *The Anti-Aesthetic: Essays on Postmodern Culture* (Port Townsend, Wash.: Bay Press, 1983); Linda Hutcheon, *A Poetics of Postmodernism: History, Theory, Fiction* (New York: Routledge, 1988), and *The Politics of Postmodernism* (New York: Routledge, 1989); Andreas Huyssen, *After the Great Divide: Modernism, Mass Culture, Postmodernism* (Bloomington: Indiana University Press, 1986); Fredric Jameson, *Postmodernism, or the Cultural Logic of Late Capitalism* (Durham, N.C.: Duke University Press, 1991); Heinrich Klotz, ed., *Postmodern Visions: Drawings, Paintings, and Models by Contemporary Architects* (New York: Abbeyville Press, 1985); Jean-François Lyotard, *The Postmodern Condition: A Report on Knowledge,* trans. Geoffrey Bennington and Brian Massumi (Minneapolis: University of Minnesota Press, 1984); Brian McHale, *Postmodernist Fiction*

(London: Methuen, 1987); Tania Modleski, ed., *Studies in Entertainment: Critical Approaches to Mass Culture* (Bloomington: Indiana University Press, 1986); Andrew Ross, ed., *Universal Abandon? The Politics of Postmodernism* (Minneapolis: University of Minnesota Press, 1988); Kirk Varnedoe and Adam Gopnik, *High and Low: Modern Art and Popular Culture* (New York: Museum of Modern Art, 1990); and Alan Wilde, *Horizons of Assent: Modernism, Postmodernism, and the Ironic Imagination* (Baltimore: Johns Hopkins University Press, 1981).

2. Charles Jencks has contributed several texts to the discussion, including *The Language of Post-Modern Architecture* (New York: Rizzoli, 1977), *Post-Modern Classicism: The New Synthesis* (London: Academy Editions, 1990), *What Is Post-Modernism?* (London: Academy Editions, 1987), and *Architecture Today* (London: Academy Editions, 1988).

3. Andy Grunberg, "As It Must to All, Death Comes to Post-Modernism," *New York Times*, 16 September 1990, 47.

4. For a detailed history of the concept of postmodernity, see Ihab Hassan, *The Dismemberment of Orpheus* (Madison: University of Wisconsin Press, 1982), 259–71. For Levin's analysis in particular, see "What Was Modernism? (1960), in Harry Levin, *Refractions* (New York: Oxford University Press, 1966).

5. For Leslie Fiedler, see *The Collected Essays of Leslie Fiedler* (New York: Stein and Day, 1971), 2:454–61, and *A Fiedler Reader* (New York: Stein and Day, 1977), 270–94. Whereas Fiedler was decisive for the recognition of postmodernity in literature, Venturi's work helped to shape the reconceptualization of architectural modernism. See Robert Venturi, *Complexity and Contradiction in Architecture* (New York: Museum of Modern Art, 1966), and Robert Venturi, Denise Scott Brown, and Stephen Izenour, *Learning from Las Vegas* (Cambridge, Mass.: MIT Press, 1972). For an insightful and ironic confrontation of Adorno with the rock group the Cadillacs, see Bernard Gendron, "Theodor Adorno Meets the 'Cadillacs,' " in *Studies in Entertainment*, ed. Modleski, 18–36.

6. Huyssen, *After the Great Divide*, 196.

7. Richard Rorty, *Contingency, Irony, and Solidarity* (London: Cambridge University Press, 1989) (cited in the text as *CIS*).

8. For a discussion of "metaphoric redescriptions" of nature in science, see Mary Hesse, *Revolutions and Reconstructions in the Philosophy of Science* (Bloomington: Indiana University Press, 1980).

9. See, for example, Geoffrey Broadbent, Richard Bunt, and Charles Jencks, eds., *Signs, Symbols, and Architecture* (New York: Wiley, 1980).

10. Jacques Derrida, *Of Grammatology*, trans. Gayatri Chakravorty Spivak (Baltimore: Johns Hopkins University Press, 1974), 6.

11. Richard Rorty, "The World Well Lost," in Rorty, *Consequences of Pragmatism: Essays: 1972–1980* (Minneapolis: University of Minnesota Press, 1982), 3–18.

12. "Peter Eisenman: An *Architectural Design* Interview by Charles Jencks," in *Deconstruction in Architecture*, ed. Andreas C. Papadakis (London: St. Martin's Press, 1988), 30.

13. Paolo Portoghesi, *Postmodern: The Architecture of the Postindustrial Society*, trans. Ellen Shapiro (New York: Rizzoli, 1983), 12. I am grateful to Douglas Nash for this information. See Nash, "The Politics of Space: Architecture, Painting & Theatre in the Postmodern German Landscape" (Ph.D. diss., University of Washington, 1992), 56.

14. See Marshall Berman, *All That Is Solid Melts into Air: The Experience of Modernity* (New York: Simon and Schuster, 1982).

15. Derrida, *Of Grammatology,* 24.

16. See my articles on citation and postmodernity: "Building Without Foundations: Postmodernism from Architecture to Critical Theory," in *Postmodernism and Beyond: Architecture as the Critical Art of Contemporary Culture,* ed. Marilyn F. Moriarty, David J. Neuman, and William J. Lillyman (Irvine, Calif.: Humanities Research Institute, 1989), 13–16; "The Subversive Quotation as a Postmodern Practice," *Philological Association of the Pacific Coast* 12 (1987): 212–19; "Zitat als Realität, Realität als Zitat," *Arcadia* 24 (1984): 269–77.

17. Jacques Derrida: *Of Spirit: Heidegger and the Question,* trans. Geoffrey Bennington and Rachel Bowlby (Chicago: University of Chicago Press, 1989), 31.

18. "Peter Eisenman: An *Architectural Design* Interview by Charles Jencks," 54.

19. In deliberate and explicit contrast to the writings of Le Corbusier and others, Venturi's "gentle manifesto" of 1966, *Complexity and Contradiction in Architecture,* celebrated the affirmative and liberating effects of multiplicity and contradiction. For an encyclopedic survey of the various features of multiplicity across various cultural areas, see Wolfgang Welsch, *Unsere postmoderne Moderne* (Weinheim: VCH, Acta Humaniora, 1987).

20. Helmut Heissenbüttel uses this notion to describe the construction of his text *Projekt Nr. 1. D'Alemberts Ende* (Frankfurt: Ullstein, 1981).

21. According to Guy Davenport in *The Geography of the Imagination* (San Francisco: North Point Press, 1981), "what has been most modern in our time was what was most archaic" (28). Davenport argues that Joyce, Pound, and Picasso were part of a general revitalization of the old: "the Renaissance of 1910, which recognized the archaic" (27). But the difference is that Gehry's architecture resists grandiose claims and moves closer to the representation of contingent, particular forms for their own sake.

22. Charles Jencks,"Deconstruction: The Pleasures of Absence," in *Deconstruction in Architecture,* ed. Papadakis, 19.

23. Ibid., 28.

24. "Peter Eisenman: An *Architectural Design* Interview by Charles Jencks," 55.

25. Ibid., 55–56.

26. Ibid., 59.

27. For Derrida's comments on architecture, see "Point de folie—maintenant architecture," *AA Files* 12 (Summer 1986): 64–83, as well as chapter 2 of this volume.

28. Behler, *Irony and the Discourse of Modernity,* 36.

29. Jean Baudrillard, *Simulations* (New York: Semiotexte, 1987).

B I O G R A P H I C A L

N O T E S

Ann Bergren is an associate professor of classics at UCLA and teaches architectural theory at the Southern California Institute of Architecture. She received her Ph.D. in classical philology from Harvard and is currently completing a book, *Architecture Gender Philosophy.*

Aaron Betsky is a contributing editor to *Metropolitan Home* and an instructor at the Southern California Institute of Architecture. He is also the managing editor (California office) of *Artcoast Magazine.*

Andrea Oppenheimer Dean was a writer and editor for *Architecture,* the journal of the American Institute of Architects, for more than fifteen years. She became a senior editor in 1974, and the executive editor in 1984. Currently, she is a senior editor of *Historic Preservation.* In addition to her frequent contributions to the magazine, she has written a book on Bruno Zevi.

The literary critic and philosopher **Jacques Derrida** is a professor of the history of philosophy at the Ecole Normale Supérieure in Paris, and has been a visiting professor at Yale, Cornell, and the University of California, Irvine, where he now holds a joint appointment. He is known worldwide for his numerous books and articles on deconstruction and is considered to be one of the foremost deconstructive critics.

The architect **Peter Eisenman**, FAIA, is internationally known for the blending of theory and practice in his work. He was the editor of *Oppositions,* was a founder of the New York City Institute for Architecture and Urban Studies (1967), and has taught at Cambridge and Yale. He was a participant in the "Deconstructivist Architecture" exhibit at the Museum of Modern Art in New York City in 1988.

Frank O. Gehry, FAIA, recipient of the Pritzker Prize, is internationally acclaimed as one of the most innovative of contemporary architects. He is well known for work such as the Loyola Marymount Law School, the L.A. County Aerospace Museum, and the Yale Psychiatric Institute. His work was exhibited at the "Deconstructivist Architecture" show at the Museum of Modern Art in 1988, as well as at a personal retrospective developed by the Walker Art Center in Minneapolis.

Diane Ghirardo was the executive editor of the *Journal of Architectural Education* (1988–1991). She teaches at the University of Southern California. In addition to her numerous articles on architecture, she has translated Aldo Rossi, *The Architecture of the City*. She has been a visiting critic at Rice, Columbia, the Southern California Institute of Architecture, and Yale.

Frank Israel was educated at the University of Pennsylvania, Yale, and Columbia and has been hailed as a quintessentially Los Angeles architect. The Walker Art Center featured his work in its "Architecture Tomorrow" exhibit in 1988 to 1989. He is an assistant professor in architecture at UCLA.

William J. Lillyman is a professor of German literature and the former executive vice chancellor at the University of California, Irvine. He is currently writing on the impact of Andrea Palladio on Goethe.

Jean-François Lyotard is a professor of philosophy at the University of Paris at Vincennes/St. Denis, and director of the Collège International de Philosophie. He currently holds a distinguished professorship in the French Department and Critical Theory Program at the University of California, Irvine. Besides his seminal work, *The Postmodern Condition* (1984), he is the author of *Just Gaming* (*Au Juste*) and an important philosophical work, *The Differend*. Lyotard also organized the 1985 exhibit "The Immaterials" at the Georges Pompidou Center in Paris.

The critic **J. Hillis Miller** is the distinguished professor of English and comparative literature at the University of California, Irvine. Previously, he taught for nineteen years at Johns Hopkins and for fourteen years at Yale. The author of seminal books and articles on literary criticism and literature, and considered internationally to be the founder of American deconstruction, Miller was president of the Modern Language Association in 1986.

Marilyn Moriarty is currently an assistant professor of English at Rollins College, Roanoke, Virginia. She is the 1990 winner of the Katherine Ann Porter Prize for fiction.

David J. Neuman, FAIA, is currently the director of planning and the university architect at Stanford University. Previously, he was the associate vice chancellor for physical planning and the campus architect at the University of California, Irvine. He is an adjunct professor in the Urban Studies Program at Stanford.

Educated at Williams and Yale, **Barton Phelps,** FAIA, is currently an associate professor of architecture at UCLA. He chairs the editorial boards of *L.A. Architect* and *Architecture California*. His work has received AIA design awards at the national, state, and local levels. Before starting his own practice in 1984, he was director of architecture at the Urban Innovations Group and assistant dean of the Graduate School of Architecture and Urban Planning at UCLA.

The architect **Robert A. M. Stern,** FAIA, has been a lecturer and professor of architecture at Columbia since 1970. He has been awarded numerous national and regional design honors, and organized many symposia and exhibitions, including "The Presence of the Past" (Southern California Institute of Architecture, 1980). He is the author of a wide variety of books; among his most recent publications is *Modern Classicism.*

Steven Taubeneck is an associate professor of Germanic studies at the University of British Columbia. His Ph.D. was awarded by the University of Virginia (1988); he specializes in recent German culture.

Michael Wilford, RIBA, has been a partner in James Stirling Michael Wilford & Associates, London, since 1971. He has been a professor of architecture at Rice and Sheffield universities, as well as a visiting critic at Yale and the University of Toronto.

Since 1976, **L. Paul Zajfen,** RAIC, AIA, has been the director of the IBI Group, Newport Beach, Calif. A graduate of McGill University, he has received numerous design awards and served as a guest critic at UCLA; the University of California, Berkeley; California Polytechnic State University, Pomona; and the University of Southern California.